Studies in Childhood and Youth

Series Editors: Allison James, University of Sheffield, UK, and Adrian James, University of Sheffield, UK

Titles include:

Karen Wells, Erica Burman, Heather Montgomery and Alison Watson (*editors*)
CHILDHOOD, YOUTH AND VIOLENCE IN GLOBAL CONTEXTS
Research and Practice in Dialogue

Rebekah Willett, Chris Richards, Jackie Marsh, Andrew Burn
and Julia C. Bishop (*editors*)
CHILDREN, MEDIA AND PLAYGROUND CULTURES
Ethnographic Studies of School Playtimes

Studies in Childhood and Youth
Series Standing Order ISBN 978–0–230–21686–0 hardback
(*outside North America only*)

You can receive future titles in this series as they are published by placing a standing order. Please contact your bookseller or, in case of difficulty, write to us at the address below with your name and address, the title of the series and the ISBN quoted above.

Customer Services Department, Macmillan Distribution Ltd, Houndmills, Basingstoke, Hampshire RG21 6XS, England

Childhood, Mobile Technologies and Everyday Experiences

Changing Technologies = Changing Childhoods?

Emma Bond
University Campus Suffolk, Ipswich, UK

palgrave
macmillan

First published 2014 by
PALGRAVE MACMILLAN

Palgrave Macmillan in the UK is an imprint of Macmillan Publishers Limited, registered in England, company number 785998, of Houndmills, Basingstoke, Hampshire RG21 6XS.

Palgrave Macmillan in the US is a division of St Martin's Press LLC, 175 Fifth Avenue, New York, NY 10010.

Palgrave Macmillan is the global academic imprint of the above companies and has companies and representatives throughout the world.

Palgrave® and Macmillan® are registered trademarks in the United States, the United Kingdom, Europe and other countries.

ISBN 978–1–137–29252–0

This book is printed on paper suitable for recycling and made from fully managed and sustained forest sources. Logging, pulping and manufacturing processes are expected to conform to the environmental regulations of the country of origin.

A catalogue record for this book is available from the British Library.

A catalog record for this book is available from the Library of Congress.

This book is dedicated to my children – Amelia, Harriet, Florence, Zach and Jemima – and to their childhoods, now past; to the changing contours of our lives, for their patience and understanding when times were challenging and for their love and belief in me as their mother; and to my newly arrived granddaughter – Molly – whose childhood is already beginning to fascinate and delight us all

Contents

Acknowledgements

First, my sincere gratitude must go to my parents – Michael and Molly Bond – who have been tremendously supportive to me throughout my career and have always been on hand to help out with the roller coaster of family – well, my family – life! I would like to thank Professor Sonia Livingstone, whose work has inspired me since I undertook my PhD at the University of Essex, and whose extensive research with the EU Kids Online network has informed many of the discussions within this book. I would also like to thank Professor Eamonn Carrabine, who first suggested and encouraged me to write this book, and to Andrew James and the editorial team at Palgrave Macmillan for their advice and patience. Most importantly, my grateful thanks must go to my friend and colleague Stuart Agnew, at University Campus Suffolk, who not only offered guidance on the content, but also whose practical help at work enabled me to actually get it written and without whom this book would never have reached completion. Thank you.

Finally, my gratitude must be extended to the hours I spent in the Suffolk countryside whilst writing this book, to the love I found in the landscapes in which I sought solace and to the folly and fields of Freston.

1
Introduction

This book is essentially about childhood. In fact, it is about childhood and the relationship between mobile technologies and childhood, highlighting children's everyday experiences in growing up with mobile internet technologies. It is an attempt to explore the changing nature of late-modern childhood and the relationship between childhood, as a social and cultural construction, and the plethora of mobile internet technologies which have become ubiquitous in everyday life, and certainly in most children's everyday lives. According to recent research by Mascheroni and Ólafsson (2013), smartphones are devices that most children are likely to own (53 per cent) or use at least once a day to go online. By mobile internet technologies, I include here, of course, not only mobile phones and smartphones but also post-PC tablets, netbooks and e-readers. As the authors (2013, p. 5) point out, however, 'there is much current discussion of mobile media, there is scope for different definitions at this point in time as well as changing definitions over time if, like the internet itself, mobile media are a moving target as new technologies and applications are continuously developed'. My analysis here examines what Rich Ling (2012) calls the 'taken for grantedness' of mobile technologies and how mobile communication devices have become embedded in society. Ling (2012, p. 6) uses the term 'social mediation technologies' in that they 'are legitimated artifacts and systems governed by group-based reciprocal expectations that enable, but also set conditions for, the maintenance of the social sphere'. I have, however, chosen to use the phrase 'mobile internet technologies' in this book as it is a clear reminder of the mobility, connectivity and technological affordances (see Hutchby, 2001a) that these personalised devices combine. Because they are now a taken-for-granted part of everyday life, it is easy to forget, even as adults whose childhood experiences were not played out through interactions with mobile internet technologies, what life was like before we had these smart pocket-sized bundles of digital capabilities in our pockets and handbags. In our everyday lives, they have indeed become taken for granted (Ling, 2012), and also implied by 'taken for granted' is that we are almost constantly contactable by and connected to our family, friends, colleagues and the wider society through the internet. What implications does this have on our family lives, friendships, relationships and working lives? We can contact others in a variety of ways – call and talk to them, send a text message or a picture message, we can talk face to face and see each other, we can send a video or we can email, update our status and get in touch on Facebook or tweet – to name but a few. We can communicate from wherever we are – on a bus or train, the street or beach, or even from the middle of a field – provided we are connected in some way to a network. Arguably, this provides us with a sense of security as a result of our constant connectivity. In turn, we can also be reached by our families, friends and partners, but if we cannot get in touch with people or if they do not respond almost immediately, in some instances, a sense of doubt and insecurity often sets in: 'Why haven't they texted me back?' or 'I haven't heard from them in days – I hope that they are OK'. So, whilst we are reassured and gain security through mobile internet technologies, they simultaneously make us feel insecure and incite anxiety (Bond, 2010). Furthermore, we can also play games, find out the latest news, check football scores and weather forecasts; we can buy things whilst on a train or walking down the street; we can watch videos, catch up on missed television programmes and download podcasts whilst waiting for a bus or sitting in the dentist's waiting room. According to Mascheroni and Ólafsson (2013, p. 11),

> the place where children are more likely to use their smartphones at least once a day is actually their own bedroom (39%) or another room at home (37%). This suggests that children value privacy and convenience more than mobility – perhaps because the smartphone is always 'at hand' and doesn't need to be turned on.

Through these mobile internet devices, we have become both constant consumers and producers of media and digital artefacts, as we can now take, upload and share videos and images from virtually anywhere, all at the touch of a screen and within seconds. The most private spaces and our most intimate thoughts can now be made public by sharing them online with our network of family, friends and the wider networked public instantly.

Just considering our own use of mobile technologies in our everyday lives reveals a highly complex and complicated network of relationships between people, things, devices and software and digital content and media. But these activities are all carried out within other local and widely changing sociopolitical, technical and cultural contexts. Changing norms and values in relation to technology use are much debated and discussed; for example, the acceptability of using mobile internet technologies at mealtimes or in meetings is often context-specific and also depends on the type of meal, whom it is with or the nature and purpose of the meeting. Even organising our day-to-day lives now often depends on digital calendars that sync with laptops, phones and tablets via a cloud-based storage facility. How did we live without them?

As adults, the chances are that we may remember life pre-mobile internet connectivity and almost certainly will recollect a childhood (at least some of it!) without the plethora of mobile internet devices that have become taken for granted in most children's everyday lives today. Even from a very young age, children are given smartphones and tablets for entertainment and amusement purposes. Any trip around a supermarket will show the aisles adorned with toddlers sitting in supermarket trolleys with a touch-screen mobile device in their hands as they swipe at various characters and interact with one of the hundreds of apps designed for pre-school children and the very early years of childhood. According to Mascheroni and Ólafsson (2013), 'Children are using the internet and get a mobile phone or a smartphone at ever younger ages' (p. 6). The age at which children are able to interact with mobile internet technologies is, indeed, getting lower and lower as touch-screen technology has now negated the need for literacy skills in performing tasks, and, coupled with the advances in software design, children are using mobile internet technologies, albeit ones belonging to their parents, before they are out of nappies. The purpose of this book is not to examine the interaction of children and mobile technologies from a developmental or an educational perspective but rather to examine the quotidian nature of mobile internet technologies in childhood.

Children and adults have very different perceptions of the internet (Livingstone et al., 2011a), and, in relation to contemporary childhoods, the only people who understand what it is like to be a child and use mobile internet technologies in their everyday lives are children themselves. This is especially apparent when considering the rapid technological advances and adoption patterns that we have seen in the last few years. What I set out to do in this book is to examine the complex interrelationships between childhood, as a social and cultural construction, mobile internet technologies and children's everyday and, perhaps, seemingly mundane experiences. In considering the 'unnoticed' (see Jacobsen, 2009) and the taken-for-grantedness (Ling, 2012), I explore and aim to make visible the embeddedness of mobile internet technologies in contemporary childhood, and also consider an analysis of children's everyday lives and offer theoretical explanations. Inspired by James et al. (2010) and others, and the social studies of childhood paradigm, I draw on theoretical approaches in childhood studies to explore the changing nature of childhood in late modernity and on socio-technical studies to discuss the nature of children's everyday interactions with mobile internet technologies in late modernity.

The structure of the book

In the next chapter I provide some background developments in my approach to the analysis offered here in framing the debates helpful to understanding the context of childhood studies itself and the theoretical frameworks helpful to understanding childhood. As part of the *Childhood and Youth* series published by Palgrave Macmillan, this book aims to provide a critical analysis of childhood, mobile internet technologies and children's everyday experiences and thus contribute to the continually growing body of literature in childhood and youth studies. Arguably, any consideration of present-day childhoods should not only address technology in the wider sense but also specifically consider mobile internet technologies, as few childhoods remain untouched by them. Also, the analysis presented in this book mainly rests on contemporary childhoods. Chapter 2 also outlines the importance of understanding childhood from a historical perspective in order to contextualise children's experiences and to illustrate how both social and cultural constructions of childhood and also children's lived experiences are influenced by a myriad of different elements, including time and space. Just as, historically, wider socio-economic and political agendas have underpinned both constructions and reconstructions of childhood, so the same is also true of contemporary childhoods and children's lived realities. By considering the history of childhood and historical approaches to understanding childhood, we can gain an in-depth understanding of how some of the dominant ideologies we associate with, and still to some extent value in, childhood today came to be so influential. The dominant ideologies of innocence, incompleteness and vulnerability impact not only how childhood is understood but also how children are treated by adults, other children and the society in general. I draw on both theories of childhood and also broader sociological explanations to outline late to modern childhoods and wider social change to consider childhood in late modernity. The analysis includes an examination of the *risk society* thesis (see Beck, 1992, 2009; Giddens, 1990, 1991) to consider how risk and risk anxiety are central and not only contemporary constructions of childhood (Scott et al., 1998). These debates are drawn upon further in Chapter 6, which considers children and online risk. The importance of understanding space and how theories of understanding childhood have been influenced by the increasing importance of children's rights and the conceptualisation of children as active social agents and experts in their own lives have also been considered. Finally, Chapter 2 considers an explanatory framework for exploring children's everyday experiences and reviewing what Qvortrup (2011) describes as the multiplicity of childhoods in themselves.

The chapter offers a developmental trajectory for how technology has been studied and understood previously, just as Chapter 2 did in relation to childhood. My approach to initially separate out childhood and technology is a deliberate one, in order to make the separate entities of my overall analysis visible in the explanations that emerge in the later chapters of the book. Again, the importance of the historical context is emphasised here as I examine the evolution of the television and the telephone as two very different technologies, before moving on to consider the internet. As argued in the opening paragraphs of this Introduction, mobile internet technologies are highly complex and even a brief consideration reveals the complexity of the technology under discussion in this book. The approaches to understanding television (one-to-many), the telephone (one-to-one) and the internet (as an interactive, networked public) are all essential to understanding converged networked mobile technologies. I draw on a variety of theoretical approaches to understanding technology and media in this chapter, as it is not just the technological functionality of the device that is under scrutiny here but also the digital content. According to Siapera (2012, p. 6), 'the central question regarding (new) media and technology concerns the nature of their relationship with people and society'. Using Matthewman's (2011) call for theoretical pluralism, I set out previous frameworks of explanation for technology and society and finally reconsider theorising childhood, technology and society.

Having examined approaches for understanding childhood in Chapter 2 and for understanding technology in Chapter 3, Chapter 4 combines both childhood and technology to examine how they are studied, examined and understood and the different methodological approaches used in research. The development of more participatory child-centred research methods, influenced by the social studies of childhood (James et al., 2010) and children's rights (Alderson, 2008; Kellet, 2005a, 2005b) has changed the way childhood is studied. The prominence of 'scientific' approaches which were previously dominated by developmental psychology and the traditionally adult-initiated education studies has more recently been challenged in favour of trying to understand children's own viewpoints and their lived experiences through the adoption of more ethnographic approaches and a qualitative turn. Ethical considerations and reflexivity in research are also examined in order to be able to interrogate methodologically the research and relevant studies published on children and mobile internet technology. There is, however, still relatively little which specifically examines mobile internet technologies (Livingstone et al., 2011a). I have, however, been able to draw extensively in this book on the most up-to-date and comprehensive study of children, young people and the internet – the EU Kids Online research which surveyed more than 25,000 children across Europe (see Livingstone et al., 2011a) and a number of other published smaller-scale research studies on a variety of mobile technology-related topics in relation to childhood, including my own study on children, mobile phones and risk (Bond, 2010, 2011, 2013). The key themes to emerge from this analysis of the research to date are discussed in the following three chapters – 'Relationships' (Chapter 5), 'Risk' (Chapter 6) and 'Rhetoric and Realities' (Chapter 7).

The focus of Chapter 5 is childhood, mobile internet technologies and children's everyday relationships. It includes a discussion on their family relationships, relationships with their peers and also their intimate sexual relationships before providing an account of children's self-identity in relation to mobile internet technologies in their everyday lives. Children use mobile internet technologies to manage and maintain their relationships and view mobile technologies, especially the mobile phone, as essential to their everyday relationships, claiming that you cannot have friends without one. I draw on the concept of *gifting* (see Maus, 2002; Berking, 1999) as important to understanding text and image exchange in children's relationships and Goffman's (1959) *Presentation of Self in Everyday Life* to consider how young people use mobile internet technologies in their performativity of self-identity. Social media is about self-presentation (Murthy, 2012), and children are reflexive in their construction of self-identity through their interactions with others mediated through mobile internet technologies (Bond, 2010). Furthermore, mobile internet technologies facilitate intimacy in children's relationships and provide contact with parents and friends, and children actively use mobile internet technologies to maintain and manage their day-to-day relationships. An important aspect of children's self-identity is a gendered, sexual self-identity, especially as they get older, and mobile internet technologies are providing spaces – virtual spaces – for children to develop intimate, sexual relationships and explore each other's bodies (Bond, 2011).

Whilst children's intimate, sexual relationships are often viewed in adult discourses as risky, it is to the wider landscapes of risk that Chapter 6 turns. Children and adults perceive risks differently (Livingstone et al., 2011a), and it is the subjective understandings of risk, especially that of the children themselves, that underpin the debates presented in this chapter. Drawing on the findings from the EU Kids Online study (Livingstone et al., 2011a) amongst others, Chapter 6 examines the phenomena of cyberbullying – the subject of much recent media attention – before moving on to discuss the risks of sexting and pornography in relation to mobile internet technologies and children's everyday experiences. The final risk considered in Chapter 6 is that of pro-eating disorder websites as an example of potentially harmful online communities and environments, like the pro-self-harm sites, which are currently causing considerable concern. There are, of course, other related risks such as violent content and gaming, but there is not enough space within one chapter to cover all risks in detail, and this is comprehensively offered elsewhere (see Livingstone and Haddon, 2009; Livingstone et al., 2012). But, using the theoretical explanations of risk offered by Beck (1992) and Giddens (1990, 1991), this chapter argues that mobile internet technologies are blurring the boundaries of risk in late modernity and also those of childhood challenging the dominant ideologies of children as innocent victims. Such discourses on risk have, of course, important policy implications but the balance between protecting children and encouraging participation in the information society is problematic.

In Chapter 7, the educational underpinnings for encouraging participation are critically examined to propose that many policy initiatives on technology and education and, more recently, mobile internet technologies in education are deterministic (Buckingham, 2007; Selwyn, 2011a). The reality of many children's everyday lives remains far from the ideological discourses on technology magically transforming educational agendas and children's learning experiences. Whilst a review of the research to date suggests that iPads have a positive effect on children's engagement with learning opportunities (Clark and Luckin, 2013), the wider social and educational environments are extremely important but often ignored in the technology/education debates. In order to adopt a broader spectrum of analysis, I draw on Fenwick and Edwards's (2010, p. 1) suggestion that to 'take forward fresh agendas for intervening in educational research, policy and practice. Our [my] use of actor-network theory is not for telling us about educational issues; it is a way of intervening in educational issues to reframe how we might enact and engage with them'. My point here is that too often educational theory and pedagogical perspectives on technology-enhanced learning fail to acknowledge the stark realities of inequality in many children's lives. Drawing on examples of poverty and disability, I argue here that there are marked differences and hidden divides in the so-called *digital generation* that cannot and should not be ignored. We need to move towards a greater understanding of diversity in understanding childhood, mobile internet technologies and the reality, as opposed to the rhetoric, of children's lived experiences. To date, there is still very little research that explores children's lived experiences and even less in relation to marginalised childhoods. Much research, which focuses on the children's perspectives, including children living with a disability or in poverty, is needed in order to address the glaring inequalities in access to mobile internet technologies and the opportunities that online environments can afford.

By way of a conclusion, Chapter 8, as the final chapter in this account, examines the main arguments presented in the book, but it does so through a lens of children's rights. Concerns over the risks in relation to children's use of mobile internet technologies have prompted new legal and policy initiatives to protect children. However, balancing children's rights for protection from harm and simultaneously upholding their rights for participation in the information society remains problematic. Whilst childhood, mobile internet technologies and children's everyday experiences is a relatively new topic of enquiry, it is one that is currently attracting much interest. My aim in this book has been to open up some theoretical perspectives in studying childhood in late modernity, and I hope to provide readers with some alternative discussions on mobile internet technologies currently under debate. And so it is to childhood that our attention now turns.

2
Understanding Childhood

Introduction

Exemplified by the philosophical writings of Aristotle and Plato, childhood has fascinated both public and academic discourses for generations through scientific and psychological fascinations at the turn of the last century to anthropological, sociological and geographical literature that more recently contributed to the social studies of childhood. Arguably, as a social construct, the concept of childhood is relatively new. 'Childhood' as an *idea* is embedded in 'culture', and children are participants (with varying degrees of agency) in many if not all of those relationships that are governed through cultural practice (Hendrick, 2011, p. 103). Contemporary academic discourse and current debates on childhood are framed around shifting social constructions of childhood, political ideologies and changing cultural agendas. Understanding the relationship between social change and constructions of childhood has often been through the conceptual lens framed by 'structure' and 'agency', especially during the late twentieth century (Qvortrup, 2011). Furthermore, the unprecedented rapid social change associated with technologies (see Ólafsson et al., 2013a), especially mobile internet technologies, has arguably changed both the nature and expectations of childhood and children's everyday experiences. In fact, how we understand 'childhood' or, indeed, 'the child' or 'children' is open to changing and often challenging ideas about what 'childhood' is or should be, what it means to be 'a child' and how children are viewed and treated in society. Gittins (2009, p. 37) observes that 'the concept of "child" concerns an embodied individual defined as non-adult, while the notion of "childhood" is a more general and abstract term used to refer to the status ascribed by adults to those who are defined as not adult'. The concepts of 'the child' and 'childhood' in history through to late modernity are considered in detail in this chapter and how these concepts shape our understanding of children's everyday lives, and of contemporary social worlds in relation to mobile internet technologies.

Theoretical approaches to understanding childhood are important to understanding the relationship between childhood, mobile technologies and everyday experiences. This chapter sets out to contextualise how they have been developed and used in relation to academic advances in understanding childhood as a historical, social and cultural construction, and to situate the debates on childhood, mobile technologies and everyday experiences within the broader academic context of the study of childhood itself.

The increasing significance and globalisation of children's rights has an impact on all aspects of children's lives, from their relationship with their parents to their participation in school and other social institutions, and, more recently, their relationships with mobile internet technologies and new social media. Prout (2005, p. 57), for example, outlines the development of childhood studies from the Darwinian legacy rooted in biology to the social constructivist position, developed towards the end of the twentieth century, which 'hailed childhood as a more or less purely social and cultural phenomenon' to argue that 'childhood might be thought of as a heterogeneous assembly in which the social, technical and biological aspects of childhood are already "impure" entities'. His argument is highly pertinent to the discussions presented in this book as the usefulness of Actor Network Theory (ANT), which, according to Fenwick and Edwards (2010, p. 1), honours 'the mess, disorder and ambivalences that order phenomenon' is considered as a conceptual lens for understanding childhood and children's everyday experiences.

The final part of this chapter considers the possible implications of considering aspects of ANT for the future of studying childhood itself (see Prout, 2005) and also in the following chapter for understanding technology (see Latour, 1999). This chapter focuses on how childhood has come to be understood through wider historical, geographical, social and political concepts, and how these understandings underpin contemporary discourses in relation to children's lives. 'The concept of everyday life has been central to a range of theoretical developments in sociology, cultural and media studies' (Longhurst, 2007, p. 7) and there is an increasing recognition that understanding everyday life from a social science perspective, based on the practices of how and where technologies are used, has had an important impact on the wider scientific community (Pink, 2012). The paradigm of childhood sociology, emphasising children's positions as social actors, as creative and inventive users of the world around them, has nurtured blossoming conceptual and empirical explorations of children's competency and agency in a range of diverse settings (O'Brien et al., 2000). However, there remains an uneasy relationship between participation and protection, especially in relation to mobile internet technologies (see also Chapter 7 for a more critical evaluation), which is influenced by the dominant discourses of risk and late modernity.

This book explores late-modern childhoods, everyday experiences and mobile technologies but the discussion begins, as many analyses of childhood do, with Philippe Ariès and conceptions of childhood in the Middle Ages in order to examine how contemporary understandings are influenced by shifting historical, cultural, social and political values. As Gittins (2009, p. 38) observes, childhood is a historical construction and 'needs to be understood in relation to ideas about what children should be and have meant to adults over time, and why such ideas and beliefs have changed'.

Histories of childhood

Historical perspectives on childhood illuminate how childhood is socially and culturally constructed, and how this influences children's everyday experiences of childhood. Historical perspectives on childhood provide a lens through which to consider critically current discourses on contemporary childhoods.

> We know nothing of childhood; and with our mistaken notions the further we advance the further we go astray. The wisest writers devote themselves to what a man ought to know, without asking what a child is capable of learning. They are always looking for the man in the child, without considering what he is before he becomes a man. It is to this study that I have chiefly devoted myself, so that it my method is fanciful and unsound, my observations may still be of service. I may be greatly mistaken as to what ought to be done, but I think I have clearly perceived the material which is to be worked upon. Begin thus by making a more careful study of your scholars, for it is clear that yon know nothing about them; yet if you read this book [Emile] with that end in view, I think you will find that it is not entirely useless.
>
> (Taken from the author's preface to *Emile* by Rousseau, written originally in 1762, reprinted 2009)

However, the everyday experience of medieval or Elizabethan children, for example, is no longer available for us to listen to, or to observe, and there are few surviving documents from these and other early periods of history. It is the material artefacts that have remained which provide evidence and insight into the childhoods of the past, but the study of the history of childhood highlights that caution is required in relation to reliability and some of the assumptions that have been made through the interpretation of the materiality of past childhoods.

Childhood has a history and it is a very important history, especially to childhood scholars. The idea that in the Middle Ages childhood did not exist, the central tenet of Ariès' (1962a) thesis, has been disputed and debated by most childhood historians but, whichever line of argument is taken, his ideas have been fundamental in shaping current understandings of childhood as a socially constructed concept. Ariès' (1962a) main argument was that current notions of childhood as 'a special life phase gradually emerged during the early modern period'; there is evidence of toys and clothes specially for children from the sixteenth century onwards and, as children came to be viewed as vulnerable beings in need of adult protection, the combined forces of family and school eventually withdrew children from adult society (Gaffney, 2011, p. 3). Ariès relied on artwork as evidence for his research and he suggests that 'medieval art until about the twelfth century did not know childhood nor attempt to portray it' (Ariès, 1962b, p. 9). The artefact – material and now digital – has a significant role to play in understanding both historical and contemporary childhoods, and aspects of material culture and practices of childhood representation have influenced our knowledge of childhood and continue to do so. Although Ariès argued that art pre-thirteenth century lacked child morphology, de Mause (1974) claimed that it realistically represented children (O'Brien, 2003) and both Shahar's (1990) and Orme's (2001) works dispute many of Ariès' original claims (Gaffrey, 2011). Although Ariès' thesis has been the subject of considerable criticism and debate, most notably due to its methodology, since its publication it has, according to Lohmann and Mayer (2009, p. 2), 'done more than any other publication to stimulate public and academic interest in the historical discovery of childhood as a phenomenon'.

This interest in childhood as a phenomenon, as exemplified in the use of images and visual representations, remains to the present day, and it has influenced anthropological and ethnographic approaches to studying childhood and youth, which are clearly apparent in contemporary social analyses of childhood. Pink (2007, p. 21) observes: 'images are everywhere... They are inextricably interwoven with our personal identities, narratives, lifestyles, cultures and societies, as well as with definitions of history, space and truth'. The image, now digitised, remains central to conceptions of childhood and underpins much of the current debate in relation to childhood and mobile internet technologies. It is important to remember that when considering childhoods past, however, our understanding of what childhood was like is subject to interpretation and speculation when surviving images are scarce, as few remain intact. This has been challenging to historians and social scientists alike, and O'Brien (2003, p. 363) suggests that 'the ontological ambiguity inherent in artworks gives rise to interpretive plurality'. Further evidence for understanding childhood and children's everyday experiences in the past comes from archaeology (see Society for the Study of Childhood in the Past (SSCIP) – online). Archaeologists have drawn upon evidence from material artefacts and used everyday objects to gain knowledge and understanding of childhoods and children's everyday lives in the past (Wood, 2009), but, as Lewis (2009, p. 105) observes, 'we have wiped the sticky fingerprints of children off our views of the past' as historical evidence of children's lives has frequently been overlooked or lost in a wider or less child-centred approach to archaeology. These approaches may appear historically removed from current understandings of childhood, but they are highly relevant to contemporary perspectives because they underpin much of the social studies of childhood (see James et al., 2010) and the ethnographic trend in contemporary approaches to childhood research (see Chapter 4 for further discussion).

The importance of history in understanding childhood is outlined by Cunningham (2003) as knowledge in relation to the actual experience of childhood, the policies adopted in relation to children and the ideas in relation to childhood in a specific societal context in a specific time. Furthermore, it was the changing norms, values and attitudes in relation to children and child-rearing practices that had a significant impact on children's experiences of childhood. Clarke (2010) outlines how childhood came to be seen as a natural and universally acknowledged phase of life, and details Stones' (1977) analysis of the seventeenth century to suggest that, influenced by the Puritan view of the child as inherently sinful, relationships were emotionally detached, and children's experiences dominated by strict discipline and punishment. A brief read of historical accounts of childhood through previous centuries, for example, will encounter the dominance of religion and religious values influencing how children are treated. The rise of Puritanism during the sixteenth century has attracted attention from historians who used records of religious sermons to illustrate how 'parents were exhorted by religious leaders to be severe with even the youngest of children in order to eradicate the sin that they believed was innate in everyone from birth' (Gittins, 2009, p. 41). It is important to remember, as Lee (2005) suggests, that even when values are related to childhood, children do not always benefit from them. However, the influence of romanticism and the Enlightenment view that children were endowed with a natural innocence as depicted in *Emile*, published by Rousseau in 1762, became widespread, especially in the middle classes during the eighteenth century (Clarke, 2010). The influence of the Enlightenment, the Age of Reason and the development of the Scientific Revolution in early modern European history began to infiltrate a conceptual shift from the dominance of religious thought, and Locke's emphasis on the influence of nurture over nature challenged the idea of children being born with 'original sin' and argued for providing children with educational opportunities instead (Hendrick, 2011). As Cunningham (2005, p. 58) also observes:

> Framed by the writings of John Locke at its beginning and of the romantic poets at the end, and with the strident figure of Rousseau at centre stage, there seems in the eighteenth century to be a degree of sensitivity to childhood and to children lacking in previous centuries. Some people began to see childhood not as a preparation for something else, whether adulthood or heaven, but as a stage of life to be valued in its own right.

Understanding the history of childhood is important to understanding how it is these notions of childhood that still influence more modern understandings. It is the concept of the *innocent* child that underpins many child-centred educational initiatives, nursery provision and individualised child-rearing practices that continue to be familiar aspects of contemporary westernised discourse in relation to childhood (James et al., 2010) and which are associated with the idea of childhood as a time free from care and responsibility (Prout, 2005). These constructions of childhood form the basis for legislation of child protection policies and also, for example, legislation on child employment in the UK (McKechnie and Hobbs, 1999). The ideology of the innocent child in need of adult care and protection is fundamental to understanding how childhood came to be separated from the world of work and the world of adults, and, indeed, the late-modern discourses of childhood in relation to protecting children from online risk via mobile internet technologies.

However, whilst romantic notions of childhood began to filter into the consciousness of the middle classes, the lived experiences of working-class children of the eighteenth century depicted a very different reality. Industrialisation reoriented many children's childhoods away from a traditionally rural, family orientated experience with their gradual entry into the world of work in the urban, often brutal and sometimes fatal employment in factories. Described by Cunningham (2005, pp. 88–89) as 'a black moment in the history of childhood', he outlines how, in the late eighteenth century as a consequence of industrialisation, which 'began to shift the location of the textile industries from home to factory, it was natural to look to children as a key component of the workforce'. This historical example demonstrates how wider political and economic changes, and dominant ideologies of childhood can have a significant impact on how children experience their everyday lives, how they are viewed and how they are treated. Heywood (2005, p. 171) traces the impact of the developments from the eighteenth century:

> Finally, one can discern a growing momentum to social and cultural changes affecting children from the eighteenth century onwards. Philosophers, poets, novelists, educators, doctors and others produced an increasing volume of works devoted to childhood. Reformers in private charities and state bureaucracies founded a range of institutions dedicated to child welfare. Families became smaller and more child-orientated. And school took over from the farms and work-shops as the principal site for the work of children.

Cunningham (2005, p. 359) points out that, until the nineteenth century, the focus of policy in relation to children had been either for redeeming their soul or for ensuring that the manpower needs of the state were met, but, during the late nineteenth and early twentieth centuries, a new ideology of childhood based on 'a concern to save children for the enjoyment of childhood' began to emerge and influence both public discussion and policy discourse. Literature, poetry, art and the use of image in considering the conditions of childhood, and recording and documenting childhood and children's lives comes to the fore at this time. In his photographic account of childhood from 1850 onwards,

Merritt (2006, pp. 63–64) notes how 'by the turn of the century photography had woven itself into the fabric of everyday life' and 'the conventional divisions of [labour] dictated that children belonged in the day-to-day world of women, many male photographers found their inspiration in their children, often making them subjects of their best work'. Read (2010, p. 422) considers how the influence of the romantic writings, art and images at the time 'presented a view of childhood, which was adopted as normative by their middle class audience' and these 'romantic notions located the child not in the gutter of a city street but in the natural environment of the field and forest. In the context of the city, relocation of the child was to be within a garden'. Thus, these romantic associations of childhood eventually expanded to working-class children, and free kindergartens began to open from 1900 offering their services to a very different group of children who went to the fee-paying kindergartens in existence 50 years earlier (Read, 2010). Schooling was seen as a socialisation mechanism to accept discipline and a structured attitude to work, but there were significant variations in the curricula and educational provision for boys was given a far higher priority than for girls (Long, 2006). According to Prout (2005, p. 35), 'by the end of the nineteenth century, conceptions of children as innocent, ignorant, dependent, vulnerable, generally incompetent and in need of protection and discipline were widespread'. This notion of innocence had, according to Lee (2005), important consequences for the ways in which children came to be valued as parents' investment, children and heritage, and children as state investments.

'Schooling, in particular mass compulsory schooling, has been influential in shaping our understanding of childhood' and it was 'through the introduction of mass compulsory schooling that modern childhood started to take shape' (Wyness, 2012, pp. 152–53). In the 1860s, approximately one-third of children in England and Wales did not go to school at all, and in 1881, there was no legislation requiring children to attend. At what ages and for how long children actually attended school is not precisely known, but Long's (2006) analysis suggests that there was greater availability of schools in urban areas and the probability of attendance peaks at about eight years of age and declines after the age of 11 in 1851. However, in 1918, legislation on compulsory schooling was extended and the school leaving age rose to 14. Spencer (2004) notes that there has been considerable sociological and historical interest on the impact of extending secondary education in the UK, which reflects wider concerns in relation to social class, gender roles and employment opportunities. Inequalities based on socio-economic background, gender and geographic location have persisted through three-quarters of the twentieth century and many remain today.

Twentieth-century childhoods

The twentieth century – widely regarded as 'the Century of the Child' – witnessed an increasingly 'close identification between childhood and the destiny of the nation' (Cunningham, 2006, p. 178). Triggered by concerns over children's welfare as a result of the ravages of two world wars, childhood became increasingly a site for both state investment and intervention. Furthermore, the simultaneous development of scientific, medical, psychological and educational knowledge gave rise to a broad body of professionals that could both stimulate and manipulate children's bodies and minds during the twentieth century. These advances had profound implications for the surveillance of childhood, child-rearing practices and children's everyday experiences.

At the beginning of the twentieth century, the primary focus for both parents and the state alike was keeping children alive, as infant mortality rates had remained high throughout the nineteenth century. However, by 'the middle of the twentieth century the death of a baby was something few parents would experience, where as in all previous centuries it had been something that parents would have been lucky to avoid' (Cunningham, 2005, p. 173). Concerns over children's health at the beginning of the twentieth century were not related to the well-being of the children themselves but related to the quality of the health of soldiers recruited to fight in the Boer War (1899–1902), and the devastating societal consequences of World War I. The increasing concern over the general health status of children was also influenced by the 1920s' growth of interventions based on a new interest in early years; for example, Arnold Gesell's guidance nursery school and interventions programmes for 'troubled children' (Safford and Safford, [1996] 2012). According to Turmel (2008, p. 178), there was a keen interest in IQ scoring at the very beginning of the twentieth century and the emphasis given to behaviourism during the 1920s gave rise to the more psychodynamic approaches of the 1930s 'which put emphasis upon emotional factors within the child'. At the same time there was what Cunningham (2005, p. 174) terms 'the growing professionalization for medicine for children' and, together with the introduction of compulsory schooling and testing, concerns about children's well-being linked to inadequate standards of living due to poverty gave rise to the introduction of physical-exercise routines in school, school meals, the school dentist and school nurses. The increasingly interventionist role of the state transformed social, legal and cultural constructions of childhood and children's everyday experiences through what Foucault (1977) identifies as 'disciplinary networks'.

> In applying such contentions to the historical process within which childhood has been constructed and reconstructed, the synthesis of power and knowledge within professional discourse and the consequent development of what Foucault calls 'regimes of truth' or 'disciplinary networks' are of central importance. The professionalization of childhood and the emergence and development of discrete specialisms – each with its own corpus of knowledge and power – demands, maintains and reproduces a process whereby 'technicians' (doctors, psychiatrists, psychologists, teachers, social workers) have been able to penetrate and regulate the social world of the child.
>
> (Goldson, 1997, p. 16)

Wider societal shifts, such as changes in family size through the widening availability and acceptability of contraception together with improved sanitation and hygiene standards accelerated the rapidly changing constructions and reconstructions of childhood, and of concerns relating to children's welfare. The end of the nineteenth century and the beginning of the twentieth century saw a societal shift in attitude towards how children were treated. Cunningham (2005, p. 182) suggest that 'poverty, child labour and schooling were the central elements of policy making with regard to children, but they did not define it' and issues related to child protection as well as concerns over child delinquency led to the development of the Children Act 1908. 'In the 1936 Halley Stuart Lecture, Sir Percy Alden argued that there could be no solution to the many problems connected with social and community welfare unless one began with the child' (Pinchbeck and Hewitt, 1973, p. 347). The reform of the Poor Law, enacted in 1929, passed responsibility for child protection to local authority health departments and the Poor Law Act of 1930 required county and borough councils to have a public assistance committee, which provided services for children in Poor Law Care, and these legal statutes directly contributed to the development of specialised children's services (Pinchbeck and Hewitt, 1973). In addition, the introduction of the welfare state after World War II represented 'an important strategy for the delivery of welfare' in the UK and it was developed as a 'comprehensive set of set of systems' (Spiker, 1995, pp. 65–66). Post-war Britain was also apprehensive about children's psychological well-being after the trauma of the war and the effects it had on children. Providing spaces for children to play became an important part of community planning and development, and saw the introduction of play areas in local geographies – urban spaces, in particular – for the first time. With increasing concerns for children's safety in the public realm in relation to car accidents, these play spaces were viewed as 'safe' spaces for children to play and 'play practices evolved with the growing influence of psychology' (Kozlovsky, 2008, p. 182). Kozlovsky (2008, p. 187) points out:

> The analysis of the adventure playground as a strategy of power and a narrative for reconstruction uncovers the contradictions of the postwar welfare state. The playground was originally part of a utopian project to reconstruct a peaceful and more stable postwar society through policies and practices directed toward each individual child, in his or her capacity as a future citizen. It was predicated upon investing play with the capacity to heal society and purge itself of the wartime manifestation of violence. Postwar society was fascinated with the play of children in ruins and put play on display as a metaphor for regeneration, all the while confirming a tragic and mythical conception of violence as rooted in human nature.

These utopian aspirations – freedom, equality, goodwill, peace and prosperity – were engendered by modernity (Jenks, 1996) and for the post-war 'welfare state, childhood, and therefore, actual children, carried the hopes for a new Britain united around an improved education system, universal health care and security benefits' (Holland, 1996, p. 156). However, such utopian aspirations have all long been recognised for their unattainability and their ideological content; the late-modern condition is one of avoidance or minimisation of distopias (Jenks, 1996) exemplified through Thatcherism, and the development of the Children Act 1989 saw the 'scapegoating of single parent families' and a rising number of moral panics related to debates on state intervention, the child and the changing construction of risk (Winter and Connolly, 1996, p. 31) (see Chapter 10 for further discussion on risk). Furthermore, the importance of the *Gillick* judgment in 1985, which challenged the previously dominant parental rights agenda, is also significant to understanding contemporary constructions of childhood as it enshrined the notion of the 'competent' child into UK social policy, but there remained much ambiguity in relation to children and sex (Pilcher,

1996), which arguably underpins much contemporary debate in relation to children, mobile technologies and sex.

> ... first, children mingled with adults in everyday life, and any gath-
> ering for the purpose of work, relaxation or sport brought together
> both children and adults; secondly painters were particularly fond
> of depicting childhood for its graceful and picturesque qualities... of
> these two ideas one strikes us as out of date, for today, as also towards
> the end of the nineteenth century, we tend to separate the world of
> children from that of adults; the other foreshadows the modern idea
> of childhood.
>
> (Ariès, [1962b] 2012, p. 12)

It is this very separateness of childhood that underlies many current protectionist debates, especially the concerns regarding children and mobile internet technologies in that childhood is no longer separate. Children have access to and participate in 'adult' worlds of information, knowledge, sexual content and online violence, for example, and they themselves are becoming producers of such content. These changing conditions of childhood threaten the previous constructions of child-hood as a time of innocence and separateness. Previously fixed internet access limited children's interactions online and a higher degree of con-trol and moderation was possible either via the schools or parental supervision, but with the increase of, in what Livingstone et al. (2011a) describe as mobilised, privatised access often possible 24 hours a day and seven days a week, children are constantly connected and this control is highly problematic. Mascheroni and Ólafsson (2013, p. 5) emphasise this point, commenting:

> This privatisation of access and use is accompanied by the pervasive-
> ness of the internet in children's daily lives and implies the creation
> of different social conventions of freedom, privacy, sociability, and –
> not least – supervision by parents and adults.

This brief journey through the history of childhood is intended to pro-vide a foreground for the more contemporary debates set out in this book, which are key to understanding the complex relationship between childhood, mobile technologies and everyday experiences. The debates presented in the following chapters also require an understanding of how childhood has come to be understood as a social and a cultural construction, and that these constructions and values associated with childhood in a given context have implications for children's everyday lives. As Prout (2005, p. 8) proposes:

> This context is rooted in the political, economic, technological, social and cultural changes that took place in Europe from about the eighteenth century onwards, which gave rise to the belief that history was entering a distinctive 'modern' era. This complex set of interlocking changes, part material practice and part mode of thought, has come to define what it meant by modernity.

Late-modern childhoods

It is to modernity that this chapter now turns and the modern context of childhood which, as the previous section established, is understood as a social construct (Jenks, 2005). Giddens (1990, p. 1) defines modernity as 'modes of social life or organisation which emerged in Europe from about the seventeenth century onwards and which subsequently became more or less worldwide in their influence'. Analyses of childhood in late modernity illustrate how images of childhood based on notions of innocence, naivety and dependence have led to increasing protection of and control over children (Prout, 2003), and the concept of risk itself is central to contemporary constructions of childhood (Scott and Jackson, 2000) as well as to modern discourses on children and mobile internet technologies. Recent sociological perspectives highlight how the concept of the child and childhood in late modernity shape our understandings of children and influence both policy and, more generally, adult control over contemporary children's social worlds. A central feature of modernity was the idealisation of the private sphere of the home (Slater, 1998), the expulsion of children from the public sphere, and the segregation of children and childhood into the home (Roche, 1999). However, the rapidly changing technological landscapes have blurred the boundaries between public and private spheres, and therefore dramatically altered the contours of risk in relation to childhood.

The relationship between modernity, risk and childhood thus underpins the analysis presented in this book which centres on childhood, everyday experiences and mobile internet technologies. As sociologists of modernity, the work of Beck (1992) and Giddens (1990, 1991), in relation to modernity and the *risk society*, is helpful here in terms of offering a theoretical framework for an explanation of a contemporary view of the world, its hazards and social change which shape and influence the lives and futures of individuals in contemporary society.

Beck's (1992, p. 19) argument is summed up in his opening lines:

> In advanced modernity the social production of wealth is systematically accompanied by the social production of risks. Accordingly, the problems and conflicts relating to distribution in a society of scarcity overlap with the problems and conflicts that arise from the production, definition and distribution of techno-scientifically produced risks.

It is the concept of distribution that is important to the argument presented here as 'innovations in information and communication technologies (ICT), intertwining with the field of culture and media, have opened a number of questions in understanding the nature of distribution, consumption and production of (cultural) goods and services' (Primorac and Jurlin, 2008, p. 71). Beck's (1992) claim that modernity is radically changing from an industrial society to a risk society stems from two historical developments: first, that genuine material need is reduced with human and technical productivity and through legal and welfare state provisions; second, that manufactured risk is an unintended consequence of industrialisation, as production in modernisation has led to unfamiliar hazards and potential threats. His ideas surrounding unfamiliar and potential hazards are highly apparent in current discourses on childhood and mobile technologies, which are framed in terms of risk. Risk is defined as:

> a systematic way of dealing with hazards and insecurities induced and introduced by modernization itself. Risks, as opposed to older dangers, are consequences which relate to the threatening force of modernization and to its globalization of doubt.
>
> (Beck, 1992, p. 21)

There are remarkable similarities between the work of Beck (1992) and Giddens (1990, 1991, 1999), and both describe high consequence risks which are 'not only undelimitable in space and time, but also in their incidence across social and economic divisions as characteristic of this historical phase' (Benton, 1999, p. 50). Giddens' background, however, is in sociology and psychology, and he is especially interested in the relationship between modernity and the individual's management of self-identity (Jary and Jary, 1995), which is helpful to gain an understanding of children's self-identity (see Chapter 5). Giddens (1990) concentrates on the central themes of security versus danger and trust versus risk, and outlines institutional transformations associated with modernity. He describes the greater opportunities created by social institutions within modernity, but, under a greater threat of conflict, as *a double-edged phenomenon*. Giddens (1991) explores these themes further, arguing that globalising tendencies of modern institutions are accompanied by a transformation in social life with profound implications for personal activities. He describes how institutionally structured risk environments, with rapidly developing and often contradictory specialised knowledge portrayed through media channels, contribute to the risk society. As awareness increases with the dynamic nature of knowledge, the notion of risk becomes central to society and to individuals as they reflexively construct their own life biographies. Risk is 'a more or less ever-present exercise, of a partly imponderable character...the risk climate of modernity is thus unsettling for everyone; no one escapes' (Giddens, 1991, p. 124).

The concept of risk is central to understanding childhood. Childhood is constructed as a time of innocence, vulnerability and dependence (Jenks, 2005), and, as argued earlier in this chapter, it is such images of childhood that are influential in shaping children's identities in public life (Harden, 2000). Scott et al. (1998, p. 690) suggest that risk anxiety 'managed through everyday practices provides a useful means of analysing contemporary fears about children and childhood'. Abstract conceptions of risk thus impact on children's everyday worlds though risk-management strategies employed by adults. Day-to-day family life and family relationships are marbled with differing constructions of risk. Backett-Milburn and Harden's (2004, pp. 445–46) study, for example, found that everyday family interactions 'shape, create and recreate how parents and children construct risk and risk anxiety', that they negotiated risk on an everyday basis and that their 'definitions of risk were fluid, contingent and contextual'. These negotiations are central to understanding childhood and mobile technologies as parents attempt to mediate their children's participation online (Ólafsson et al., 2013).

The importance of understanding risk in relation to understanding childhood has been emphasised by a now well-established body of literature that explores children's everyday experiences, as well as the more recent work on their everyday experiences online. For example, in 2001, the ESRC programme 'Children 5–16: Growing into the 21st century' published its findings and the research into aspects of child poverty was used to create better indicators of social change. The most comprehensive research on children and online experiences is the EU Kids Online research (see Livingstone et al., 2011a), which surveyed more than 25,000 children across Europe to investigate children's perceptions of risk in relation to the internet and how families view risks online. Hood et al. (1996a) suggested that parents and children conceptualise risk within public and private spheres, and Harden (2000) found that children are reflexive in their conceptualisations of risk. Arguably, perceptions of online risk now permeate contemporary family life and children's everyday experiences:

> In sum, contemporary families must negotiate a rapidly changing society without the traditional resources of established relations between generations, with parents neither benefiting from the experience of their own childhood nor having the moral right to impose rules and sanctions without democratic consultation.
>
> (Livingstone, 2009, p. 7)

Furthermore, risk and risk-management strategies have profound implications for self-identity as, through risk-profiling and adopting risk-taking behaviours, children achieve identity as individuals and as members of cultural groups (Green, 1997a). Therefore, 'the perception of "risk" is predicted on cultural, social and historical factors' (Lohmann and Mayer, 2009, p. 1). Stevens and Hassett (2007, p. 136) highlight the complex relationships in risk analyses and argue that, whilst not specifically dealing with complexity, the risk society analysis of 'Beck and his colleagues gives a sociological view that supports complexity concepts such as dissipative systems and working at the edge of chaos', which may be helpful in developing a more effective approach to child protection. This approach is also key to understanding approaches to protecting children online when considering the complexity of the relationships between people, mobile internet technologies and social media (see Chapter 6). Furlong and Cartmel (1997, p. 1), in their comprehensive examination of young people, risk and individualisation, argue:

> The life experiences of young people in modernised industrialised societies have changed quite significantly over the last two decades. These changes affect relationships with family and friends, experiences in education and the labour market, leisure and lifestyles and the ability to become established as independent young adults ... As a

consequence of these changes, young people today have to negotiate a set of risks which were largely unknown to their parents; this is true irrespective of social background or gender, moreover, as many of these changes have come about within a relatively short space of time, points of reference which previously helped smooth processes of social reproduction have become obscure. In turn, increased uncertainty can be seen as a source of stress and vulnerability.

As suggested above, it is the notion of vulnerability that has underpinned the drive for protection and, as perceptions of risk change, so do responses to risk management. The concept of individualisation associated with modernity has two very apparent consequences for current constructions of childhood – the individualisation of childhood and attitudes towards having children have also changed which has, arguably, altered family dynamics and relationships. It is, according to Giddens (1999, p. 60) 'a decision guided by psychological and emotional needs'. In late modernity, family structure has altered as a consequence of individualisation, and people are driven into bonding in a partnership, which is not a primeval need, but one which grows with the losses that individualisation brings (Beck, 1992). Parents who recollect a childhood unhindered by many of the concerns facing today's parents are anxious about traffic and stranger danger, and, indeed, worry about most aspects of their children's lives (O'Brien et al., 2000); and whilst parents are concerned about risks online, they are often unaware that their child has actually encountered risk (Livingstone et al., 2011a). As a consequence of individualisation, there is greater diversity in family types (Beck and Beck-Gernsheim, 2002) and Beck (1992, p. 118) suggests that the child is the 'source of the last remaining, irrevocable, unexchangeable primary relationship' and 'becomes the final alternative to loneliness'. Thus, late-modern society appears to have readopted the child as the site or the relocation of discourses concerning stability, integration and the social bond, and 'children are now seen not so much as "promise" but as primary and unequivocal sources of love, but also partners in the most fundamental, unchosen, unnegotiated form of relationship' (Jenks, 2005, p. 107).

In individualised society, qualitatively, new types of personal risk arise and today's risks derive from internal decisions that depend simultaneously on scientific and social construction: 'the social effect of risk definitions is therefore not dependent on their scientific validity' (Beck, 1992, p. 32). Livingstone and Haddon (2009) identified a complex spectrum of online risks associated with children's internet use and found that the risks that children identify as worrying them were often not those that adults were concerned about. (Un)successful risk-management strategies impact on identity as a bad/good parent (Green, 1997b). Increasingly, letting children roam or play outside unaccompanied in physical space is becoming a marker of neglectful or irresponsible parenthood (O'Brien et al., 2000), as also now in relation to online spaces and virtual worlds too and mediating children's activities online is associated with being a good parent (Ólafsson et al., 2013). Scott et al. (1998) suggest that discourses around parental responsibility heighten parental anxiety as parents are held responsible for their children's well-being and conduct, and are, thus, held accountable if their children are victimised or, indeed, if they victimise others. According to Elias (1994), members of an established group are hardly ever indifferent to the opinion of insiders, in whose monopolistic control they participate and with whom they share a common pride in the group charisma. However, Furedi (2002) argues that many aspects of what he terms *paranoid parenting* have little to do with the reality of children's lives, arguing that:

> This obsessive fear about the safety of children has led to a fundamental redefinition of parenting. Traditionally, good parenting has been associated with nurturing, stimulating, and socializing children. Today, it is associated with monitoring their activities. An inflated sense of risk prevails, demanding that children should never be left on their own and that preferably they should be within sight of one of their parents at all times.
>
> (Furedi, 2002, p. 5)

In contemporary society, we live our everyday lives amidst the almost constant reflexive monitoring of risk, which pervades our sense of how to manage ourselves and the world (Scott et al., 1998). Both parents and children conceptualise public space in terms of risk, and parents balance and negotiate the immediate with the longer-term risks in managing and controlling their children's lives (Hood et al., 1996a). Children are concerned about moving outside the private and local spheres physically (Harden, 2000; O'Brien et al., 2000) and about a variety of risks online (Livingstone et al., 2011a).

James et al. (2010) suggest that the opportunities for contemporary children to mix, socialise and learn face-to-face are restricted to institutional settings, which may have a profound effect on children's social interaction and social learning. O'Brien et al. (2000) argued previously, however, that, although modes of parental sponsorship create a closeted lifestyle where children are spatially segregated and chaperoned, this is one of the adaptations particular parents and children make to living in a more insecure world, and the general elaboration of the modern home has created a socio-sphere of enrichment rather than entrapment for many contemporary children. Online, children balance a diverse range of opportunities and interact, socialise and learn with a variety of risks (Livingstone and Helsper, 2010). Beck's (1992, p. 118) claim that 'the importance of the child is rising' is compounded by the social construction of childhood as a time of innocence, vulnerability and dependence (Jenks, 2005), and the child appears for public consumption as a victim (Roche, 1999). Children, the object of a great deal of social concern and increasing anxiety about risk, superimposed on a protective discourse, are located as vulnerable innocents to be shielded from the dangers of the wider social, implicitly adult, world (Scott et al., 1998) and now also the dangers of the online world.

Spaces of childhood

It is the notion of vulnerability that shapes the nature and the consequences of adult concerns and behaviours towards children in late-modern society, and which underpins much current discourse on childhood and mobile internet technologies. 'Children have become a source of our concerns about the nature of identity in a rapidly changing world' (James et al., 2010, p. 205) and the brief foray through the literature on the history of childhood detailed above clearly illustrates that the way in which childhood is understood and how children's everyday experiences have undergone radical changes over the centuries. It is important to remember, however, that historical analyses are specific to particular geographic, social and economic contexts, and that 'within any particular historical and social context there will be a normative and hegemonic concept of childhood against which children themselves are compared as individuals and collectives' (Wells, 2009, p. 16). Read (2010, p. 421) observes how the geography of urban spaces simultaneously began to obey the 'philosophy of separate spaces' and, whilst there are various recurring themes which dominate the cultural history of childhood in Western societies, one clear undisputed consequence of the changing constructions of childhood has been the 'separateness of childhood from the world of adults, with the young cooped up in schools, playgrounds, their own rooms and so on' (Heywood, 2005, p. 170). Children and adults have different perspectives on different environments, yet rarely can children challenge the dominant adult and established viewpoints; however:

> The poet, the artist, the sleuth – whoever sharpens our perception tends to be antisocial; rarely 'well-adjusted,' he cannot go along with currents and trends. A strange bond often exists among anti-social types in their power to see environments as they really are. This need to interface, to confront environments with a certain antisocial power, is manifest in the famous story, 'The Emperor's New Clothes.' 'Well-adjusted' courtiers, having vested interests, saw the emperor as beautifully appointed. The 'anti-social' brat, unaccustomed to the old environment, clearly saw the emperor 'ain't got nothin' on.' The new environment was clearly visible to him.
>
> (Emphasis in the original, McLuhan and Fiore, 1967, p. 88)

Access to online environments, social media and the availability of mobile technologies has changed the landscapes of childhood, and, according to Jones (2010), the complex interplay between space and identity has been the topic of much recent debate in relation to childhood. The following section of this chapter examines the 'taken for grantedness' of childhood as something separate from adulthood in relation to understanding contemporary discourses, and argues that the very separateness between childhood and adulthood is changing as the boundaries between the previously defined spaces of adulthood and childhood are becoming increasingly blurred. There has been much interest in the geographies of childhood in both the UK and in international contexts which interrogate both the separation and the integration of children and young people within diverse socio-spatial contexts (Holt, 2011).

The discussion here is around childhood and everyday life. Crouch (2010, p. 12) contends that 'space becomes highly contingent, emergent in the cracks of everyday life, affected by and affecting energies both human and beyond human limits'. Longhurst (2007) suggests that everyday life is sociologically significant and that social studies should focus on the mundane and the ordinary. However, 'there is widespread agreement among sociologists that everyday life is indeed difficult to capture, delimit and define, and that "the everyday" therefore continues to occupy an uncertain ontological position in social science' (Jacobsen, 2009, p. 9). Pink (2012) discusses considering how the places and practices of everyday life illustrate how it is situated within social, material, virtual, sensory and environmental contexts. The concept of childhood itself, when combined with the many different and varying spaces of childhood, intersects across the realities of children's experiences and emerges as a diversity or a multiplicity of childhoods. Ideas associated with the rural countryside, for example, exemplify how idealised discourses shape conceptions of childhood, and parents see it as a safer place to grow up, preferable to urban landscapes (Holloway and Valentine, 2000). Such idealised and often sentimentalised ideas remain faintly reminiscent of the thinking which underpinned the evaluation of children from the cities during World War II, but they are often in contrast and in contention to the perceptions that many contemporary young people hold in relation to the environments. Matthews and Tucker (2007, p. 105), for example, found that 'many rural villages in the Minority world are desolate places for young people, characterised more often by spatialities that exclude, marginalise and persecute'.

It is well acknowledged that there is a close relationship between space and place, which Massey (2005) highlights how it is through spaces and places that the social is constructed in the negotiation of relations in multiplicities. Cresswell (2004, p. 11) discusses the notion of place as a way of understanding and suggests that 'place is also a way of seeing, knowing and understanding the world. When we look at the world as a world of places we see different things. We see attachments and connections between people and place'. This way of using place as a viewing lens offers a useful metaphor for considering a further aspect to the complexity of childhood. 'Place is more than a geographical location – it is a space imbued with social and cultural meanings' (James and James, 2008, p. 131) and there is no starker example of the impact of place on experiences of childhood than the discourses on globalised childhoods (see, for example, UNICEF, 2012). The increasing inequalities of childhood and the realities of the lived experiences of children globally in the majority South and the minority North are examined by Penn (2005, p. xii), who argues:

In raising these contradictions and paradoxes I try to discuss how childhood is recognised, defined, catalogued and understood across the North and the South and in transitional countries. Early childhood in the North is commonly viewed as a time of playfulness and curiosity. However this perception co-exists with toleration of political and economic conditions that grossly undermine or evenly prematurely terminate the lives of millions of young children in the South.

Understanding childhood, therefore, is intersected with global and national as well as local and domestic conditions (Scourfield et al., 2006), such as urban and rural, poverty and inequality, and embodied with gender, (dis)ability and ethnicity, which all provide further compounding variables in both conceptualising childhood and children's lived experiences. There is not sufficient space here to offer an in-depth exploration of each of these categories of analysis and there are other volumes which do this well (see, for example, James and James, 2004; Prout, 2005; Qvortrup et al., 2011). However, the importance of contextualising the specific debates examined in the later chapters in this book within these broader, globalised and often political processes cannot be emphasised enough, and it is essential to recognise, as Aitken et al. (2007, p. 4) observe, 'the myriad of contributions of young people to global processes and the many ways that these contributions are hidden, subverted, or contrived through adultist machinations at the global and local level'.

James et al. (2010) contend that, in late modernity, the child remains a victim of public space where the outside is considered a risky place to be and, as I have already argued, debates on the spaces of childhood are underpinned by perceptions of risk which structure contemporary constructions of childhood and children's everyday lives. James and James (2001) suggest that contemporary moral discourses are tightening the Net of social control on children's lives to the extent that children have increasingly become the subjects of overt and covert regulation. Valentine (1996) suggested that opportunities for children to be relatively free from adult control have been greatly reduced and Ungar (2001) argued that, conceptually, the shifts in social control processes and in the nature and targets of social reactions are probably the most significant sociological developments associated with the risk society. As a result:

> the focus on safety has led to two contradictory results: the child is a victim who must be placed under surveillance for protection; and the child is an anti-social threat who must be placed under surveillance to protect society. From either perspective, the richness of the child's lived experience is lost.
>
> (Steeves and Jones, 2010, p. 187)

Holloway and Valentine (2000) highlight how the debates about spatiality in childhood are associated with places, sites in everyday life and the spatial imagery in ideologies of childhood generally. Public space has come to be defined as adult space, and children's participation in public space is controlled and limited by adults in a number of ways, from formal, often legal, restrictions on where children are allowed to go, parental restrictions on children's participation in and access to public life, restrictions on children's behaviour in public spaces, and many public amenities are geared towards adult use in terms of size (Harden, 2000). Elias (1994) is helpful here in furthering understanding of how the exclusion and stigmatisation of an outsider group by an established one can be powerful weapons adopted by an established group to maintain its identity, assert superiority and keep the outsider group firmly in its place. Jenks (2005) develops Foucault's ideas of spatial control to suggest that the exercise and manipulation of space is a primary example of adults controlling the child's world, and suggests that the postmodern diffusion of authority has not led to democracy but to an experience of powerlessness, which is not a potential source of identity but a prescription for victimisation, and children figure largely as symbolic representations of this welter of uncertainty, both literally and metaphorically.

Parents are becoming increasingly afraid about a diversity of social and environmental dangers to their children lurking in the public realm, not least dangers from other children, which means that parents are now seeking to prevent their children from having contact with anything but the most controlled and sanitised of public spaces (Philo, 2000). Online, many parents actively mediate their child's internet use, which is, in turn, related to lower risk and, therefore, lower harm (Duerager and Livingstone, 2012). However, Scott et al. (1998) argue that risk anxiety, engendered by the desire to keep children safe, frequently has negative consequences for children themselves and curtails children's activities in ways which may restrict their autonomy and their opportunities to develop the necessary skills to cope with the world. In relation to online use, Duerager and Livingstone (2012, p. 1) state: 'parental restrictions work by limiting children's internet use in general. Thus they also reduce children's online opportunities such as learning, communication, participation and fun'. In the wider context, however, Prout (2000) observes that only a few children are so tightly controlled in this parenting process and suggests that, for many children, it involves a high degree of negotiation with parents keen to protect their children from the real and supposed dangers of the street but also anxious to maximise their children's accumulation of informal cultural and social capital. Interestingly, in Duerager and Livingstone's (2012, p. 2) analysis of parents, '89% impose rules about whether their child can give out personal information online; 82% talk to their children – especially their daughters – about what they do on the internet; and 59% stay nearby when their child is online'.

Whilst anxieties about risk may be shaped by public discussions, it is individuals who cope with these uncertainties and central to this is the individual reflexive monitoring of risk. However, it is possible to question, in relation to children, whether all individuals are regarded as equally reflexive. Public debates on risk rarely include children's own opinions, and risks to children are defined and managed by adults on children's behalf, and, therefore, the element of choice, responsibility and reflexivity accredited to adults in relation to risk is frequently denied to children (Harden, 2000; Roche, 1999). The discourses on risk now extend to virtual spaces and the online digital places that children inhabit (Buckingham, 2007; Livingstone, 2009; Livingstone et al., 2011a). Spaces of childhood are changing and children are spending more and more time online. 'Nearly half of European children go online in their bedroom, and one third go online on a mobile phone or hand-held device. Given the rise of privatised and mobile access, it is difficult for parents to closely regulate their children's safety' (Duerager and Livingstone, 2012, p. 1). This is highly pertinent to the analysis presented in this book as conceptually the shift in the separateness of childhood from the adult world associated with modernity based on protecting the innocence of childhood and managing risk in public space has come to bear on the virtual world also. Livingstone's (2002) examination of the complicated interplay between social change, children, public anxieties and new media, suggests that the growing body of research in this area is increasingly informed by children themselves. However, the terms associated with work in this area – audiences, children and young people, users and contexts of use and new media – she suggests, remain somewhat contested and her discussion emphasises the complexity of contemporary media environments and children's everyday lives:

> We can no longer imagine living our daily lives – at leisure or at work, with family or friends – without media or communication technologies. Nor would we want to. As we enter the twenty-first century the home is being transformed into the site of a multimedia culture, integrating audiovisual, information and telecommunication services. There is much more discussion of the potential benefits of the ever-more significant, ever-more multifunctional electronic screen. Media headlines regularly focus on the possible

consequences – e-commerce, the virtual classroom, global consumer culture, cyber-democracy, and so forth. And public anxieties keep pace, reflecting a widespread concern with the kind of society that today's children will grow up to live in as adults. Hence, there is a speculation about 'the digital generation', 'children in the information age', 'computer nerds', 'innocents on the net', the 'digital divide' and 'addicted surfers'.

(Livingstone, 2002, pp. 1–3)

Valentine and Holloway (2001) emphasise that there have been two dominant themes which support two sides of the technology debate in relation to young people: the highly optimistic and positive approach taken by Tapscott (1998); for example, dominated by notions of the future currently reflected in the UK government's approach to ICT in education; and, conversely, the negative, very pessimistic viewpoint voiced early in the debate by Postman (1993) that technology is putting children at risk and destroying childhood itself. These debates form the basis for the discussion in Chapter 6, which examines risk and the consideration given in Chapter 7 on learning and the diversity of children's everyday experiences. Given the range of competencies and functions required of a complex modern society, children must be encouraged to develop a range of evaluative and interpretative skills (Smith, 2000). However, inequalities in children's lived experiences remain. Green (1997a) suggests that to deny responsibility for risk management would be to deny competence as an individualised expert in the risk society. The technological contexts of contemporary everyday lives are blurring the boundaries of the notion of expert (Keen, 2007). Roche (1999) argued that children are social actors with much to contribute here and now, and that the language of children's rights is about respecting and valuing the contribution children make, and have to make, to the world children and adults share, a world hitherto defined and imagined primarily in adult terms – it is about power. Their arguments are represented in the methodological developments in researching childhood, technology and children's experiences outlined in Chapter 4, but also have a bearing on the argument presented in understanding childhood as:

Being a child is no longer, even if it ever was, simply a matter of being shaped by adult controlled institutions. If individualization processes continue then children will become ever more recognised as the active interpreters and co-producers of their own lives and hence of the communities and societies of which they are part.

(Prout, 2000, p. 313)

Theorising childhood

'The idea that children have rights is a modern one' (Archard and Macleod, 2002, p. 3) and O'Brien et al. (2000) and Honig (2011) suggest that the globalisation of children's rights has had an impact on all aspects of children's lives, from their relationship with their parents to their participation in school and other social institutions. Developments in standpoint feminism and the influence of individualisation as 'the tendency for contemporary children to be seen as having a voice in determining their lives and shaping their identity' are important aspects of recent advances in studying childhood (Christensen and Prout, 2005, p. 53), and it is now well recognised that children generate their own understandings of the world and of culture in response to the structures and images which surround them (James et al., 2010).

Much recent literature explores how children see the world, their values and priorities and the ways in which they themselves feel marginalised – and the child has become a research subject (Roche, 1999 and Chapter 4, this book). In their critique of the socially developing child (the child viewed through the lens of developmental psychology and socialisation theory as incomplete – the becoming adult), James et al. (2010) propose four new ways or discourses of seeing 'the child' – the social structural child; the socially constructed child; the tribal child and the child as a minority group. These are not conceptualised as separate but more as an analytical framework which views the child as being, 'a person, a status, a course of action, a set of needs, rights or differences – in sum, as a social actor' (James et al., 2010, p. 207). 'Sociology has, historically, been comfortable to study "being", understood as full members of the social world, while developmental psychology has studied the "becomings", each of which is understood to have at least a toe in raw, unprocessed nature' (Lee, 2008, p. 58). Arneil (2002, p. 75) observes that 'children's rights theorists have attempted to overcome the status of children as "becomings", arguing that children, like adults, are "beings" or in Kantian terms "ends in themselves" '. Indeed, James et al. (2010) argue that, rather than thinking of children as *becoming* adults, they are now finally beginning to be understood as *beings* in their own right and the notion of the adult as the expert in children's lives has been interrogated. In their discussion of the development of the social studies of childhood, for example, Gallacher and Kehily (2013, p. 239) suggest that:

> by the turn of the twenty-first century, the new social studies of childhood had become an established framework for the sociocultural study of childhood. It could no longer be reasonably referred to as a 'new' or 'emergent' paradigm struggling against dominant models of 'socialization' or 'development'; it had become the dominant paradigm in the field. As a result, a set of critiques of this, now dominant, paradigm began to emerge and scholars began to investigate ways of proceeding in the light of them.

The social studies of childhood as an international and interdisciplinary field of research is now well established and well recognised in the scientific and public policy community (Qvortrup, 2005), and the influence of children's rights, according to Honig (2011), was an important element in its success. The conceptual shift attributed to the social study of childhood has not only challenged the previous dominance of developmental psychology in studying childhood but has also brought about a reflexive turn in *how* we study early childhood (see Chapter 4), and contemporary anthropologists have been heavily influenced by the United Nations Convention of the Rights of the Child (UNCRC) (Montgomery, 2013, p. 186).

The children's rights debate also extends to online as Savirimuthu (2011) suggests the current and developing policy initiatives and educational awareness programmes in relation to e-safety have both legal and social obligations that adhere to the principles of the UNCRC. Yet, as with wider philosophical debates in children's rights, the relationship between the child-protection discourses and participation is often problematic.

James (2010) argues that childhood studies was at a 'crossroads' and that future directions need to be interrogated in light of the critique put forward by Qvortrup (2005) and others on the complexity and multiplicity of the diversities of childhoods. James (2010, p. 497) uses the metaphor of weaving, of recognising the different elements of 'warp' and of 'weft' that constitute different patterns of fabric and suggests:

> The conceptualisation of childhood studies in this way might therefore offer a way forward for childhood studies as an interdisciplinary project, offering the prospect of a structure within which currently competing and even politically contradictory perspectives can be

woven into the fabric of childhood studies, in a way that enables the apparent tensions between them to make a constructive contribution to the structure of the fabric. It also provides a framework within which we can confidently engage in the analysis of some of the more difficult issues, such as the significance of different ages within childhood, without jeopardizing the project as a whole. In the process, it will ensure the continued academic rigour and theoretical development of childhood studies, without the need for creating and sustaining false dichotomies, or sacrificing the potential political power that comes from the recognition of childhood as a single social category, which must be distinguished from adulthood.

Previously, in *The Future of Childhood*, Prout (2005) argued that understanding childhood, a complex phenomenon, is limited by dualistic discourse and that contemporary childhoods in postmodernity are marked by dissolving boundaries and heightened ambiguity, and that new conceptual frameworks are required in the study of childhood. One such framework, he suggests, is offered by ANT. Actor-network terms and concepts influence many disciplines; for example: organisational theory, geography, medical anthropology and psychology (Brown and Capdevila, 1999). ANT has had an impact on social science and the sociology of scientific knowledge (Prout, 1996), the social shaping of technology (MacKenzie and Wajcman, 1999 and Chapter 4, this book) and education (Fenwick and Edwards, 2010). As already proposed, there is a complex relationship between childhood, mobile internet technologies and children's everyday experiences, and in current child-protection debates (Stevens and Hassett, 2007). Strathern (1999) demonstrates the applicability of ANT models to the practical understanding of what otherwise would seem a heterogeneous collection of materials and, according to Murdoch (2001), an apparent ambition of ANT is interdisciplinary thinking. Gomart and Hennion (1999) suggest that the notion of 'actants' facilitates exploration of the heterogeneity of elements, which impact the course of things, and, in allowing the types of relations between the elements of a network to multiply far beyond traditional sociological terms such as power, domination, strategy etc., ANT has exceeded sociological explanations in which action refers to structures within the agent (cognitive, psychological) or structures which surround the agent (social class, cultural paradigms).

'ANT is committed to demonstrating that the elements bound together in a network (including the people) are constituted and shaped by their involvement with each other' (Lee and Brown, 1994, p. 774). This concept of *network*, according to Prout (2005), offers a language of ordering that stands between the polar oppositions put forward by modernist social theory. In following these networks along their length, 'network theory is quite simple' and provides a grounded theory approach (Murdoch, 1997, p. 322). Both natural and social entities come into being as a result of the complex relations (or networks) that link them together and, in viewing the world through this prism of the (heterogeneous) network, ANT attempts to demonstrate that nature and society are 'outcomes rather than causes and these great and powerful categories emerge from a complex set of relations' (Murdoch, 2001, p. 120).

Roche (1999) suggests that children, despite being social actors, are often rendered silent and invisible by the attitudes and practices of adult society. Childhood, as discussed earlier in this chapter, remains a form of social subordination (Scott and Jackson, 2000) and, as Scott et al. (1998) point out, children's participation in constructing their own everyday world takes place within the constraints set by their subordinate location in relation to adults – as children's understanding of what it means to be a child has been shaped by their interaction with more powerful, adult social actors with pre-existing, albeit negotiable, ideas about childhood and children. ANT incorporates the question of the nature of belonging into different domains and it allows the concepts of dependency and belonging to be applied recursively (Lee and Stanner, 1999). Drawing on Latour's (1993) approach to modernity as a form of belonging, guaranteed through excluding certain characters (hybrids), ANT dissolves boundaries imposed to bring the 'other' back into belonging and endorses democracy (Strathern, 1999) as it does not exclude the 'other' in its attempt to cross ontological boundaries in recognising the rights of non-human entities. If we recognise that within a network of interdependencies each actant plays a role in the production of reality, we should work towards an inclusive network (Lee and Stanner, 1999). Law (1999, p. 9) notes 'what is interesting are matters, questions, and issues arising out of, or in relation to, actor-network, and the various approaches to thinking materiality, ordering, distribution and hierarchy with which it interacts'. Recent social changes have, according to Prout (2003), altered the conditions and experiences of childhood, destabilising previous ideas, and the current climate offers a context for understanding the emergence of the children's voices. As Latour (1999, p. 19) observes, 'actors know what they do and we have to learn from them not only what they do, but how and why they do it', thus making it possible for new actors (actants) to define the world in their own terms, using their own dimensions and signs. Carrabine (2008) argues that this shift towards the local within an increasing awareness of diversity and the acceptance of multiple realities perspectives reflects Stones' observation on postmodernist approaches:

> for respecting the existence of a plurality of perspectives, as against a notion that there is one single truth from a privileged perspective; local, contextual studies in place of grand narratives; an emphasis on disorder, ?ux and openness, as opposed to order, continuity and restraint.
>
> (Stones, 1996, p. 22 cited in Carrabine, 2008)

Conceptually, therefore, these arguments would appear to be beneficial in supporting some of the key aspects which emerged from within the social studies of childhood paradigm viewing children as experts in their own lives, the children's rights-based approach to participation and the development of new research methodologies towards such participation and inclusion (as outlined in Chapter 4). Furthermore, in examining the acknowledgement of the rise of childhood agency, (as discussed by James et al., 2010), Latour and Law developed through ANT a useful explanatory framework (Lee, 2001a). It suggests that the more agency and independence a person appears to have, the more dependent they are on a network for their power and identity (Lee, 1998). Similar to Law's (1994, p. 384) view on agency that it is not something that people possess but an effect generated by a 'network of heterogeneous, interacting materials', Latour's (1999) account of Louis Pasteur illustrates how the concept of agency and independence is challenged, and paradoxically accounted for, by dependence and incompleteness, and since agency is no longer conceived of as a simple possession it is exposed to empirical study and analysis. A helpful example of this is provided by Lee (2001b, p. 130) in his analysis of the role of technology in enabling children to give evidence in court through video:

> The child witness becomes more agentic and can pass as more self-present as more 'actors' are added to their network. Video camera, videotape, television screens, and the police and social workers who help children to produce their testimony all contribute to redistributing the burden of childhood ambiguity so that it does not all come to rest on child witnesses' shoulders.

Whilst children cannot be seen as entirely autonomous (Craig, 2003), by adopting the metaphor of network, childhood can be seen as a 'collection of different, sometimes competing and conflicting, heterogeneous orderings' (Prout, 2005, p. 71). Aspects of ANT, therefore, will be helpful to the debates that are presented in this book and to our understanding of childhood, mobile technologies and everyday experiences. Social processes and technology are, thus, interrelated and we need to understand the complex relationships between children's social worlds, childhood as a cultural phenomenon and technologies (Hutchby and Moran-Ellis, 2001). However, as argued above, childhood is not given but open to continual revaluation and vulnerable to changing definitions of what is normal and acceptable, and changing concerns indicate the process of understanding and reconstructing childhood is not a continuing but 'continually novel historical phenomenon' (Smith, 2000, p 4). Lee (2001b) illustrates how children have become separated through a set of practices, people, policies and protecting them from undesirable influences:

> Children under preservation became part of the network that linked them to reasons of state and challenged their agency into their development, socialization and education. The conventional view of children as dependent that emerged was part of this actor network.
>
> (Lee, 2001b, p. 132)

Conclusion

This chapter has outlined how childhood, as a social and cultural construction, is understood as a complex phenomena. The debates presented in this book concur with Gane's (2004) argument that the social, technological and natural processes that characterise contemporary social life all intersect and hybridise profusely. According to Cloke and Jones (2005, p. 313), 'childhood is a highly differentiated category, varying across and between culture, age, gender, class, ethnicity, family structure, individual disposition and so on' and they draw on Deleuze to suggest that the spaces of childhood should be viewed as 'constantly ebbing and flowing contested constructions and deconstructions'.

This chapter has examined how the changing social and cultural constructions of childhood, that ebb and flow with space and time, are central to understanding the context of contemporary children's everyday lives. Historical analyses illustrate how conceptions of childhood are influenced by dominant ideologies, wider political and economic forces, and prevailing social conditions. Globalised influences associated with the risk society and the increasingly recognised importance of the UNCRC have changed both academic approaches to and political perspectives on childhood, but these developments intersect with more micro-level and localised economies and social structures. Thus, it is understood in terms of diversity, inequality and multiplicity, and it is argued that the individualising tendencies of late modernity have also altered understandings of childhood and (some) children's social position in society and in academic discourse as summarised eloquently by Prout (2005, p. 2):

> Childhood, then, like all phenomena, is a heterogeneous, complex and emergent, and, because this is so, its understanding requires a broad set of intellectual resources, an interdisciplinary approach and an open-mined process of enquiry.

This chapter set out to examine some examples drawn from a wide set of seemingly relevant intellectual resources and it has attempted to adopt such an interdisciplinary perspective. Inspired by previous approaches to understanding childhood and technology (for example, see Buckingham, 2000; Livingstone and Bober, 2004; Livingstone et al., 2011; Selwyn, 2003), the analysis presented here recognises the interrelationship between children and technology and perceptions of risk, and considers the implications of understanding aspects of an ANT lens (see Latour, 1999; Law, 1991; Callon, 1999) to understanding childhood, mobile internet technologies and everyday experiences. It is to technology that the next chapter turns and it is argued that there can be no distinction between social relations and technology, as they are mutually exclusive and inextricable.

3
Understanding Technology

Introduction

Rule (2002, p. 242) outlines key theoretical models that have previously shaped knowledge of communication technologies, and proposes that 'if we are to grasp the role of technology in the changing social world, it helps to take stock of where the concepts for understanding that role come from'. Drawing on his suggestion, this third chapter explores the theoretical literature on technology to broaden the previous conceptual framework on understanding childhood, outlined in Chapter 2, and clarifies emerging themes and categories in light of other social phenomena. The rapidity with which children and young people are gaining access to online, convergent, mobile and networked technologies is unprecedented in the history of technological innovation and diffusion (Ólafsson et al., 2013, p. 6). In order to understand the claim made by Ólafsson and her colleagues above, some consideration of the history of technological innovation and diffusion is required, and theoretically how this history has been and is understood. This approach is important as, rather than consider each technology as a separate entity with different characteristics, Rice (1999) argues that it is important to have a broader understanding of media technologies and that it is essential to consider both the consistencies and the inconsistencies. He suggests that it is beneficial to study attributes of media in general, and the paradoxes created by both new and familiar media. ' "Media" is a term that refers to technologies (print, radio, television, sound recording and such like) through which content created for groups or consumers is moved and organised' (Küng et al., 2008, p. 7).

The previous chapter discussed perspectives on understanding childhood and considered how childhood, understood as a social and cultural construction, is a complex phenomenon. It argued that the concept of risk and risk anxiety are important to understanding the social construction of contemporary childhood and children's everyday lives. MacKenzie and Wajcman (1999) contend that everyday life is entwined with various technologies which are fundamental to the contemporary human condition and, according to Kellner (1995, p. 3), 'media culture has come to dominate everyday life, serving as the ubiquitous background and often highly seductive foreground of our attention and activity'. This chapter reflects on aspects of contemporary everyday life and how previous approaches to studying various technologies have influenced both contemporary debate and current approaches to understanding media, culture and mobile internet technologies and childhood.

The term 'technology' is in itself, however, difficult to define, but usually it is based on the idea that a technology is an application of scientific knowledge for practical purposes. There is a growing plethora of mobile technologies – smartphones, tablets, e-readers and laptops, for example – which can access the internet, and have an array of applications (Apps) and downloaded media content, such as text, images, sound and video. These mobile technologies can also produce content – user-generated content (UGC), which can be uploaded, published online and shared for others to view and/or download or comment on. 'The term "user-generated content" was first used in 2005, reflecting the various kinds of media content produced by users, uploaded online and publically available' (such as blogging, podcasting, videos and so on) (Varbanova, 2008, p. 167). Thus, 'digital culture is described as participatory culture where users do not only consume information but also contribute to it in a variety of ways' (Uzelac, 2008, p. 17). Lyon (1995) actually questions whether the defining technology idea is even appropriate for the purposes of social and cultural analyses, and Jin (2011) proposes that we need to change the narrow way that we think of technology to thinking about it in a broader sense and he distinguishes between 'hard technology' and 'soft technology':

> Simply technology is the means and tools of 'problem solving'. There are two types of 'problem solving': one is concerned with tangible things such as products, and the other is concerned with intangible phenomena such as processes. We can call the former 'hard technology' and the latter 'soft technology'.
>
> (Jin, 2011, p. 45)

Arthur (2009) is also concerned with the often overlapping and some-times contradictory meanings associated with the term 'technology' and he draws on a wide range of technologies to argue that they are both mechanistic and organic simultaneously. Technology is understood to be blurring the boundaries between time and space, public and private, human and non-human in late modernity, but further consideration is needed here in terms of what we actually mean by 'technology'. Küng et al. (2008), for example, helpfully distinguish between the terms 'digital' and the 'internet'. They suggest that 'the term "digital" refers to a technology that stores data in binary form' . . . 'the term "internet" refers to a distribution of information' . . . 'and "digitalization" means mathematically reducing all types of information into a binary form' (Küng et al., 2008, p. 3). The term 'convergence' is associated with new media and the late-modern condition, and it is, they argue, digitalisation rather than the internet which enables convergence. 'Digitalization has triggered many changes in the last two decades' and 'with the convergence of (tele)communication and information technologies, new possibilities for interaction are being established. These possibilities allow the swift flow of symbols across borders that cause (among other things) processes of hybridization of cultural forms and (local) cultural change' (Primorac and Jurlin, 2008, p. 71). Lyon (1995) proposes that the phenomenon of technological convergence is significant, and Jenkins (2006, p. 2) suggests that convergence is 'the flow of content across multiple media platforms, the cooperation between multiple media industries, and the migratory behaviour of media audiences who will go almost anywhere in search of the kinds of entertainment experiences they want'.

Appadurai's (1996) notion of the complexity of mediascapes, which refers to both the global distribution of media and the images/ideologies conveyed through media and cultural landscapes based on the complicated interplay between economy, culture and politics, is also helpful to the analysis presented here. Furthermore, 'cultures are made up of communication processes' (Castells, 2000, p. 403) and the nature and purpose of the first section of this chapter is to outline the development of older but still-familiar technologies, drawing on the development of the telephone and the television as examples. According to Buchner (1988), they represent two basic types of communication – public/private and one-way/two-way – and consideration is given to the main differences and similarities in their adoption and use within everyday life. This chapter also looks at the history of the internet before considering theoretical perspectives on understanding technology. Jin

(2011, p. 15) suggests that 'in the twenty-first century, human beings have entered into an era of the integrated development of the humanities, social sciences and the natural sciences resulting in the elevation of human awareness of knowledge'. The approach adopted throughout this book is one of plurality – a multidisciplinary plurality – which does not attempt to sit entirely within a particular body of literature. This analysis draws on approaches from socio-technical studies as well as media studies, sociology, geography and anthropology. This chapter outlines previous academic approaches to understanding technology and everyday life. I draw on Matthewman's (2011) preference for 'theoretical plurality' to argue that children's experiences with new mobile technologies cannot be understood as 'online' or 'offline' or 'virtual' or 'real'. Küng et al. (2008, p. 17) also suggest that a multi-lensed approach is beneficial as it has 'been shown to yield richer and deeper understanding of complex phenomena'. The approach presented here also endeavours to strive to overcome what Prout (2005) describes as unhelpful dualisms associated with childhood and technology, and it acknowledges that children are using multiple platforms of mobile communication and social networks often simultaneously and interchangeably. It is these complex everyday experiences which need to be understood. Castells (2000, p. 4) states that:

> we must treat technology seriously, using it as the point of departure of this inquiry; we need to locate the process of revolutionary technological change in the social context in which it takes place and by which it is shaped; and we should keep in mind that the search for identity is as powerful as techno-economic change in charting the new history.

The importance of the historical

Krug (2005) discusses the differences between technologies of communication in the past and in the present, and Matthewman (2011, p. 81) argues that 'technological activity is a process informed by past performances and reactions to them', and that discourses arise from technological knowledge, performances and responses.

> This move from 'old, traditional, mass media' to 'new, digital and interactive' media, from passive and homogenised audience towards active, fragmented audiences, and their influences on the conceptualization of the public sphere, are some of the crucial concepts that

need to be viewed from a historical perspective in order to understand the ways in which these seemingly dichotomous categories interplay in a manner of continuity.

(Popović and Hromadžić, 2008, p. 44)

Thus, 'technology and society do not coincide. History undermines ontology' (Silverstone, 1999, p. 10) and the study of media is older than is generally recognised (Briggs and Burke, 2001). It is argued that media culture is important to understanding the human adventure and 'individuals spend tremendous amounts of time listening to the radio, watching television, going to see films, experiencing music, going shopping, reading magazines and newspapers, and participating in these and other forms of media culture' (Kellner, 1995, p. 3). However, 'technologies do not simply appear on the scene, fully developed and ready to be implemented' (Croteau and Hoynes, 2003, p. 314) and 'even old media were at one time new' (Stöber, 2004, p. 484). Parker (1973) claimed that, in order to understand the social history of communication, contemporary and ongoing changes, socio-technological analyses should take account of the historical context, and Oudshoorn et al. (2004) draw on the concept of path dependence to highlight the importance of history on future developments.

Willmore (2002) describes how the development of modern systems of information and communication began with the Gutenberg printing press in the fifteenth century, progressing through the pre-paid postal system, electric telegraph and telephone in the nineteenth century, radio and television broadcasting in the twentieth century and, most recently, the internet, and he discusses government responses to these developments. 'Mass knowledge and mass "truth" had their origins in the rise of the newspapers of the nineteenth century' (Krug, 2005, p. xiv). As such, technology 'weakened the ability of governments to control access to literature and news and the challenge of the internet, therefore, is much the same as the challenges of earlier innovations in ICT, beginning with the printing press in the fifteenth century' (Willmore, 2002, p. 96). Consideration of the political, economic and social climate is essential to illustrate how 'a technology system is shaped by politics, regulations, and economic circumstances within prevailing social conditions' (Kim and Sawhney, 2002, p. 299).

Thus, 'the new emerges out of the past but also in a disruptive relation to it' (Poster, 1999, p. 12), and Lehman-Wilzig and Cohen-Avigdor's (2004) natural life-cycle model of new media evolution emphasises the interaction and strain between old and new media. This notion of social transformation resulting from change in the productive system is not new and, although it was central to Marx's argument that technological developments are fundamental to capitalism and associated aspects of social life, others 'have been more sceptical about the social and political progressive qualities attributed to science and technology' (Smart, 1992, p. 30). For Matthewman (2011), however, Marx's theoretical contribution is significant in that he proposed a materialist approach and highlighted the role of technology in industrial capitalism. He was, according to Matthewman (2011, p. 47), 'amongst the earliest social theorists to consider the politics of artefacts, and to give due attention to the crucial issues of technological ownership and control' and 'contemporary actor-network theorists' writings seldom eclipse Marx's descriptions of the ways in which machines help to structure social relations of production'. Fischer (1992) also discusses the liberating aspects of technologies and how concerns and moral debates around new technologies that mark Western modernisation have historically arisen and are associated with wider concerns about modernity itself. In his book *Taken for Grantedness*, Ling (2012) uses the examples of the clock, the car and the mobile phone to examine how technical systems have become embedded into our society. My approach here is also to use familiar examples in examining the social adoption of familiar technologies – that of the telephone, the television and the internet – the following section compares previous perspectives to examining technologies in society before exploring the strengths and limitations of the approaches adopted. McLuhan (1964, p. 24) differentiates between 'hot' and 'cold' media and suggests:

> There is a basic principle that distinguishes a hot medium like radio from a cool one like the telephone, or a hot medium like the move from a cool one like TV.... hot media are, therefore, low in participation, and cool media are high in participation or completion by the audience. Naturally, therefore, a hot medium like radio has very different effects on the user than a cool medium like the telephone.

The telephone

Informed by an interest in teaching deaf children, the artificial reproduction of vowel sounds and an understanding of electricity and magnetism, the telephone was invented by Alexander Graham Bell and patented in 1876. Bell's perception of the telephone as a conversational rather than a broadcasting device resulted in the telephone system that still exists today (Etheredge, 1998). According to Dant (1999, p. 161), 'telephones are ordinary, practical objects that do nothing else but mediate by allowing humans to communicate through the auditory channel by talking'. Its developmental history is, however, characteristically slow, uneven and divided – a pattern that remains in contemporary developing countries (Walsham, 1983). Whilst the social effects of technologies are complex and contingent (MacKenzie and Wajcman, 1999), 'historians, social scientists, journalists, and current commentators have given us very few significant forecasts or analyses on the telephone's social effects' (Pool, 1997, p. 185). A key element of material culture, both functionally and emblematically (Fischer, 1992), originating from *tele* (at a distance) and *phonic* (sound), the telephone is a 'pervasive, yet unstudied communication medium' (Wellman and Tindall, 1993, p. 64). The telephone is of fundamental importance in everyday life and has become a taken-for-granted two-way communication, but it has remained largely invisible to scholars (Moyal, 1995) and there has been, surprisingly, a remarkably small amount of social science research on the telephone (Rice, 1999).

A review of the relevant literature, including Fischer's (1992) comprehensive account of the introduction of the telephone, how people use it and its role in everyday life, suggests that the telephone signified a radical change in personal communication. Pool's highly influential analysis of the telephone as a technology of freedom outlines three eras of communication during the past 150 years: traditional methods of communication in pre-modern or peasant societies, one-way mass communication to national audiences and the emerging era of telecommunications (Etheredge, 1998). During the emerging era, Bell's creations, although inspired, were met with dichotomous responses from the press, ranging from appreciative amazement to substantial anxiety and uncertainty (these reactions are also visible in more contemporary debates on mobile internet technologies' uptake and usage), and, according to Pool, some key lessons on the impact of new technologies and whether the 'effects' differ in different periods depend on saturation of new technology and other available technologies (Etheredge, 1998).

The telephone's invention alone did not chart its future trajectory as many other additional inventions were needed. Artle and Averous' (1973) theoretical analysis of the telephone system shows a self-sustaining growth process in demand, explained in the distribution of income and by the 'public-good' aspect of the telephone system, yet concerns over access versus no access and issues of equity were raised. In the UK, the telephone remained a luxury (Etheredge, 1998) confined to the elite upper classes and it was not until the birth of the public call office, which brought the telephone, in a cabinet located in public places, to members of society to whom the telephone had been little more than a rumour. Whilst this development widened access to the telephone service, Marvin (1988) observes how telephone subscribers were against the idea of public telephones; of allowing others to join the network and the invasion of the privacy of their homes. Interestingly, these points, although relating to the historical development of the telephone, are also reflected in more recent accounts in particular contexts. Zimmerman Umble (1992), for example, details the concerns over the intrusive nature of the telephone by unwanted outsiders on family life, which continue within the Amish community where telephones remain a community resource positioned in a public space and not within family homes. The wider social, cultural and political context of everyday life, therefore, is significant in understanding both the adoption and everyday use of technology.

Singh (2001), however, argues that the telephone is seen as a tool for personal communication and not a technology. This observation is important as the technological network requires the human-network function. It is important to remember the human-factor link in the success of the telephone. Crabb (1999) points out that the very usefulness of the telephone network depended on people obeying the rule to answer and reliability in answering the telephone, occasioned by a technological necessity, became the social norm. Zimmerman Umble (1992) draws on Marvin's (1988) conception of new technologies, not as objects of transformation either positive or negative, but as social interactions which are altered and adapted with the introduction of a new method of communicating. During the development and take-up of new media, people attempt to fit new media into old conventions or build up new ones (Rice, 1999). Whilst, initially, it was feared that, in introducing the telephone into homes, face-to-face interaction would be pushed aside in favour of quicker, easier means, in telephone use a pattern merges of augmentation and the telephone is viewed as one of several means to achieve sociability (Robinson and Kestnbaum, 1999).

The telephone mediates between people in different places (Dant, 1999). Telephone conversations are usually private one-to-one exchanges and, whilst the telephone plays an important role in social networks, this role is complex and multifaceted, as the telephone is used by different people in different relationships and in different circumstances for different reasons and purposes (Wellman and Tindall, 1993). Kline and Pinch (1999) suggest that it is important to show how social groups shape technology and also how the identities of social groups are reconstituted in the process. In her study of women's use of the telephone in Australia, Moyal (1995) claims that the female culture of telephone use forms a key dynamic of society. Fischer (1988) explores gender differences in telephone use and the social meaning of understanding those differences, and argues that some technologies have been exploited by women for gender-linked, social and personal ends. He suggests that 'women "appropriated" a practical, supposedly masculine technology for distinctively feminine ends and that this "gendering" of the telephone may have simultaneously reinforced gender differences' and also 'amplified women's abilities to attain both their normatively prescribed and personally preferred ends' (Fischer, 1988, p. 212). Women used the telephone not only for their role as homemaker, but also for their own social purposes to converse with family and friends. Also of note here is Smoreda and Licope's (2000, p. 238) claim that 'women's inclination to use the telephone at home has generally been explained by the gender distribution of family role and by women's investment in private life and intimate relationships' but many factors, including 'division of household labour, division of family roles, and differences in composition of social networks, gender identities and interaction styles, contribute to the gender specific use of the telephone'. Their research suggests that it is not only gender that influences telephone use, but also variations in topic and relationship.

From the brief historical account of the telephone presented here, it is apparent that both historical and cultural contexts shape the meaning of the telephone for different groups in society. Zimmerman Umble (1992, p. 183) observes that 'the meanings of technologies, old and new, are culturally constructed and negotiated in the service of particular values and needs'. It is this notion that also further informs current discourse and the debates set out in later chapters of this book, and that, as Myerson (2001, p. 7) suggests, 'however obvious it may sound, what is occurring is the mobilisation of that old telephone'.

The television

By way of comparison, the television model is also historically familiar, an economically successful model, and an important 'control mechanism for the production, distribution and consumption of information' (Kim and Sawhney, 2002, p. 228). However, by way of contrast to the telephone, emerging as the dominant medium during the 1940s and 1950s (Miller, 2002), television rapidly achieved widespread ownership and domination of leisure time to become the leading and most significant form of mass communication, creating a mass medium par excellence and remaining the most 'ubiquitous cultural industry' (Lewis, 2002, p. 4). The rapid adoption of television, faster than any other household appliance, did not simply change home life but was adapted to fit in with domestic life and also tried to shape domestic practices to promote television as a central component of domestic life (Croteau and Hoynes, 2003). 'Television completes the cycle of the human sensorium. With the omnipresent ear and the moving eye, we have abolished writing, the specialized acoustic-visual metaphor that established the dynamics of western civilization' (McLuhan and Firoe, 1967, p. 125). According to Lewis (2002, p. 4), 'the cultural primacy of television as a form of mass communication has, understandably, captured a great deal of attention among those interested in the study of mass media'. Unlike the telephone, which received little attention from social science, the television has been the subject of much research and academic interest, and a review of the literature reveals a plethora of controversy and debate.

Taken from a simple perspective, television is viewed as a one-way mechanism for transmitting visual information to large audiences but, from a broader perspective, it denotes a complex communication system that is interrelated with other technologies (Kim and Sawhney, 2002). Important to our understanding of new media is the way they all interconnect (Croteau and Hoynes, 2003). In the case of television, it can be seen that it 'acted as a Trojan horse through which other modernising forces have affected nations on every part of the globe'; it is fundamental to common cultural and social attitudes and to the consumption and distribution of other goods and services (Moran, 1994, p. 41). However, Hay (2001, p. 222) highlights the contradiction in debates on television between the assumption that television is subsumed into other media and the notion that television is an object with a distinct use and history, and he argues for a spatial materialism of the televisual as a strategy in challenging the assumption that only now has television 'become appended to other media, other technologies'.

Television does not, however, afford the type of individual attention that the telephone does; yet, it is frequently on, and can be background, whereas the telephone (in terms of communication) cannot (Dant, 1999). Morley's (1986) adaptation of Radway's work on the act of media use demonstrates how the domestic context of viewing television is embedded in the social relations within the household. According to Morley (1995), television is about entertainment. Moran (1994, p. 39) suggests that, not only does television content carry social meanings and symbols that 'become part of the mental imagery of the audience', but that the 'technologies of home entertainment also impact on social life in the material sense' and 'the changing physical nature of the object implies their intended location within different physical networks in the home at different points in time'. Morley, (1986), according to Dant (1999), was also interested in how the television, as a physical object, fits into the domestic space and discusses the notion of 'radio with pictures' in its early development, so that women could continue with household chores, and notes the ability of people to follow a television programme whilst carrying out other tasks. Early television content, shaped by cultural practices and traditions about family life, was aimed at women, who were considered to have a great deal of leisure time within the home, and was marketed as something that would entertain women whilst they carried out daily household chores (Croteau and Hoynes, 2003).

As also depicted in the account of the telephone above, gender appears as an important concept in understanding patterns and differences in perceptions and everyday uses of technology. Morley (1995) describes the differences in gender viewing of television associated with the different positioning of men and women within the domestic sphere of the home and outlines male dominance of power in viewing choices. Morley's (1986) study, however, focuses on relatively 'traditional' families which may have had more clearly defined gender roles (Croteau and Hoynes, 2003). Morley himself admits that the participants in his sample were traditional lower-/working-class families with more traditional gender roles and a decade later may see a different pattern with many television households. Interestingly, the male domination of viewing-choice power was also reflected in Gillespie's (1995) account of viewing practices amongst South Asian families in West London, where viewing Indian films was a way of maintaining and strengthening traditional values and culture. Livingstone (1999) suggests that television, as the *oldest* screen medium, has been entrenched in domestic routines for generations, but claims that Morley's (1986) traditional notion of 'family television' is associated with gender and generational hierarchies and is rapidly becoming obsolete in contemporary homes with the proliferation of television sets in different spaces in the home. Not just reliant on the possession of a television set, the proliferation of devices including mobile devices and mobile phones which enable television viewing via the internet has further transformed and altered family viewing practices and media consumption in the home.

'The medium provides global coverage of events, while social relations are lifted from an immediate interactional setting and stretched over global time and space' (Denney, 2005, p. 96). Beck (1992, p. 132) suggests that television 'removes people from traditionally shaped and bounded contexts of conversation, experience and life. At the same time, however, everyone is in a similar position. They all consume institutionally produced television programmes'. Ang's (1992, p. 134) work on television viewing in domestic space provides useful insight into how the domestic context of the home makes understanding television consumption difficult as it can be carried out alongside other activities and the two types of consumption – programmes and advertisements – merge into one activity 'watching television', and attempts to measure television viewing has relied on 'simplistic methods of information gathering'.

> It is a complex practice that is more than just an activity that can be broken down into simple and objectively measurable variables; it is full of causal, unforeseen and indeterminate moments which inevitably make for the ultimate unmeasurability of *how* television is used in the context of everyday life.
>
> (Ang, 1992, p. 139)

Thus, the debate on television, the individual and society continues in contemporary discourse. Moran (1994, p. 42) claimed that television 'reinserted individuals into a social network' with entertainment, communication and information, carrying 'an image of reality at a time when the legitimacy of older institutions, such as religion and politics, is being eroded'. These debates are important to the analysis presented in the later chapters of this book. Just as television is recognised to be a 'medium which disembeds and displaces social relationships' (Denney, 2005, p. 96), young people's use of mobile internet technologies similarly disembeds and disenchants but also re-embeds and reintegrates (Thomson, 2007). Thus, at various times, television has been understood as both harmful and harmless (Moran, 1994), just as the internet, through mobile technologies, is viewed today.

The internet

The history of the telephone and the television offer illuminating insights into landscapes of adoption and integration into everyday life and how they influence current understanding of technology and society. It is to the more current use of technology that this chapter now turns and to the internet, as no discussion of contemporary society could be complete without a consideration of the internet.

> The technical history of the internet can be briefly summarised. The internet began as a small, publically owned computer network established in 1969 in the United States. This network expanded with the development of a shared computer language and set of protocols. E-mail (or network mail, as it was first called) was introduced in 1972. The term 'internet' emerged in 1974 as a simple abbreviation for interworking between multiple computers.
>
> (Curran, 2012, p. 34)

Croteau and Hoynes (2003, p. 150) propose that it is difficult to disagree with the claim that 'cyberspace permits new forms of interaction and challenges our assumptions about the nature of mass-mediated communication'. The internet is a global network of interconnected computers and the World Wide Web is a 'user-friendly' interface for the internet (Gauntlett, 2004). Poster (1999) discussed the 'World-Wide Web' and notes that it provides the transmission of text, images and sound simultaneously.

On creating the internet, Berners-Lee (2000, p. 133) wrote:

> The Web is more of a social creation than a technical one. I designed it for a social effect – to help people work together – and not as a technical toy. The ultimate goal of the Web is to support and improve our weblike existence in the world. We clump into families, associations and companies. We develop trust across the miles and distrust around the corner. What we believe, endorse, agree with and depend on is representable and, increasingly, represented on the Web. We all have to ensure that the society we build with the Web is of the sort we intend.

The internet, a media-based public sphere (Devereux, 2007), has become a ubiquitous technology – an often taken-for-granted source of information, social interaction and community in everyday life. 'In both popular and scientific media, there is currently circulating an idea to the effect that the use of the Internet has grown exceptionally fast, exceeding that of radio by almost an order of magnitude and grown four times faster than television' (Hannemyr, 2003, p. 111). In fact, according to Livingstone (2009, p. 19), 'by the mid 1990s, the internet was fast becoming an everyday technology, reaching sizable proportions of homes, schools and workplaces in the developed world'. In the UK, use of the internet rose from 59 per cent in 2005 to 79 per cent in 2011, and accessing the internet from a smartphone from 30 per cent in 2010 to 44 per cent in 2011 (Ofcom, 2012a). Furthermore, in just one UK county alone, young people's access to the internet via a smartphone doubled between 2011 and 2012 (Bond and Carter, 2013). 'A technological revolution, centred around information technologies, began to reshape, at accelerated pace, the material basis of society' (Castells, 2000, p. 1). Much recent research is concerned with the nature of identity online, and with risk and trust, and there has also been considerable social science interest in researching the internet and online environments (see, for example, Hine, 2005). Research approaches to understanding the World Wide Web were initially more quantitative in nature and included measuring 'hits' – a strategy, Buzzard (2003) suggests, transferred from the economic model employed by the television industry to categorise and map. The more recent approaches reflect the more qualitative turn in social science research and include developing critical visual methodologies and exploring new ways of understanding the social formations that have come about through people using email, mobile phones and websites, as well as other mediated forms of communication (Hine, 2005). Dutton (2013, p. 1) examines the rise in internet studies as an emerging field of academic study which has global significance:

> Internet Studies draws on multiple disciplines covering political, economic, cultural, psychological, and other social factors as well as computer studies, information sciences, and engineering. The emergence of this field has given a focus to theory and research on questions concerning social and cultural implications of the widespread diffusion and diverse uses of the Internet, the Web, and related information and communication technologies (ICTs). The field has grown in step with the rising significance of the technology for its expanding global user community. It has offered a framework within which academics from the many related disciplines have joined with interdisciplinary scholars to form growing communities of researchers.

Castells (2000, p. 381) uses the notion of the networked society and suggests that 'the capacity of the network of networks (the Net) is such that a sizable proportion of the communication taking place on the Internet is still largely spontaneous, unorganised, and diversified in purpose and membership'. Mah (2006, p. 364) offers a detailed analysis of internet connectivity and suggests that there are many assumptions made about internet connectivity often based on the comparisons with early telephony and the pre-internet online services industry, and proposes that challenges remain for policymakers and regulators to translate what is known about internet connectivity into 'positive policy prescriptions grounded in a specific social, political and economic context'.

'The new communication system radically transforms space and time' (Castells, 2000, p. 406) and fundamental to this transformation is the globalisation of online spaces. Globalisation, it is argued, has become 'a virtual synonym for the network society' (Burnett and Marshall, 2003, p. 43). As a globalised phenomenon, 'the interaction between the internet and society is complex' (Curran, 2012, p. 59) as, whilst the way that the internet is conceptualised is, indeed, globalised, it is also simultaneously understood as localised and individualised. Popović and Hromadžić (2008) examine the social and cultural changes associated with media technologies and consider the societal dis/integration of media users through media technology to argue that through new information and communication technologies there is increasingly a fragmentation and heterogeneity of audiences. The internet has also given rise to the phenomenal growth in social networking sites (Fenton, 2012), and this is reflected in the burgeoning interest in identity and communities in online environments and how identities are constructed in virtual space. 'Digital media, and the internet in particular, are transforming our means of gathering information and communicating with each other and contributing to both these practices through creative production' (Fenton, 2012, p. 123). Murthy (2012, pp. 1060–61) considers sociological approaches to understanding emergent social media and, using historical analysis to examine the example of Twitter, observes:

> Though these broad historical arguments reveal similarities of emergent social media to older communication technologies, what makes Twitter distinct is also its departures from the telegraph. Specifically, it is free to use, public (or perhaps semi-public), multicast (i.e. many to many), interactive, and networked. The power of Twitter and other social media is also they are designed to provoke and call forth regular updates from their users.

Unlike previous technologies, like the telephone and television outlined above, social media have and continue to evolve rapidly, often without prior warning, and this can have significant implications for both those using the technology and those researching it and, as such, the emphasis for social media researchers is to describe both the social-technical context and the technological artefact they are analysing (Ellison and boyd, 2013). Changes in the design and diversity of the softer technologies of new social media and the digitisation of culture and society, coupled with transformations in hard technologies in technological capabilities, have brought about the increased mobilised and privatised access to online environments, and access to the internet is now increasingly possible from private and public spaces via a handheld mobile device. It is worth noting from Love (2005, p. 7) that:

> The growth of mobile phone usage and the development in mobile phone technology has probably had the most significant impact on the way we communicate with each other (with the exception of the Internet) over the past 10 years or so.

Theorising technology

According to Uzelac (2008), the highly complex and sophisticated technologies which are being discussed here cannot be simply understood as tools that help us overcome problems, but as environments. 'The goal, then, is to understand how media technologies develop, how people use them, and what this means for broader patterns of social communication' (Croteau and Hoynes, 2003, p. 319).

> The appearance of new digital media has once again changed the way of understanding media audiences, the public sphere and forms of interaction enabled by the medium. The rapid development of various information and media technologies over the past couple of decades has led to the rise of theories concerning the democratic potential that the new digital media carries, as well as towards constructions of new forms of public spheres mediated by contemporary media technologies.
>
> (Popović and Hromadžić, 2008, p. 52)

Yet, according to Baudrillard (1971, p. 164), 'there is no theory of the media'. Whilst post-structuralist and postmodernist theory were influential during the 1980s, as were neo-Marxist debates about the public sphere through the 1990s, audience reception theory and effects research have remained dominant, although, more recently, debates around new media have introduced new theories and there has been a revived interest in earlier technological perspectives (Williams, 2003).

Different approaches to understanding technology use over time have been concerned with the effects on people (Rakow, 1999). However, as Miller (2002, p. 6) observes:

> The early development of mass communications research was, there-fore, partly as a response to a vast range of social, political and cultural concerns about the impact of mass media and centred on the effects of media which were found to be minimal... it only sanctioned the development of the mass media as a force compatible with (rather than antithetical to) democratic culture but informed a liberal, pluralist philosophy of mass media.

Culturally, a mass medium for delivery of information in the form of news, entertainment and advertisements – from one to many – the audience has been conceptualised as a mere passive media receptacle and television was 'characterised as an idiot box and the audience as couch potatoes' (Kim and Sawhney, 2002, p. 233). The *effects* model assumes that the audience is passive and it is concerned with what the media does to the audience. By contrast, the *uses and gratifications* model is concerned with what the audiences do with the media. Furthermore, the effects model is interested in critiquing capitalist/mass culture, whereas the uses and gratifications model is interested in patterns of consumption and choice. Sterling (1995) argues that the effects research approach, developed in the context of anxiety linked to negative consequences of mass communications, conceptualises the mass audience as a passive homogenous group and fails to acknowledge the active audience. More sophisticated than the effects model, the uses and gratifications approach was premised on a functionalist sociological model in which media power was scrutinised much more for its role in contributing to deviant behaviour, rather than its role in reinforcing the status quo (Miller, 2002). As television became part of the cultural environment, without becoming a tool of mass propaganda or causing major upheavals to the social order, the uses and gratifications approach saw the influence of the media in the way it was used to gratify people's needs to be entertained or informed (Miller, 2002). Associated with the uses and gratifications model, approaches which have developed more recently emphasise media consumption as an active process in both the choice of media selected and in their different uses, and how the audience interpret and 'decode' them (Morley, 2008). Morley

(2008, p. 1098) suggests that Hall's 'encoding/decoding' model of communication 'attempted to incorporate, from the uses and gratifications perspective, the idea of the active viewer, who makes meanings from the signs and symbols that the media provide' and focused on ideological and cultural power to consider how meaning was produced. The encoding/decoding model also moved away from content analysis and the idea of a single ideology to propose a more hegemonic dominance.

> Because messages are interpreted and 'read' differently, depending on the social context and the individual, personal experience of the 'reader', the media audience could no longer be comprehended in a singular form, but in the plural. In addition, the analysis of particular media practices showed diverse modes of media usage in the context of everyday practice.
>
> (Popović and Hromadžić, 2008, p. 50)

The importance of context underpins cultural approaches and, according to Miller (2002), despite being written in a pre-television era, Walter Benjamin's *Art in the Age of Mechanical Production*, published in 1935, was one of the more sophisticated attempts to come to terms with the mass production of information and culture, and, unlike others, Benjamin did not see the consumer of mass culture as a simple functionary; for him, the citizen was capable of engaging with new forms of communication. Inglis (2009, p. 376) outlines the development of cultural studies from the 1950s and proposes that it has an emphasis of conceptual openness and fluidity:

> Cultural studies has been pre-eminently a critical discipline, seeking to combat what it sees as outmoded approaches to the comprehension of human life and replacing them with new, more vital and more engaged forms of analysis and understanding.

The dichotomy between the active citizen and the passive consumer has remained, however, and been repeated at various points in various forms in the history of mass communication studies (Miller, 2002). Rakow (1999, p. 76) claims:

> From 'uses and gratifications' research on the liberal side of communication scholars to 'interpretative communities' on the part of cultural studies and post-modern critics, we have had a scholarly conversion to respecting the audience and the audience's creative,

resistive, and meaningful accounts of how they use media and make sense of media text.

Drawing on the different epistemological and ontological perspectives adopted, Tudor (1995) considers the two dominant approaches in understanding mass communication – the media research perspective on how they are understood to cause effects in individual behaviour: first, effects research, and, second, a cultural studies approach linking 'text' to individuals and social transformations. Tudor (1995, p. 97) is, however, critical of both these approaches, arguing that they need to 'rethink the epistemology and social ontology on which they are founded'.

'Different times call for different theorists' and McLuhan's claim that the medium is the message caused considerable contention and subsequent debate, but his suggestion that different media have different effects remains influential according to Matthewman (2011, p. 126). 'Electronic technology fosters and encourages unification and involvement. It is impossible to understand social and cultural changes without a working knowledge of the media' (McLuhan and Fiore, 1967, p. 8). McLuhan argued that content confuses our understanding of technology and its future (Burnett and Marshall, 2003). In Moran's (1994) discussion of key theorists, he suggests that, whilst McLuhan's (1964) theory of media emphasised the importance of media as a technology in the development of human society, it was deterministic and he has accorded much criticism because of this. Siapera (2012, p. 7) suggests, however, that a theoretical interrogation of the relationship between the media and society typically begins with Marshall McLuhan. Moran (1994) argues that it is Raymond Williams' Marxist viewpoint, which emphasises the role of social agency and practice, that has been the most influential to a contemporary understanding of television and other media. However, this approach, which views technology as symptomatic, and an embodiment of cultural ethos, assumes technologies are a consistent coherent whole and that the effects are similar on all people and 'its holism may conceal and confuse matters more than the piecemeal nature of technological determinism' (Fischer, 1992, p. 16).

Fischer (1992) outlines technological determinism and technology as symptomatic, as the two dominant intellectual approaches in understanding technology and society, and suggests that both are problematic. Under technological determinism, the sociology of technology focuses on an analysis which centres the social consequences of technological development (Bucchi, 2004). In media and communication studies, the concept of technological determinism is often used to describe power of technology over a culture and is, therefore, according to Burnett and Marshall (2003), useful in understanding the current power of the Web and where that power originates from. Although technological determinism is 'the single most influential explanation of the relationship between technology and society', it views technologies as neutral and changes in technology as the most important cause of social change – technology in this view impinges on society from the outside (Wajcman, 1994, p. 3). Technological determinism is partly right as a theory of society (technology matters not just physically and biologically, but also to our human relations with each other), but it fails to acknowledge the political aspects of society (MacKenzie and Wajcman, 1999). Matthewson (2011, p. 37) actually suggests that 'theorists are called technological determinists as a term of abuse'. But determinism also does not account adequately for the social embeddedness of technology.

The theoretical approaches to understanding technology are important to the current debates on mobile internet technologies. We need to understand the concept of the socio-technical network and how technologies 'do not exist apart from institutions, exerting an external impact, but are part and parcel of them' (Warschauer, 2003, p. 208), and Krug (2005) argues that technologies are systems, and that these systems are always linked to other systems.

> All media work is over completely. They are so pervasive in their personal, political, economic, aesthetic, psychological, moral, ethical and social consequences that they leave no part of us untouched, unaffected, unaltered. The medium is the message. Nay understanding of social and cultural change is impossible without a knowledge of the way media work as environments.
>
> (McLuhan and Fiore, 1967, p. 26)

Social media, for example, are related to traditional media but 'this new medium is designed to facilitate social interaction, the sharing of digital media, and collaboration. Social networks are also important to social media – especially in their ability to disseminate' (Murthy, 2012, p. 1061).

> *Technology does not determine society*. Nor does society script the course of technological change, since many factors, including individual

inventiveness and entrepreneurialism, intervene in the process of scientific discovery, technical innovation and social applications, so the final outcome depends on a complex problem of interaction. Indeed the dilemma of technological determinism is probably a false problem, since technology is society and society cannot be understood without its technological tools.

(Castells, 2000, p. 5)

Silverstone (1994) highlights the role of television as a 'transitional object in the building of human subjectivity in advanced capitalist countries, as well as ideas of how television is part of the management of ontological security' (Longhurst, 2007, p. 9). The home is increasingly portrayed as the centre of a web of technologies (MacKenzie and Wajcman, 1999) and is a key focus of the relationship between technology and privacy (Shapiro, 1998). 'Media are, in essence, part of our lives and must be understood in the context of the relationships that constitute our lives' (Croteau and Hoynes, 2003, p. 289). Schwarzt Cowan (1999) outlines the technological revolution in the home and suggests that it has transformed the conduct of our daily lives in unexpected ways. She draws on functionalist theory and claims that 'under industrialisation the family is much less important' (Schwarzt Cowan, 1999, p. 281). Linked to the debates presented in Chapter 2 in relation to the family in late modernity, MacKenzie and Wajcman (1999) explore Parsons' (1956) argument that the functions of the family, through industrialisation, have decreased. 'The number of social functions they perform is much reduced, until almost all that remains is consumption, socialization of small children and tension management' (Schwarzt Cowan, 1999, p. 282). Crabb (1999, p. 669) argues that:

Future telecommunications technologies will pose new problems for individuals and households as they try to identify and follow appropriate norms of social interaction and privacy regulation and research examining these processes is critical to understanding social environments that are increasingly mediated and defined by technological systems.

As previously suggested, defining technology is problematic and Kline (1985) considers technology as socio-technical systems of manufacture and socio-technical systems of use. Myerson (2001, p. 9), using the example of the telephone, observes that 'the phone is an object and a technology. But it is also part of a system of ideas, even a way of looking at everyday life. The phone has become part of an idea of the family, of intimacy, emergency and work'. Matthewson (2011) defines technology as objects (virtual or actual), activities, knowledge, modes of organisation and socio-technical systems, and Popović and Hromadžić (2008, p. 46) suggest that 'with the emergence of electronic media, their spread and rise of popular culture, new concepts and approaches' are needed.

> Actor network theory is a form of relational materialism that codifies a body of ideas developed in the sociology and history of technology. At its centre is a non-dualistic account of the relation between 'society' and 'technology'. In this view society is produced through the mutually constituting interaction of a wide range of human and non-human entities (including machines and technologies).
>
> (Prout, 1996, p. 198)

Law (1991) distinguishes between the previous sociological approaches to society and technology as technological determinism (technical acts as explanation) or social reductionism (expression of social relations), and argues that it is a mistake in sociological practice to ignore the networks of heterogeneous materials that constitute the social. ANT is critical of sociological approaches which adopt a dualistic approach to explaining social life and argues that the latter cannot be understood as either human or technical, as neither human nor technology controls the resulting patterns of relationships. Furthermore, Murdoch (2001) suggests that, in traditional sociological approaches, the conceptualising of divisions between humans and non-humans limits a more in-depth and detailed understanding of both environmental and social problems. However, that is not to say that ANT has little in common with traditional sociological approaches as it has commonalities with theoretical approaches, including social constructionism, symbolic interactionism, semiotics and Foucauldian approaches to power, but it is distinct in one respect in that it rejects the assumptions that society is constructed through human action and meaning alone (Prout, 1996). As ANT allows entities to define and construct one another and focuses on the role of technical devices and scientific skills in performing the collective, it highlights the importance of material devices, natural science and social sciences in general (Callon, 1999).

A form of relational materialism, ANT draws on semiotics, social constructionism and symbolic interactionism in order to consider the materials from which social life is produced and the processes by which these are brought into relationship with each other (Prout, 2005).

'Symbolic internationalism is a way of thinking about how our selves and social worlds are formed via the meanings we give to them and to the actions of others' (Holmes, 2010, p. 143). Descola and Palsson (1996 in Latour, 1999, p. 21) observe how ANT 'slowly drifted from a sociology of science and technology, from a social theory, into another enquiry of modernity – sometimes called comparative, symmetrical, or monist anthropology'. Furthermore, it is related to, and absorbed by, and reflects other points of origin; for example, cultural studies, social geography, anthropology and organisational analysis (Law and Hassard, 1999). However, whilst accepting the importance of discourse, ANT is thoroughly materialist, and Prout (1996) suggests that the recent interest in both the history and the sociology of technology has grown enormously, giving rise to new theoretical ideas and wide-ranging areas of empirical research.

Actor-network terms and concepts influence many disciplines; for example, organisational theory, geography, medical anthropology and psychology (Brown and Capdevila, 1999), and, according to Murdoch (2001), an apparent ambition of ANT is interdisciplinary thinking. ANT has had an impact on social science – the sociology of scientific knowledge (Prout, 1996), and Strathern (1999) attempts to demonstrate the applicability of ANT models to the practical understanding of what otherwise would seem a heterogeneous collection of materials.

If the social world cannot simply be divided into things, on the one hand, and the social, on the other (Bingham, 1996), it becomes necessary to understand the 'intricate and mutually constitutive character of the human and the technological' (Prout, 1996, p. 198). Murdoch (2001, p. 114) suggests that ANT directed sociology to 'confront a new "hybrid" world'. Drawing on the historian of technology Thomas Hughes' (1983) analysis, Law (1991) suggests that the difference between the human and the non-human, although there, is superseded by the desire to explore the development of a complex socio-technical system which is determined neither by the technical nor the social alone. 'Machines came to be seen as produced in and by a heterogeneous mixture of influences including earlier technologies and a variety of social and economic interests' (Prout, 1996, p. 201). Murdoch (2001, pp. 113–15) suggests that sociology, traditionally, has ignored the role of nature as an active entity and 'merely provides the context of human action or it falls victim to human endeavour', and that ANT, in seeking to identify how relations and entities come together, approximates an 'ecological sociology' in which 'abstract distinctions between the natural and the social are redundant'.

The ANT approach gives non-human entities the position of actant and, according to Lee and Brown, (1994) the argument presented by Callon and Latour is clear and cogent, and transgresses the dualistic tendencies of traditional sociological understanding. Latour (1999), for example, suggests that one of the most useful contributions of ANT is that, whilst it never wanted to enter the debate between structure and agency, it does not separate the roles of agency and society but conceptualises them as faces of the same phenomenon. Additionally, Michel (1996, in Brown and Capdevila, 1999) highlights how ANT examines the construction of identity in non-dualist terms. According to Dugdale (1999), we often treat materials as background and, therefore, unimportant to analysis but, through an ANT approach and drawing on perspectives from feminist sociology, she argues that it is clear that materials are crucial in producing the bodies that are combined as subjects. Furthermore, Prout's (1996, p. 198) analysis of the Metered Dose Inhaler (MDI) demonstrates how ANT can facilitate an understanding of sickness and healing which 'can encompass the performative interactions of both human beings and technologies'.

ANT – the Actor and the Network

In conceptualising society as produced by and through networks of heterogeneous material, it is made up through a variety of shifting associations and dissociations between human and non-human entities (Prout, 1996). ANT describes actors as associations of a myriad little elements, human and non-human (Gomart and Hennion, 1999). According to Lee and Stanner (1999), for Latour the problem was one of formally recognising the role that objects play in human networks and the hybrids he discusses are so called because, within the networks, they cannot be called 'natural' objects. 'ANT is committed to demonstrating that the elements bound together in a network (including the people) are constituted and shaped by their involvement with each other' (Lee and Brown, 1994, p. 774). This concept of network, according to Prout (2005), offers a language of ordering that stands between the polar oppositions put forward by modernist social theory. In following these networks along their length, 'network theory is quite simple' and provides a grounded theory approach (Murdoch, 1997, p. 322). Both natural and social entities come into being as a result of the complex relations (or networks) that link them together and, in viewing the world through this prism of the (heterogeneous) network, ANT attempts to demonstrate that nature and society are 'outcomes rather than causes and these great and powerful categories emerge from a complex set of relations' (Murdoch, 2001, p. 120). In seeking to describe the actions of humans and non-humans symmetrically, ANT seeks to depict the composition of heterogeneous elements in networks which produce emerging action from an indeterminate source; objects have been turned into networks and, therefore, have been radically redefined (Gomart and Hennion, 1999).

A clear example of these complex network relationships is offered by Moser and Law (1999) in their case study considering the continuities and discontinuities of subjectivity. They discuss both technology and dis/ability in terms of a set of specificities, which are specific because they come in the form of networks of heterogeneous material, and they claim that, if the networks are in place, ability is achieved but, if the networks are not in place, then disability arises. It is the character of the materials, Moser and Law (1999) argue, that enable passages and ways which secure or do not secure them. Technology use becomes an embodied skill and 'the competent subject is indeed one that can count, can calculate, can plan, can exercise discretion and so take responsibility for the decisions it has taken' within a paradigm of subjectivity (Moser and Law, 1999, p. 213). Additionally, Prout's (1996) analysis of the MDI illustrates how ANT enables the device to be understood as a complex, hybrid association, simultaneously social and technical, and involving a whole series of natural, technical and human elements brought together and packaged into a particular device.

Entities are conceptualised by Latour (1993) as hybrids, as quasi-objects and quasi-subjects, and the distinction between human and non-human is constantly changing and being renegotiated. However, Benton and Craib (2001, p. 71) observe in their discussion of ANT that 'Latour's desire to find terms which link humans to non-humans into seamless networks leads to metaphorical excesses which carry little conviction' and that his key concepts are based on already established meanings which contravene his own methodology. Dugdale (1999) explores the specificities and materials in women's decision-making in relation to their use of a contraceptive technology and how these settlements are reached to suggest that ANT facilitates a rethinking of both the notions of negotiation and closure. In her discussion of decision-making and informed consent, she illustrates how as women (centred) are inserted into multiple logics, the centred and the decentred subjects are, therefore, mutually dependent, as choice is located within information and everyday knowledge.

A tension between self-realisation and control has always been a feature of modernity (Giddens, 1990, 1991), and, according to Latour

(1999), the main difference between ANT and the reflections on modernity, including post-, hyper-, pre- and anti-modernity, is that it incorporated all the aspects of what Latour terms 'modernist predicament' simultaneously. Dugdale (1999) also discusses the pluralistic and multiple character of postmodernism in the negotiations and compromises that function in the legitimacy of power in each perspective and, drawing on Foucault's arguments, she claims that if power is to work then it has to appear in and be constantly reorganised in the course of negotiations. As Thrift (1996, p. 1485 quoted in Holloway and Valentine, 2003, p. 13) comments:

> The actors in these actor networks redefine each other *in action* in ways which mean that there are no simple one-to-one relationships from technology to people but rather a constantly on-going, constantly inventive and constantly reciprocal process of social acquaintance and re-acquaintance.

In his example of the MDI, Prout (1996) suggests that, in using the device, parents and children are enrolled into ongoing interaction in which technologies and people mutually constitute each other but, as Strathern (1999) points out, whilst ANT analysis implies people are always negotiating their relationships with others, relations also achieve divisions as relationships separate out capabilities for action and difference is constantly being created in the conduct of social life. Old social divisions are used to create new ones. Lee and Stanner (1999, p. 95) state: 'we produce the modern world by mixing natural and cultural things into productive hybrids who can then be promptly ignored thanks to the purifying tendencies of modern thought'.

Basalla (1988, p. 217) examines 'artefactual diversity' and proposes a theory of technological evolution to suggest that the artefacts are related to each other, that 'the reformulation of technological progress should be acceptable to the opponents in the technology-versus-society debate and still satisfy the condition that evidence for progress not be gathered across technological and cultural boundaries and over a long period of time'. Strathern (1999, p. 157), however, draws on Latour's (1993) suggestion to argue that 'humanity should never have been constructed in opposition to extensions of itself, an axiom', she suggests, that Bruno Latour 'has extended to all kinds of societies and circumstances'. ANT, therefore, offers an analytical framework for social analysis to explore the nature of the 'dynamic of the interplay between technological artefacts and people' that can overcome the limitations of many previous approaches and, used as a descriptive methodology, allows actants to speak for themselves (Cordella and Shaikh, 2006, p. 5).

Whilst the language of ANT is one of equality, fluidity and hybridity, it should be borne in mind that different technologies have different characteristics and perform different functions and roles in everyday life. Thus, our ability to understand technology would not be complete without due consideration of their *affordances*. Hutchby (2001a, p. 26) develops Gibson's concept of affordances to argue that 'different technologies possess different affordances, and these constrain the ways they can be read. The physical capabilities of aeroplane and bridge are different and, because of this, they afford different though overlapping ranges of meanings'. It is the changing nature of the affordances associated with mobile technologies that are significant to the analyses presented in this book. In empirical terms, Hutchby and Moran-Ellis (2001, p. 3) suggest that 'the significance of technology lies not in what an artefact "is", not in what it specifically does, but in what it enables or affords as it mediates the relationship between its user and other individuals'. It is through close consideration of the affordances of technology, which are closely intertwined with agency (Lee, 2001a) that in ANT terms are seen as distributed agency, which constitute the basis for current debates on contemporary discourses about childhood, mobile technologies and everyday life.

In spite of considerable attention, questions remain in attempting to understand the interrelation of social and material worlds (Rappert, 2003) and 'the concept of diversity, which stands at the beginning of evolutionary thinking, is basic to an understanding of technological evolution' (Basalla, 1988, p. 208). Technology, therefore, should not be understood as fixed but as a flexible process used differently by different groups of people (Berg, 1999). Kline and Pinch (1999) contend this point, drawing on the Social Construction of Technology (SCOT) to argue that various different social groups associate different social meanings with different artefacts, leading to, what they term as, interpretative flexibility appearing over the artefact, as the same artefact can mean different things to different social groups of users. This is especially important when we are considering mobile internet technologies, as Stokes (2010, p. 321) observes: 'conceiving of the "web" as a dimension of reality rather than as a separate space frees us from the traditional false dichotomies found in social science (anthropology's "the other", "the researched" and "the researcher") and the false geographic analogy of "virtual" and "real"'.

Conclusion

This chapter has examined approaches and perspectives in understanding technology, considering historical trajectories of the telephone, the television and the internet in outlining the key debates in how they have come to be understood. There are many theoretical approaches which offer to illuminate different aspects of technology use in everyday life, which Matthewman (2011, p. 15) helpfully summarises:

> There have been a wide variety of ways of theorizing technology, change and agency. We can impose a sense of order on them by separating them into three broad schools: 1) anti-humanist ones that privilege the role of technology in social explanations; 2) humanist ones that privilege the role of society; and 3) posthumanist ones that refuse to privilege either.

How the audience is understood has also been explored through different perspectives and approaches. Approaches which privilege the role of technology have viewed the audience as passive and consider technology to influence society, but the approaches focusing on media effects have been criticised and alternative viewpoints put forward. By contrast, uses and gratifications theory is an audience-centred approach which considers what people do with media. Hall (1980/2006, p. 166) argued, however, that effects, uses and gratifications are in themselves 'framed in structures of understanding, as well as produced by social and economic relations, which shape their "realization" at the reception end of the chain and which permit the meanings signified in the discourse to be transposed into practice or consciousness'. ANT neither privileges technology nor society, and there has recently been a revival of ANT-inspired approaches to understanding education, literacy, policy and educational technology (Fenwick and Edwards, 2010). This chapter has presented a variety of theoretical approaches to examine former distinctions in related sociologies and media studies by drawing on appropriate heterogeneous material without deliberately giving priority to any particular perspectives. The approach adopted here is not to seek for laws or regularities, as the networks of childhood and technologies remain changeable and unstable in postmodernity; as Law (1999, p. 10) argues: 'nothing is purely technical. Neither is anything purely social. And the same can be said for the economic, the political, the scientific, and all the rest'.

The importance of context has, however, been emphasised and, in consideration of previous analyses of technology and society, Matthewson (2011, p. 21) points out that 'an important lesson is to be drawn: technologies cannot be abstracted from the environments which they help to create'.

As this chapter concludes the debates on understanding technology towards the further exploration of childhood, mobile technologies and everyday experiences in this book, careful consideration of the wider (technical) context is required. Currently, much research is focused on the convergence of new media technologies and the relationship between changing technologies and childhoods. As Jenkins (2006, p. 259) notes:

> Welcome to the convergence culture, where old and new media collide, where grassroots and corporate media intersect, where the power of the media producer and the power of the media consumer interact in unpredictable ways. Convergence culture is the future, but it is taking shape now. Consumers will be more powerful within convergence culture – but only if they recognise and use that power as both consumers and citizens, as full participants in our culture.

Whether or not this conceptualisation of consumers and citizens also applies to children is questionable and explored by Livingstone (2009), and in more depth in Chapter 7 in this book. Certainly, it seems to be well acknowledged that children are consuming technologies, but to what extent they are considered to be citizens remains open to debate. The changing access and increased ownership of personalised, mobilised technologies (Livingstone et al., 2011) is altering the landscapes of how online spaces are used and understood:

> While the internet has often entered homes intended for communal use in the living room, it too is migrating to more specialised and personalised locations around the home. In terms of space, the decision for many households is no longer whether to have the internet but rather how many connections to have and where to locate them in the home, facilitated by a continual process upgrading and recycling existing technologies through the household. As desktops give way to laptops, mobile and other platforms, even these decisions become unnecessary as access becomes ever more flexible.
>
> (Livingstone, 2009, p. 22)

4
Researching Childhood, Mobile Internet Technologies and Everyday Experiences

Introduction

As outlined in Chapter 2, until relatively recently childhood was either neglected by mainstream social theory, or considered and researched within areas such as education or the family (see, for example, Brannen and O'Brien, 1995; Corsaro, 2011). Much of this research has accorded criticism for conceptualising children as incompetent, unreliable and incomplete, as mere objects to be studied (Hill et al., 1996). This chapter sets out to consider the more recent methodological perspectives in researching childhood and children's everyday experiences as informed by the social studies of childhood and the increasing influence of Article 12 of the UNCRC. It examines the philosophical underpinnings of research perspectives and considers both quantitative and qualitative approaches to researching childhood, mobile t internet technologies and everyday experiences.

> The present communication age imposes relentless change as standard. The rapid development of information connectivity, communication and availability, facilitated by ever-emerging means/mediums of new technology and digital culture, is racing ahead in a challenging way which suggests numerous issues for research and analysis of its impact and social relevance.
>
> (Bušnja and Jelinčić, 2008, p. 127)

The blurring of the boundaries between 'offline' and 'online' in understanding virtual media spaces, as discussed in Chapter 3, is also important to the debates presented here, especially those which consider notions of reality. Recent research on childhood and technology is critically considered in order to offer the reader an up-to-date review of the relevant key literature and methodological approaches employed. The concept of knowledge has traditionally excluded children from research, as adults tend to be viewed as having greater knowledge and understanding than children. Theoretical developments in understanding childhood which position the child as an active, competent and knowledgeable expert have led to methodological developments in childhood research which draw on these characteristics and celebrate children's unique viewpoints. There is increasing recognition that it is the young people themselves who are expert in their own lives and not the adults (who have previously dominated the role of the expert). This is especially pertinent in understanding mobile internet technologies, as it is the children themselves who are experiencing their childhoods and using mobile internet technologies in their everyday lives and no adult can currently share in this unique phenomenon.

The chapter discusses how the concept of competence in children's participation in research has been interrogated through creative research methods (for example, Clarke and Moss, 2001; Lancaster, 2003). Influential to the research presented in the discussions which inform the subsequent chapters in this book is Kirby's (2002) account of the developments in childhood research from being dominated by developmental perspectives to the child-centred participatory approaches becoming increasingly recognised and used in contemporary research. In exploring the methodologies that draw on young people's strengths, rather than focusing on what they are unable to do, the chapter argues that issues of power and social exclusion can be addressed and also, for example, in relation to disabled children's experiences, that children's active participation in researching mobile internet technologies can be facilitated and their voices allowed to be heard.

The developments outlined above are becoming increasingly recognised as important to both research agenda and policy initiatives, as Lansdown (2011, p. 5) so eloquently observes:

> Adults do not always have sufficient insight into children's lives to be able to make informed and effective decisions on the legislation, policies and programmes designed for children. Children have a unique body of knowledge about their lives, needs and concerns, together with ideas and views which derive from their direct experience. This knowledge and experience relates to both matters affecting them as individuals and matters of wider concern to children as a group. It needs to inform all decision-making processes

affecting children's lives. Decisions that are fully informed by children's own perspectives will be more relevant, more effective and more sustainable.

Whilst Greene and Hogan (2005) suggest that epistemological and methodological issues do not require reappraisal when researching children, Barker and Weller (2003) argue that traditional research methods, which do not directly involve working with children, have been criticised for carrying out research on, rather than with, children. Developments in standpoint feminism and the influence of individualisation as 'the tendency for contemporary children to be seen as having a voice in determining their lives and shaping their identity' are also considered in this chapter, as they are important aspects of recent advances in undertaking research with children and are associated with the social studies of childhood (Christensen and Prout, 2005, p. 53).

Children's rights and research

Kellett et al. (2004) highlight the importance of the impact of Articles 12 and 13 of the UNCRC in encouraging children to receive information on, and being involved and consulted in, all activities affecting their lives. However, in spite of the increasing academic literature on the role of children in social science research and a rising awareness which has led to an increased involvement of children as participants and co-researchers, much research remains adult-initiated, as well as led, designed and understood from adult perspectives (Kellett, 2005a). Morgan et al. (2002), for example, observe how the increasing acknowledgement of children's rights has encouraged research aimed at understanding children's views and experiences which demonstrate the divide between children's and parents' views and concerns. They argue that 'it is neither theoretically nor methodologically appropriate to rely on proxies to represent the views and experiences of children...children's views can and ought to be taken seriously' (Morgan et al., 2002, p. 146). This approach also includes even very young children (Alderson, 2008) if the relevant methodological approach is understood and appropriate methods adopted.

Furthermore, it is argued that an interest in researching children's experience can 'be allied to a moral perspective on the role and status of children which respects and promotes their entitlement to being considered as persons of value and persons with rights' (Greene and Hogan, 2005, p. 3). The UN defines children as persons under 18 years of age, and Barker and Weller (2003, p. 34) suggest that 'contemporary research undertaken within the new social studies of childhood is very much influenced by, and contributes to, the children's rights movement'. Grover (2004) suggests that, whilst the right of children to be active in the research process has not been a main theme in academic debate, it is an idea that has been brought forward in sociology and is enshrined in current legislative frameworks (for example, the UNCRC and the Children Act 1989/2004). 'From a rights-based agenda, the perspective of children as social actors places them as a socially excluded, minority group struggling to find a voice!' (Kellett et al., 2004, p. 330).

The next section of this fourth chapter examines different approaches to researching children, mobile technologies and their everyday experiences. I use the term 'approaches' here rather than attempting to set out the intricate and often well-worn debates over positivism versus interpretivism, quantitative versus qualitative and subjectivity versus objectivity. The tension between these dualisms, and whether they necessarily should exist at all, are not the topics of debate here and have been covered in detail elsewhere (see Greig et al., 2012; Benton and Craib, 2001; May, T., 2011).

> 'Approaches' is a general term, wider than theory or methodology. It included epistemology or questions about the theory of knowledge; the purposes of research, whether understanding, explanation or normative evaluation; and the 'meta-theories' within which particular theories are located. It takes in basic assumptions about human behaviour; whether the unit of analysis is the individual or the social group; and the role of ideas and interests.
>
> (della Porta and Keating, 2008a, p. 1)

As already considered in Chapter 2, the UNCRC has had a significant impact on contemporary conceptualisations of childhood and, subsequently, on changing paradigms of child-centred research. Much contemporary research seeks to address and support children's participation in social research and to ensure that their voices are heard. However, understanding children's perspectives is crucial not only in theory, but also in practice (Hagerman, 2010, p. 63). As such, there is a 'range of important methodological considerations when doing research with young people and these vary according to the methods being used, the particular groups of people involved and the topics being researched' (Hopkins, 2010, p. 32). France (2007) observes that both social theorising and empirical research have been changed by modernity and discusses how post-structuralists have rejected modernist ideas of structural dominance to consider the importance of agency, diversity and subjectivity. Plummer (2001, p. 264) argues that 'the telling of a life can be both a humanist and a postmodern project' and Christensen and James (2008, p. 2) suggest these developments have meant that research is done with children rather than on them, and that children, as social actors, are viewed as subjects rather than objects of enquiry, but that these recent developments have also brought new ethical and 'theoretical problems into the methodological debate'. These points are essential to understanding the trajectory of this chapter, as the research context is vitally important to the following analysis of understanding childhood, mobile technologies and everyday experiences. 'Scholars in both technology studies and media studies have been arguing for the importance of analysing in a grounded way the broader web of social and cultural connections that determine the shape and meaning of new media and technologies' (Ito, 2009, p. 14), and these contexts include how they are researched and understood, which, therefore, requires an understanding of the shifting social research agendas and approaches.

The nature of social research

Within social science there are research strategies each with a definite set of interrelated epistemological, ontological and practical foundations. Key methodological questions, therefore, shape the character of research inquiries and the overall nature of research methodology shapes how each method is used. Methodology refers to philosophies, ideologies, principles and values that inform the research process (Roberts-Holmes, 2011). According to Pawson (1999, p. 20), sociological methodology is said to have the task of 'developing and amalgamating the principles and practice of social research'. Social research is inevitably based on some dimension of the intellectual tradition of Western knowledge, and alternative views of reality lead to different propositions about what reality is (ontology); different ways of establishing what can be accepted as real (epistemology); different strategies for validating our claims about reality; and different techniques for collecting data (Hart, 1998). Corsaro (2011) considers different types of research approaches in understanding childhood – macro-level approaches, micro-level approaches and, what he describes as, non-traditional approaches.

The relationship between the natural and social sciences, however, is not a straightforward one (Epstein, 2012). Different research strategies have different strengths, but also limitations, and it is not the intention of this chapter to offer a critical evaluation of approaches adopted, but more to highlight the plurality of research designs and methodological perspectives in understanding children and mobile technologies in their everyday lives. According to Hart (1998), different philosophical traditions need to be appreciated for what they are and not for what they are assumed to lack from another standpoint. Bryman (2012) points out that there are many different and sometimes opposing influences on conducting social research, which include theoretical approaches, ontological and epistemological perspectives, values and practical considerations. In relation to the social contexts of research with children, Lange and Mierendorff (2011, pp. 79–80) helpfully set out four central dimensions:

(1) the cultural, societal and political contexts in which the generational order structures the power relationship between children and adults;
(2) the ongoing interactions amongst children and adults or amongst peers in private, informal and institutional areas;
(3) the permanent reproduction of children's so-called culture within the culture of a society (or more and more of globalised 'world society'); and
(4) children's views on the social world in which they are permanently involved.

Positivism, for example, originating in the natural sciences, assumes that there is an objective reality which can be accurately measured (Hogan, 2005). It adopts the use of natural scientific methods with social science and aims to be objective, produce generalisable knowledge and explain behaviour in terms of cause and effect (May, T., 2011). Epstein (2012) suggests that naturalists view phenomena as natural and that society can be studied, like nature, scientifically and objectively. 'If we can now deploy positivistic methods in measuring and comparing various aspects of children's lives rather than simply their rate of development, then we are starting to recognise children as full members of society' (Wyness, 2012, p. 204). As such, macro-level methods of research, including large-scale surveys, can offer comparisons between communities, generations and over time (Corsaro, 2011). Madden et al. (2013) conducted a nationally representative survey of 802 teenagers aged 12–17 and their parents in the US. They found that 78 per cent of teenagers had a mobile phone, almost half (47 per cent) of whom owned smartphones, which translates into 37 per cent of all teenagers who have smartphones, up from just 23 per cent in 2011. They also found that one in four teenagers (23 per cent) had a tablet computer – a level comparable to the general adult population. Another study of this type, also conducted in the US, was based on a survey of 1,030 13–17-year-olds, conducted online by Knowledge Networks in 2012. They suggest that:

> almost all teenagers in America today have used social media. Nine out of 10 (90 per cent) 13 to 17 year-olds have used some form of social media. Three out of four (75 per cent) teenagers currently have a profile on a social networking site, and one in five (22 per cent) has a current Twitter account (27 per cent have never used Twitter).
>
> (Rideout et al., 2012, p. 9)

In Europe, the most comprehensive research programme is the EU Kids Online network, which is a multinational thematic network investigating children's online uses through a multi-method approach. Livingstone et al.'s (2011a, p. 2) research surveyed more than 25,000 European children and their parents in 25 countries, and found that:

> internet use is increasingly individualised, privatised and mobile: 9–16 year old internet users spend 88 minutes per day online, on average. 49 per cent go online in their bedroom, 33 per cent go online via a mobile phone or handheld device, and most use the internet at home (87 per cent) and school (63 per cent).

In the UK, Ofcom (2012b) used quantitative tracking surveys in its research and found that, since 2011, smartphone ownership had increased amongst all children aged 5–15 (28 per cent as compared with 20 per cent in 2011), primarily driven by a 21 percentage point increase amongst children aged 12–15 (62 per cent in 2012 as compared with 41 per cent in 2011), and that from the age of 12 onwards smartphone ownership outstrips ownership of other mobile phones (Ofcom, 2012b). These large-scale quantitative research studies, and others of a similar nature, have provided detailed evidence of both shifting patterns of ownership and patterns of usage in relation to the rapidly developing technological landscape of mobile devices. Furthermore, research on mobile technology use suggests that personalised post-PC devices are being used more and more in educational contexts and, recently, Clark and Luckin (2013) reported from a comprehensive review on the available research and literature on iPads in the classroom that they are generally viewed positively by students and can contribute to the learning environment in a number of ways.

In contrast to the predictive understanding outlined in the paragraph above and advocated by positivists, interpretativists favour Max Weber's (1964) empathetic understanding known as *verstehen*, which is: 'the attempt to understand social action through a kind of empathetic identification' (O'Connell Davidson and Layder, 1994, p. 31). My own work, for example, conducted a few years ago with 30 young people in the UK, considered children's perceptions of risk and mobile phones. The study, which explored children's thoughts, feelings and ideas about risk within their social worlds, sits within an interpretative framework (see Bond, 2010, 2011). Interpretivism tends to emphasise the meaning of human conduct to the exclusion of practical involvements and causal conditions, and fails to examine social norms in relation to asymmetrics of power and divisions of interest in society (Giddens, 1976). In discussing the realism versus relativism debate, however, Pawson (1999) argues that such a dualism in research methodology is an oversimplification. Concerns are often raised from a positivist perspective over the lack of objectivity, small sample size, the use of anecdotal evidence and the difficulty in replicating and generalising from interpretive studies, but these are, according to Miles and Huberman (1994), common disadvantages associated with qualitative research.

Experience is about interpretation (Greene and Hogan, 2005) and research which adopts a social constructivist approach seeks to collect subjective accounts and perceptions in order to understand the participants' experiences and constructions of their everyday lives (see Sikes, 2004). According to Greig et al. (2012), the social constructivist researcher views children as subjective, contextual, self-determining and dynamic, and endeavours to understand how the worlds of children operate by describing and analysing the contextualised social phenomena found there. In adopting an empiricist approach, in that the facts are assumed to exist prior to the theories that explain them (Silverman, 2012), studies adopting this approach are based on the notion that factual knowledge comes from factual research based on direct experience gathered through the senses (see Sarantakos, 2005). Grover (2004, p. 82) considers the value and importance of phenomenological data in social research and its implications regarding power issues in research with children and suggests that 'phenomenological material is thus a valuable addition to the research endeavour and ought not to be excluded as supposedly "unscientific"'.

O'Leary (2010) explores aspects of post-positivist research as participatory and collaborative, inductive, dependable and auditable, which seeks findings that are idiographic, valuable and qualitative. Greene and Hogan (2005) suggest that qualitative methods are appropriate for investigating children's unique experiences. My research (Bond, 2010, 2011) on children's perspectives of risk and mobile phones, which explored children's subjective experience of their social world, lies within the framework of qualitative research (see Atkinson, 1993), which implies an emphasis on meanings and stresses the socially constructed nature of reality (Denzin and Lincoln, 2005). The study set out to explore how children themselves actually use mobile phone technologies and understand risk in their everyday lives, and found that the children were reflexive in their understanding of risk and mobile phones and in the construction of their individualised life biographies. Their accounts highlighted the complex, multifarious relationships of the heterogeneous networks of the technical, the social and the natural that constitute children's everyday lives. The methods used by qualitative researchers exemplify a common belief that they can provide a deeper understanding of the social phenomena than would be obtained from purely quantitative data (Silverman, 2012) and the rich detail they provide assumes an interpretivistic approach (May, T., 2011).

Much of the growing body of child-centred research is derived from a social constructionist perspective that 'social reality is a creation of the interaction of individuals and groups' (Giddens, 2006, p. 1034). It sets out to produce qualitative data and stems from an interpretative framework (Benton and Craib, 2001) which has historically argued for the uniqueness of human inquiry (Denzin and Lincoln, 2005). Within childhood studies, the 'by now widely adopted, and constituting somewhat of a new research orthodoxy, the recognition of children as competent social actors is the place from which much contemporary anthropological research with children now sets out' (James, 2007, p. 261). These more micro-level approaches (see Cosaro, 2011) include ethnographic research, which is central to childhood research, and was originally adopted by those working with a model of 'the tribal child' (James et al., 2010). Anthropological approaches influenced by ethnography highlight the many different ways of viewing and thinking about children, and Lancy (2008, p. 373) argues that 'perhaps the most significant insight gained from using anthropology's lens to study children is to appreciate their value'.

Ethnography is central to qualitative approaches in the social sciences (Bray, 2008) and combines a number of different methods (Allan, 2012). Hammersley and Atkinson (2007, p. 2) propose:

In short, 'ethnography' plays a complex and shifting role in the dynamic tapestry that the social sciences have become in the twenty-first century. However, this term is by no means unusual in lacking a single, standard meaning. Nor does the uncertainty of sense undermine its value as a label.

In spite of the recent developments in anthropological approaches and the growing influence of ethnography in childhood research, certain aspects of children's lives remain under-represented on the research agenda. Wyness (2012, p. 205) suggests, for example, that the greater number of educational ethnographies of children's lives compared with ethnographies of the family and/or home highlights how 'a culture of secrecy and privacy still pervades family life'. The concepts of private and public space, and the blurring of these boundaries in late modernity, are also important to understanding contemporary approaches to researching mobile technologies and everyday life (as considered in Chapter 5).

Wyness (2012, p. 209) suggests that, compared with ethnography, 'in turning to other less intrusive research techniques such as interviewing, less stress is placed on the impact of the researcher within the research community'. According to Hopkins (2010, p. 35), interviews are 'verbal exchanges where the interviewer attempts to elicit information from a young person' and 'interviews can be useful for assessing deep understandings and experiences, exploring complex behaviours and motivations and, through being individual, they give priority to individual young people's experiences'. Verbally engaging children in research can challenge traditional assumptions of children's experiences (Carney et al., 2003) and interviews offer rich insights into people's experiences, opinions, aspirations, attitudes and feelings (May, T., 2011). Grover (2004, p. 84) suggests that when children are allowed to talk meaningfully the data 'provided is rich and complex'. Additionally, an unstructured approach allows the researcher greater flexibility (Coolican, 2009) and has the ability to challenge any preconceptions held by the researcher, and would, therefore, have a qualitative depth in providing a greater understanding of the children's perspectives (May, T., 2011). Thus, 'conversational techniques are central to a qualitative approach, for they highlight the respondents' understandings of themselves and their social worlds' (Wyness, 2012, p. 212).

However, unstructured interviews can lead to interviewer bias, and Frankfort-Nachmias and Nachmias (1996) suggest that differences between interviewers' innate characteristics and techniques could affect the answers. However, Greig et al. (2012) suggest that the interactive nature of unstructured interviews facilitates access to dimensions of information not otherwise available. Although interaction between interviewer and interviewee is viewed as a potential problem from a positivist perspective (Hester and Francis, 1994), from a feminist perspective it is seen as an essential component of successful interviewing (Oakley, 1990). The feminist tradition pioneered participatory approaches to research (Gilbert, 2008). Feminist research based on participatory, collaborative and non-exploitive relationships following the interpretivist/constructionist paradigm emphasises women's everyday experiences and provides women with a voice to discuss social life from their perspective, rejecting traditional research methods to reconsider the relationship between the researcher and the researched (Sarantakos, 2005). According to Truman (2000), feminist research critical of positivist-influenced approaches exposes the centrality of male power in the social construction of knowledge and challenges fundamental binaries in traditional research, such as objectivity and distance from research participants, and considers the relationship of marginalised groups in the research process. Delamont (2003, p. 60) observes how 'the debates surrounding feminist methods encompass the biggest impact feminism has made to sociology'. Feminist research views unstructured in-depth interviews as an appropriate method as they encourage subjectivity and dialogue between equals. Thus, interviews, influenced by Oakley's (1990) argument that disengagement is inappropriate, can be very informal and can, therefore, allow interaction between the researcher and research participants. Although such interaction may undermine the methodological ideal of reliability and standardisation highly valued from a positivist perspective, Coolican (2009) suggests that the use of unstructured interviews can provide research with high validity but reliability suffers and it is not easy to generalise. Whilst reliability is important for specific measures, Greig et al. (2012), therefore, suggest that it is mainly validity that matters when verbally engaging children. From an interpretivist perspective, interactionally flexible techniques are preferred in order to portray the depths of meanings of the subjects' social understandings and thus ensure 'validity' of the interview data (Hester and Francis, 1994). As Osgerby (2004, p. 65) argues:

> Generally, quantitatively-based research is ill suited to uncovering the way people make sense of media texts and give meaning to their social behaviour. Rather than employing quantitative methodologies in a bid to 'discover' laws of media 'cause and effect', many authors

have argued that a better approach is to use qualitative research methods (for example, ethnography, interviews and focus groups) to explore the various meanings and interpretations different audiences give to the media.

Qualitative data is a 'source of well-grounded, rich descriptions and explanations of processes' (Miles and Huberman, 1994, p. 1). Focus-group methods developed away from the major methodological traditions of qualitative research and remained largely overlooked in formal academic research until the late 1970s but more recently have become increasingly popular in the social sciences (Kidd and Parshall, 2000). Morgan et al. (2002) adopt child-friendly techniques to promote children's participation and suggest that focus groups are a valuable method for eliciting children's views and experiences, and, therefore, appropriate to the debates presented here. It has, however, been argued that the recent interest in focus groups is often based on practical issues such as time and cost when compared with individual interviews, but there is evidence to suggest that focus groups may be of value in studying issues in socially marginalised groups (Kitzinger, 1994; Madriz, 1998 cited in Kidd and Parshall, 2000), and would additionally focus upon group norms and dynamics around the issues under investigation (May, T., 2011). Hollander (2004, p. 605) suggests that methods of data collection are 'employed in social contexts and are subject to social influences', and that social contexts such as gender, status and relational contexts influence the course of the focus-group discussion and the responses of individual participants as they may exaggerate, minimise or withhold experiences. However, in my research, the unstructured approach using focus groups began with very open questions; for example, 'What do think about mobile phones?' or 'How would you feel without it?', which produced a wealth of rich and varied data as the children discussed their thoughts, feelings, views and experiences relating to mobile phones and risk in their everyday lives. 'One of the most consistent threads in focus group literature is the vital importance of using nondirective questions to elicit spontaneous expression among participants' as limiting discussion to a particular focus may be in contradiction to some of the underlying assumptions of grounded theory (Kidd and Parshall, 2000, p. 296). Thirty children participated in my research in 2007, and the discussions were lively and required little intervention on my part. They also produced some very interesting and worthwhile findings, especially in relation to intimacy and self-identity. I observed: 'facilitated by the use of unstructured focus groups, detailed discussions of the use of mobile phones in their relationships and in the sharing of sexual material, both downloaded and user generated, took place' (Bond, 2011, p. 588). It was probably, on reflection, the use of adopting well-established and self-selected friendship groups in my own focus groups that may have influenced the responses of the participants in, what was intended to be, a positive direction. Because the children were previously well known to each other, the power balance between the children and the researcher shifted towards the established friendship group. Discussions of shared experiences within the group were frequent and, therefore, required no further explanation. This facilitated some themes to emerge – for example, on sexuality and sexual content – that were less likely to have been discussed in the context of an individual interview.

Whilst some limitations of focus-group research are common to many other research methods, Morgan et al. (2002) outline the potential problems in focus groups with children and the tendency for children to view an adult facilitator as an authority figure. Other disadvantages of focus groups include: difficulties in following up individual views, group dynamics may affect whether participants contribute and what they actually say (Robson, 2011); they can be difficult to record and transcribe and may lead to group effects (Greig et al., 2012). Furthermore, the researcher has less control over the data produced (Morgan, 1998) and the participants' responses are not independent of one another, which may mask individual viewpoints and further restricts the generalisability of results (Kitzinger, 1994). Also, a more talkative or dominant member of the focus group may potentially bias the results as the more reserved group members may be reluctant to talk. Despite these well-acknowledged limitations, they are well recognised as a valid research method for understanding children's views on mobile technologies, and Bruseberg and McDonagh-Philp (2002) suggest that focus groups can provide detailed information about user needs that can feed directly into the design process.

Ringrose et al. (2012, p. 22) used both focus-group research and individual interviews in their UK-based study on 'sexting' but they used them as part of a multi-method approach in their qualitative research design, and they highlight the differences in adopting the two difference methods:

> Participating in an individual interview is a very different experience to taking part in a focus group so we talked through the reasons for conducting individual interviews with participants, explaining that

we wanted to explore some of the subjects raised in the focus groups and online ethnography in more depth and get to know a little more about their lives. Conducting a mix of focus groups and individual interviews allowed us to explore both the social context of 'sexting' and speak with young people about sensitive topics without their peers. The individual interviews consequently focused on the issues around sexual communication and digital technology raised in the focus groups and students' Facebook interactions online.

Child-centred techniques are methods favoured by children themselves (Wyness, 2012, p. 213); they tend to be based on non-traditional approaches (Corsaro, 2011) and these methods have been employed by a growing number of social science researchers in a variety of contexts. For example, see Barker and Weller (2006), Heath and Walker (2012) and Coombs' (forthcoming) research on children's perceptions of death using a 'Stuff in a box' method. Gillies and Robinson's (2012) research using creative methods with challenging pupils, although not about mobile technology, highlights some interesting issues for fostering participation and developing child-centred approaches, especially when displaying or publishing art work, poems and opinions. Mand (2012) also suggests that art-based methods seek to include children's voices, but that in representing and giving space to children's voices, some 'voices' are muted or lost due to spatial restrictions and adults agendas. These studies usefully highlight that, whilst the development of child-centred/non-traditionalist approaches is seen as ethical and inclusive from a theoretical perspective, these approaches can be less than straightforward in practice.

> We inevitably encountered challenges and difficulties which offer insight into some of the complexities of creative methodologies. Any research with children or young people requires careful consideration, but the use of more creative methods can generate particular ethical dilemma, particularly in terms of how to represent the material collected.
>
> (Gillies and Robinson, 2012, p. 171)

'Ethnographers have long since used photography, film and more recently video in research and representation' (Pink, 2007, p. 8), and both ethnography and visual methods are widely used in research with young people (Allan, 2012). Using a combination of visual, online and creative methodological approaches to facilitate young people's meaningful participation in research and to allow their voices to be heard whilst balancing participation with child-protection considerations using virtual methods requires careful consideration (Bond and Agnew, 2013). The use of visual methods in childhood research is gaining not only popularity but also academic acceptance as a valid research method; however, in using visual methods, the importance of other forms of communications should not be forgotten, as Pimlott-Wilson (2012, p. 146) points out:

> the importance of dialogue cannot be lost even with the adoption of visual and activity-based methods. Creative methods generate knowledge about participants' lives and social experiences, and thus their creations cannot be understood in isolation. In order for visual representations to express the meaning of their author, a level of dialogue is needed rather than researchers attaching their own interpretations to the productions made by participants. Together the combination of visual method with narration can offer deeper insights than either one can provide alone.

Carrick-Davies' (2011) study used film as a methodological approach to engage challenging and vulnerable groups of young people in his research on the risks and safeguarding issues in relation to e-safety. The young people in the Munch, Poke, Ping project were encouraged to talk about their own use of online social networking sites or their mobile phone on their own terms through focus groups, drama and film-making, and these participatory techniques were highly effective in establishing and maintaining the groups' interest and engagement in the study (Carrick-Davies, 2011). Using film and other visual methods is well established across a number of social science disciplines, and 'photography is an increasingly popular research method, used to explore a number of topics with a wide range of social groups, including children and young people'; however, 'using photography requires engagement with philosophical debates regarding the nature of the social world and how knowledge can be constructed' (Barker and Smith, 2012, pp. 91–92).

Similar philosophical debates are relevant also to the debates surrounding online methods and the nature of reality in relation to virtual worlds and online/offline identities. When researching technology, Ito (2009) draws attention to the importance of understanding the social and cultural contexts in which technological developments are embedded, as they are not separated from them. The rapidly growing interest and research practice in relation to the internet, both as an object of research and as a research tool, has transformed the range and nature of research methods available for social science studies. The internet provides a rich context for online research, including virtual ethnography, email interviews, virtual focus groups and participant observation, including covert participant observation, online social surveys, and content and discourse analysis (Bryman, 2012). My own internet-based study, which aimed to improve knowledge and understanding of pro-ana websites and online communities, was funded by Nominet Trust in 2012. It considered perceptions of risk from a variety of perspectives and notions of self-identity in relation to pro-ana online environments. The research examined how the sites offer tips and advice, support and other information, and an embodied social space for people with eating disorders. The research used content analysis of 126 online spaces to gather detailed empirical evidence using existing literature and collected data online. Both quantitative and qualitative data were analysed, including text and images gathered from selected, publicly available pro-ana websites, blogs and online forums. The relationship between the users' perceptions of risk as discussed online, self-identity and online environments was examined in order to gain knowledge and understanding of the range, uses and content of these sites (discussed in more detail in Chapter 6).

Another example of online research is offered by Davies (2009), who emphasises how, in her work research with young people in online environments, it is possible to collect data in its original form in its original context. She observes:

in the work I report here, I have 'listened in' to children and young people's voices, seeing them communicate in groups where they have chosen to participate, often *away from the gaze*, as it were, of teachers and parents. In reading texts that young people have chosen to put online, I have seen them represent themselves through different 'voices' in different contexts, experimenting with a variety of ways of being. It is hard to know what an 'authentic voice' actually is, and this may be the researcher's 'holy grail', but I believe it is possible to witness authentic play online, as well as voices that are earnest and serious.

(Davies, 2009, p. 179)

Ringrose et al. (2012) also used a variety of virtual methods in their sexting study, which included online ethnography via Facebook and also text mapping via Blackberry messaging, and Barbovschi et al.'s (2013) report outlines a number of examples of methodological innovations in undertaking research with children. Online methods are increasingly used in social science research, as Kozinets (2010, p. 1), in his account of *Netnography* (online ethnography), highlights: 'Our social worlds are going digital. As a consequence, social scientists around the world are finding that to understand society they must follow people's social activities and encounters onto the internet and through other technologically-mediated communications'. Another example of online methods is Carrington (2008, p. 151) who used blogs in a study of childhood, text and new technologies, and who argues for a view of 'text as "active" rather than as an artefact and an acceptance that children's lives are lived across multiple sites that require sophisticated blending and use a variety of literate practices'. boyd (2006) also comments on the use of blogs in her research, and highlights the role of the blog as a space for research opportunities and performing an identity. Snee (2012) also uses blog analysis very effectively as a way of accessing very rich, in-depth, naturally occurring data on young people's construction of identity through their gap-year experiences. Online gaming is also a research method that is gaining much interest in the social science community and Facer et al. (2004) investigated experiential learning through mobile gaming with children. The role of geographies of childhood and youth literature is increasingly recognised, and Crowe (2012, p. 163) examines how young people interact with technologically created environments, arguing that 'in research terms, at least – online space is sharing many of the characteristics of material space'. Weller (2012) demonstrates the role of online and digital spaces in facilitating qualitative longitudinal research with teenagers and, although doing research online is relatively new in the shifting paradigms of social research, especially in relation to social research with children and young people, it can offer more choice of methodological approaches and greater accessibility to both social researcher and participants.

To some, the online environment as a shifting research environment may feel daunting. We believe, though, that it offers an exciting shift in the possibilities for research and provided a wealth of opportunity. For example, when we think of research we typically think of researcher and participant. The internet, however, appears to be transforming the role of researcher and those being researched.

(Gaiser and Schreiner, 2009, p. 159)

Children's participation in research

Giving children a voice is a well-established concept in childhood studies but issues related to authenticity, meaningful participation and the diversity of children's individual experiences have remained somewhat problematic (James, 2007). Whilst children and young people have been traditionally passively positioned in the research process, the recent increased emphases on children's rights and citizenship have led to emphasis now being placed on children's participation in research (Veale, 2005). Thomas and O'Kane (2000, p. 825) argue that 'the use of participatory methods can help resolve a number of ethical problems in research with children, and, at the same time, can enhance validity and reliability'. Whilst the research method should fit the question that is asked (Greene and Hogan, 2005), Grover (2004) points out that there is no set way to give children a voice in social research due to the wide variety of research issues and contexts. Furthermore, participation of children in research emphasises dialogical qualities as beneficial, the researcher needs to engage with children's own cultures of communication and, in the process of research, as power moves between different actors and different social positions it is produced and negotiated in the social interactions (Christensen, 2004).

Hart (1992) considers how the unequal balance of power between children and adults can be ameliorated through the use of more child-friendly research techniques. Underpinned by an holistic ideology, which values the whole child and endeavours to understand each child within the context of their community and culture (Woods, 2005), qualitative studies often employ multiple methods of data collection which are holistic, emergent and reflective (Creswell, 2003). It is interesting to note from Kirby (2002, p. 268), therefore, how 'the growing interest in the concepts of empowerment and participation in the political arena has been mirrored by an increasing awareness for the potential of user involvement in research'. Thomas and O'Kane (2000, p. 832) outline the key principles for researching with children and suggest that research with children is improved when it incorporates and builds on children's own definitions of what is interesting or important; uses methods of communication that children find meaningful and comfortable; and acknowledges the importance of children's emotional needs.

Despite developments in social science research, which acknowledge and even celebrate child participants as competent social actors, concerns about their competencies are still seen as limitations to children's participation in research (Bucknall, 2012). 'Whilst up-to-date research has tended to assume that children are capable of playing a full research part as meaning-making respondents, a few adult researchers have experimented with using children in a researching rather than a researched capacity' (Wyness, 2012, p. 204). Kellet (2005a, 2005b) sets out the debate for children themselves being active researchers in the research process, and Kellet (2010, p. 8) develops these discussions further to consider children's rights and the notion of citizenship to consider the 'pivotal position of research *by* children' to argue for a reappraisal of children and research. Bucknall (2012) examines the theoretical and applied developments of children as researchers (CaRs), and argues that even young children can be efficient and effective researchers. 'Through sensitively judged facilitation, young researchers develop a sense of ownership which, in turn, provides the motivation they need to persevere with necessary lengthy projects, empowers them as researchers and leads to the promotion of new knowledge and understanding about children's lives' (Bucknall, 2012, p. 7).

Hill (2006) proposes four discourses that influence young people's willingness to take part in research initiatives: an interest in the topic being researched; how they may learn from participating; therapeutic opportunities to talk about issues/feelings; and empowerment opportunities to be listened to and inform policy/service provision. The shifting paradigms of childhood research underpinned by Article 12 UNCRC have led to a number of international community initiatives in which children have undertaken research that has challenged inequality and policy developments which they felt were not in their best interests (see Lansdown, 2011) but, whilst there are some celebrated examples of child-centred and child-led research, the debates on what is meant by ethical and meaningful participation continue.

One of the great imponderables is whether child-led research can continue to grow within existing adult research parameters or whether we need to begin to consider a new paradigm to accommodate it. What is clear is that research *by* children is fundamentally different from adult research *about* children and we cannot use the same norms of reference nor the same terms of measurement and assessment. The time to begin that deliberation process is now before we are overtaken by a wave of child-led research which we are ill-prepared for and have not properly considered how to receive it, measure it or value it.

(Kellet, 2005b, p. 31)

Ethical considerations

Wyness (2012) discusses the ethical dimensions and dilemmas of child research, and Kimmel (1988) suggests that a detailed reporting of ethical procedures should be required and expected in all published social research. The Economic and Social Data Service (ESDS) guidelines (available online) on legal and ethical issues in researching with children suggest that there are no legal or ethical guidelines which define the age at which a person can give consent to be interviewed or observed in a social research study, and that uncertainty remains about the nature of the confidential relationship between a child and a researcher. Ethical guidance is available from a variety of sources, including, for example, Hill (2005); Save the Children (online); Barnado's children's charity; the National Children's Bureau (NCB) online; the NSPCC; and the ESDS, also online. These guidelines suggest that access to children involves issues of informed consent, confidentiality and legal issues prior to negotiations to gain access via gatekeepers who, through their relationship with the children, have a protective role. However, it is interesting to note from Hood et al. (1996b) that gatekeepers can potentially undermine children's right to participate, and undertaking research with children and young people of any type may give rise to potential ethical issues. Thomas and O'Kane (1998, p. 336) argue that 'whilst most methodological and ethical issues that arise in work with children are also present in work with adults, there are important differences'. Aspects of child protection, the role of the researcher and questions of responsibility, confidentiality and how to deal with the potential disclosure of information, and the possibility of abuse by a researcher or possible exploitation through the research process require special consideration (Thomas and O'Kane, 1998).

Frankfort-Nachmias and Nachmias (1996) suggest that two common issues within the ethical decision-making framework are informed consent and privacy. The process of informed consent is of particular importance when researching children and young people (Mahon et al., 1996) especially when researching sensitive issues. Ringrose et al. (2012), for example, offer careful consideration of the ethical implications of their sexting research and the management of disclosures in relation to potential abuse and illegal activity, and describe how they were mindful of potential discomfort. Their study detailed careful child-protection procedures, data-storage confidentiality and informed consent. Kellett (2005a) argues that informed consent should go further than simply informing participants on the nature of the research and asking them to sign a consent form, and suggests that any research that does not go beyond this is insufficient and ethically questionable. She suggests that 'participants should be told the aims and objectives of the research, how the data collected from them will be used (especially with regard to confidentiality and anonymity) and how the findings will be disseminated' (Kellett, 2005a, p. 33). In addition, Christensen (2004) outlines the importance for researchers to be sensitive towards the issue of power. Research relationships that are based on respect and on informed consent can in some way ameliorate power imbalances between researchers and the child (Roberts-Holmes, 2011).

Robert-Holmes (2011) also suggests that the ethical values and principles which underpin child-centred methodology place children at the centre of the research process. Thomas and O'Kane (1998) argue that the ethical problems in research with children can be overcome by using a participatory approach and that by addressing ethical issues presented by qualitative research with children from a perspective that respects children's autonomy, the research methodology can be improved. 'Allowing children to be active participants in the research process enhances their status as individuals with inherent rights to participation in society more generally and the right to be heard in their authentic voice' (Grover, 2004, p. 90). Attitudes to research are, therefore, central to ethical considerations and, if the research respects children's abilities, it will use a variety of methods in order to listen to children's voices (Roberts-Holmes, 2011). Ólafsson et al. (2013a, p. 39) offer a helpful common-practice section in their 'How to research children and online technologies? Frequently asked questions and best practice':

- Seeking to safeguard the interests of all affected by the research, including considering the possible consequences of the study or the misuse of the results.
- A commitment to listening to and including the perspectives of children and young people in the research.
- Inviting freely given written consent from all children participating in the research, and from the parent or guardian of those under 16, whilst ensuring that all understand that they can refuse any question or withdraw at any time.
- Informing children and parents, through discussion and the provision of age-appropriate leaflets, what the research is about, how it will be disseminated, and how their data will be stored.

- Keeping all data confidential, removing all personal identifiers, and assigning pseudonyms where appropriate, plus storing the data in accordance with the Data Protection Act (UK).
- Informing participants that if they divulge information suggesting that they or others are at risk of harm, the researcher has a duty of care to report this and to ensure support for the child (and to inform the participant that this is occurring).
- Providing a debriefing after each research interview, leaving all participants with a written record of the researchers' names and contact information.
- Providing feedback on the research process to all who ask for it (e.g. sending a copy of the summary report to participating schools or homes if requested).

Reflexivity in research

In considering 'innovation in qualitative research, it is fundamentally important to reflect on what we, as researchers, regard as creative' (Weller, 2012, p. 130). Jones (2002, p. 140) notes that 'post-structuralist theories have been useful in aiding the reflexive process that is incorporated into the research process'. Jones (2002, p. 145) also draws on Derrida's work (which centred on a criticism on the authoritarianism of Western thought, especially in its commitment to essentialism) to observe how 'the combined practices of essentialising people as well as locating them in opposing categories results in one being considered as subordinate to the other'. This is well summed up by Allan (2012, p. 70), who argues that:

> For many academics, the emphasis that ethnographers have placed on naturalism has become increasingly problematic in recent years with the advent of post-structuralist theory, with the developments that have taken place within hermeneutic and feminist thinking, and with the 'crisis of representation' that is thought to have occurred within social science. Many began to question whether ethnography can reflect the 'reality' in any simple sense, and whether ethnographers can ever be value neutral in their practice, simply reporting on what is out there.

Wyness (2012) argues that researchers are continually made aware of the unequal power relationships between children and adults. Buckingham and Bragg (2004, p. 38) suggest that 'feminist and postmodern researchers stress the importance of reflexivity – that is, the role of the researchers in interpreting, representing and producing knowledge from the voices of research subjects'. Yet, in relation to researching children's experiences of technologies, especially online, there is, according to Ólafsson et al. (2013b), a somewhat mixed picture of approaches and outputs. They suggest that many studies conducted in this field have been undertaken at a single point in time, which makes comparisons problematic, although there are now increasing numbers of studies which are published through peer-reviewed academic journals. Many are published online and a proportion of the research is not conducted effectively, well reported or disseminated. The 'debates about recognizing and addressing power relations in the research process are part of a wider move towards reflexivity' (Barker and Weller, 2003, p. 36).

> The recognition of children's social agency and active participation in research has significantly changed children's position within the human and social sciences and led to a weakening of taken-for-granted assumptions found in more conventional approaches to child research. In order to hear the voices of children in the representation of their own lives it is important to employ research practices such as reflexivity and dialogue.
>
> (Christensen, 2004, p. 165)

Whilst this is an area of increasing interest for research in social science, Grover (2004, p. 92) argues that the research process itself may suffer if children continue to be regarded as objects of study rather than 'collaborators in telling the story of their lived experience'. In childhood and youth studies, 'reflexivity is now widely regarded as a methodological necessity in research' (Christensen and James, 2008, p. 6), and these developments have led to reflexive forms of conceptualising the research process and the researcher's role in the research. However, what remains challenging, certainly for the purposes of this text, is that in research with children and online environments 'overwhelmingly [the] focus is on fixed internet, to the neglect of mobile, convergent and emerging technologies' (Ólafsson et al., 2013b, p. 5). The most recent research (at the time of writing) is the initial findings by Mascheroni and Ólafsson (2013) and the Net Children Go Mobile study who, funded by the Safer Internet Programme, investigated through both qualitative and quantitative methods how increasingly mobilised internet access changes the landscapes of risk for children in Denmark, Italy, Romania, the UK, Ireland and Portugal.

> Good research is a thinking person's game. It is a creative and strategic process that involves constantly assessing, reassessing, and making decisions about the best possible means for obtaining trust-worthy information, carrying out appropriate analysis, and drawing credible conclusions.
>
> (O'Leary, 2004, p. 1)

Morrow and Richards (1996) raise questions about children's relationships with both the research process and the researcher, and Grover (2004) discusses involving children as active rather than passive participants in the research process. Often, children are not consulted, but even when their views and opinions are sought, their ideas may not be taken seriously (James, 2007). Christen and James (2008, p. 3) argue that 'what is important is that the particular methods chosen for a piece of research should be appropriate for the people involves in the study, for its social and cultural context and for the kinds of research questions that are being posed'. 'Culture is essentially a collective concept, applicable to social groups, consisting of shared meanings and interpretations and enabling us to get beyond explanations of social processes that are the mere aggregate of individuals' actions or, worse, statements about individual psychology' (Keating, 2008, p. 111). Thorne (2012, p. 31) suggests that 'it is not by chance that the most suggestive empirical research on children – revealing them to be complex actors, strategists, performers, users of language, creators of culture – is based on qualitative and interpretive approaches'. As summed up by Hagerman (2010, p. 98):

> By offering children new ways to communicate with adults, by listening to the authentic voices of children, and by considering children's perspectives seriously, adult sociologists provide children with a basic human right that is frequently denied to this population, the right of the child to be heard.

Towards a methodological pluralism

Therefore, for the purposes of this book, I have attempted to draw on the limited research in the field and have adopted a reflexive approach in trying to ensure that the material used is trustworthy before considering theoretically the analysis presented here. The theoretical developments in research with children presented in this chapter stress the importance of focusing on children's competence rather than children's incompetence in researching with children. Meneses and Mominó (2010, p. 198) observe how 'the latest thinking in the field has started to define and understand children and young people as hetergenenous, nonpassive, autonomous, diverse, and versatile agents actively appropriating the Internet in meaningful contexts of their everyday lives'. Grover (2004) argues that positivistic approaches do not address the subjective experiences of participants, and Roberts and Sanders (2005, p. 297) contend that 'unlike the relatively closed world of natural scientific experiments, the social world is more contingent because of the unpredictable nature of human behaviour'. In understanding the social world, Winch (1990, cited in May, T., 2011) argues that positivist methods are not applicable in the social sciences and emphasises the importance of meaning and language in research. Utilisation of two or more techniques within research of the same methodological origin and nature is known as intra-method triangulation and uses the strengths of each method to overcome the deficiencies of the other, and the intra-triangulation of research tools would achieve a higher degree of validity and reliability than a single research tool (Sarantakos, 2005). Barker and Weller (2003) offer an evaluation of innovative children-centred research techniques; for example, photographs, diaries, interviews and surveys. Furthermore, 'research is a practice that is part of social life rather than an external contemplation of it' (Christensen, 2004, p. 166) and the 'medium by which humans interpret their encounters with the world is linguistic or at least symbolic' (Greene and Hogan, 2005, p. 5). There has certainly been far more written about the qualitative approaches that seek to highlight children's own understandings in localised contexts (Wyness, 2012), and qualitative research as a longitudinal study can also highlight trends and changes over time (Weller, 2012).

However, the very nature of knowledge is a debatable concept in itself. Qualitative research of this nature lends itself to the more idiographic view of knowledge, considering nomothetic knowledge as insensitive to local meanings, and favouring understanding and interpretation as research goals (Punch, 2005). Denzin and Lincoln (2005) suggest that the social constructivist approach views knowledge as local, partial and situated. Grover (2004, pp. 84–85) further outlines how a 'phenomenological study', that allows 'subjects to communicate their experience without having it transformed by the researcher so as to alter its meaning in any significant manner', produces phenomenological data adding a dimension which has its own 'authenticity and validity'. In Plummer's (2001, p. 7) *Documents of Life 2: An Invitation to Critical Humanism*, he argues for privileging the 'active human subject' in social science research, and that it should strive to consider human subjectivity and creativity in understanding how people respond to social constraints and actively form their social worlds. He calls for a greater understanding of the diversity in people's lived experiences and for adopting a more humanistic approach to social science research. I have tried to highlight some of the diversities in children's lived experiences in the discussion in Chapter 7, but just as research on children and mobile internet technologies remains scarce, research with children with a disability or from other traditionally excluded groups is even rarer. In fact, when undertaking the research for this book, I used the European evidence database of 1,200 studies – held by the EU Kids online network – extensively, but typing *disability* into the search field revealed only one study, an unpublished Masters dissertation (Kontogianni, 2012) and *disabled* produced no results at all.

Ryan-Flood and Gill (2010, p. 1) claim that 'all research involves secrets and silences of various kinds'. The debates set out above are pertinent to my argument in this chapter in relation to researching children's views and experiences, and most especially in relation to understanding the everyday experiences of children with a disability, as 'it is no longer acceptable to exclude disabled children simply because they are considered incompetent or pose challenges to traditional research methods' (Boggis, 2011). In her study of disabled children's views and experiences of using high-tech communication aids in their everyday lives, Boggis (2011) employed what she describes as 'creativity and reflexivity' in 'designing approaches for consultation, and, to this end, "bespoke" methods were adopted and a range of data collection tools were used, including participant observation, interviews and focus groups. This multi-method approach enabled the provision of important findings relating to disabled children's everyday experiences of using high-tech communication aids'. Goggin (2006, p. 102) suggests that mobile technologies and disability have been overlooked in social science research, but that 'this is an important research agenda, not only as a matter of human rights and justice but also because these narratives unsettle our taken-for-granted theories of technology' (a fuller discussion of disabled childhoods, mobile technologies and everyday experiences is offered in Chapter 7). There is a small body of literature that considers disabled children's viewpoints using a variety of methods. For example, using case-study action research, Mavrou's (2011) research on Assistive Technology (AT) highlights how mobile technologies are used in individualised educational settings and argues for more effective AT policy frameworks. Wong and Tan (2012) used a case-study approach to explore the potential of iPhone/smartphone technology for blind or visually impaired users. However, 'additional research, of a qualitative nature, is much needed to continue developing a sociology of childhood and youth that is also interested in the specific signification that they grant to digital inclusion exclusion in society' (Meneses and Mominó, 2010, p. 206).

Conclusion

This chapter has outlined different approaches to undertaking research with children, and the methodological and philosophical developments in child-centred research related to the social studies of childhood. Christensen et al.'s (2011) recent work on using mobile phone technology as part of a mixed-methods approach also offers a useful conceptual framework through which to understand the recent developments and opportunities offered by new media technologies in understanding childhood. In their study of children's mobility, their innovative methodological approach facilitated a rich understanding of the children's everyday movements through a detailed documentation of the children's subjective experiences with systematic observations, mapping and survey data. Heath and Walker (2012) highlight recent methodological innovations in youth research using creative methods more familiar in humanities and arts, and, although they also observe that qualitative methods are more suitable for understanding children's unique experiences, Greene and Hogan (2005) emphasise the importance of considering children's lives from multiple perspectives, and observe that no single theoretical or methodological approach is preferable overall. Furthermore, Christensen et al.'s (2011, p. 3) conclude from their study that 'qualitative methods are limited in their ability to provide a systematic and accurate overview of children's everyday mobility patterns' and neither quantitative nor qualitative approaches alone provided an adequate understanding of children's everyday mobility; they combined ethnographic approaches with innovative mobile technological methods to form a methodological triangulation that they felt enhanced the validity of their study.

Lange and Mierendorff (2011, p. 78) observe that 'due to the general methodological doubts concerning the question of what we know if we look at the so-called rapidly changing "realities" – which no longer seem to be realities – and due to the growing paradigm of individualism and pluralism'. This is important for the purpose of the debates set out in this chapter. Corsaro's (2011, p. 47) claim that 'the research process reflects a direct concern with capturing children's voices, perspectives, interests, and rights as citizens' is fundamentally important, as are the values which MacNaughton et al. (2001) outline as the principles of high-quality childhood research, and they argue that research should be: respectful of children's participatory rights; critical, political and ethical; well designed, transparent and purposeful; and should reflect honesty regarding any assumptions. Wyness (2012, p. 208) observes that 'researchers use their "foreignness", their distinctiveness from the children, as a means of entering their social worlds'. Some studies have used Prensky's (2001) 'digital native' versus 'digital immigrant' distinction to undertake research with children and technologies. Brown and Czerniewicz (2010), however, are highly critical of this concept and argue that such terminology hides inequalities in digital experiences, and that instead we should be concerned with digital democracy and reclaiming the term 'digitizen' (these debates are explored further in Chapter 7). Furthermore, Veale (2005, p. 270) notes:

> In work with children, perhaps more so than with adults, there is a complex relationship between issues of power, control, responsibility and ethics in the research approach and methodology, and questions about 'participation' in child research continue to pose challenges.

In Chapter 3, I argued for theoretical pluralism in understanding childhood and technology, and this chapter considers different research agendas and approaches that have been, and could be, adopted in researching childhood, mobile technologies and everyday experiences. Greig et al. (2012) suggest that research should be cumulative and this research builds upon previous research in the social studies of childhood and the influence of the globalisation of children's rights as enshrined in the UNCRC. These changes have begun to have an impact on all aspects of children's lives, from their relationship with their parents, to their participation in school and other social institutions. The paradigm of childhood sociology, emphasising children's position as 'social actors' – as creative and inventive users of the world around them – has nurtured blossoming conceptual and empirical explorations of children's competency and agency in a range of diverse settings (O'Brien et al.,

2000). This is important to the analysis of childhood, mobile internet technologies and everyday experiences presented in this book, as is Buckingham's (2007) call for caution in using research findings to make generalised observations about technology and children's experiences, especially in relation to learning. He points out that many government-funded studies, for example, have found positive relationships between ICT and attainment in children's learning, but that other independent studies have been less than convincing that such a claim can be made and, as such, it is 'impossible to generalise about the consequences of using technology in education' (Buckingham, 2007, p. 73). This remains a relatively new area of academic study and, as such, we are only just beginning to understand the complexities of researching mobile, networked mediation technologies in an increasingly digitised society.

> Computer culture, virtual culture, cyberculture, e-culture, Internet culture, new media, convergence culture, digital culture are all relatively new terms that are toady widely used in scientific and popular literature. Scholars from various disciplines have examined the impact of the new media on various social aspects of virtual space and its impact on the real sphere and they have changed their views on digital culture many times over a relatively short periods of time... As ICT further progresses in its development towards miniaturization, the boundaries are no longer clear.
>
> (Uzelac, 2008, p. 12)

Yet, it is precisely this development towards mobilisation and miniaturisation that is the focus of this book, and, drawing on a selection of research and theoretical approaches, it sets out to do so in a way that attempts to avoid adopting a perspective trajectory. It is in having a respect for the 'plurality of approaches in social sciences' that we can recognise differences but also appreciate the 'potential for dialogue between approaches and methods' and 'identity meeting-points among the various approaches' (della Porta and Keating, 2008b, pp. 318–19). O'Connel Davidson and Layder (1994) propose that theories form part of a broad framework of ideas and play a role in a researcher's agenda. May, T. (2011) suggests that theories allow researchers to make links with other researchers within specific fields of interest and to locate their research findings within a general theory of the workings of society. As della Porta and Keating (2008b, p. 316) observe:

This also means that each good research project is indebted to the work of other scholars. We refer to other people's theories; borrow concepts that are developed (either inductively or deductively) by others; make use of previous debates on problems and solutions in data collection; apply techniques of analysis that have long histories of trial and error. Each piece of research usually only marginally improves on issues of theoretical clarity and empirical knowledge.

5
Relationships

Introduction

This chapter centres on children's everyday experiences in their relationships and their use of mobile internet technologies – their relationships with their family, friends and with wider society. It considers how children manage and maintain their day-to-day relationships through mobile technologies and the importance of *context* in their experiences.

> The term 'relationship', meaning a close and continuing emotional tie to another, has only come into general usage relatively recently. To be clear what is at stake here, we can introduce the term *pure relationship* to refer to this phenomenon. A pure relationship has nothing to do with sexual purity, and is a limiting concept rather than only a descriptive one. It refers to a situation where a social relation is entered into for its own sake, for what can be derived by each person from a sustained association with another; and which is continued only in so far as it is thought by both parties to deliver enough satisfaction for each individual to stay within it.
>
> (Giddens, 1992, p. 58)

In the light of Giddens' reflections on the term 'relationship' above, this chapter discusses children's friendships, their intimate and/or romantic relationships and family relationships to consider how the mobile technologies themselves and the sharing of content are increasingly important in children's relationships and in the construction of young people's self-identity in late modernity.

'The pure relationship', increasingly sought in late modernity (Jamieson, 1999), characterises Giddens' (1992) notion of the transformation of intimacy. The discussion here considers mobile technologies in children's sustained associations in relationships, and how these are mediated and managed through mobile internet technologies in their everyday lives. There are, however, no simple one-to-one relationships between technologies and people (Thrift, 1996 cited in Holloway and Valentine, 2003). Mobile internet technologies are simultaneously viewed as both supportive but also potentially damaging, in providing security and connectivity but also in influencing insecurity and anxiety, thus exemplifying the double-edged sword of modernity as discussed by Giddens (1990). Barns (1999, p. 163) observes that technological developments similarly both fascinate and concern us, and, that 'the meanings of technologies are significantly determined by what people make of them in the context of everyday practices, conversely it is also true that the diffusion of technologies will often subtly transform social practices, identities and relationships'. Being connected to others through mobile technologies offers reassurance in everyday relationships and in how everyday lives are managed, but these connections can also operate as a site of concern when communications are either negative or aggressive in nature or are absent. Giddens (1999) contends that emotional communication replaces traditional ties in late modernity and that sexual love and relationships, as well as parent–child relationships and friendships, are transformed. Mobile technologies connect and provide platforms to the networks in which these emotional communications are played out in young people's everyday lives. Ding and Littleton (2005, p. 97) observe that 'children's interactions with other children are important contexts for development, as it is through such interaction that children learn skills such as how to co-operate and resolve conflict, and share the task of constructing their social understanding'. Konkka (2003) makes a useful distinction between functional and emotional needs, and young people adopt different uses of mobile technologies in different contexts, with audiences and between different spaces in their everyday lives. Mobile technologies have become and are what Ling (2012, p. 35) terms 'social mediation technologies' which integrate different dimensions of the internet and the mobile internet, including social network sites, email, images, texting and talking online. From a young age, children use and appropriate digital technologies and virtual environments within the context of their everyday lives, and they play activities, frequently combining virtual interactions with fantasy play or other activities (Plowden et al., 2010, p. 63). Social mediation technologies assume a critical mass for groups of users (Ling, 2012) and, as such, the concepts of age, gender, geographic space and time are also important to an understanding of patterns of technology consumption.

Durkin (2001, p. 64) notes that an 'important aspect of the development of social knowledge is understanding social phenomena. In recent years there has been a growth of research into how children perceive and think about other people, about social relations and about the social structure'. As discussed in chapters 2 and 4, Jenks (2005) further emphasises that children's social relationships and their cultures are worthy of academic study in their own right, and should not be dependent on adults' perspectives and concerns. Children and young people use a wide variety of mobile technologies to manage and maintain their everyday relationships, and are reflexive in their use of the technologies and are often concerned with what is appropriate and expected and what is not (Bond, 2010). Durkin (2001) outlines socialisation theory and how it is through social processes that patterns and skills are developed that underpin our face-to-face interactions in life, and I argue here that these social processes are also apparent in children's mobile technology practices and behaviours, which are also subject to a socialisation process. Mobile internet technologies are increasingly important to family communication practices, family functioning, friendship formation and social support, and at a more sinister level, to less positive behaviours and bullying. Analysis of the EU Kids Online data (Livingstone et al., 2011a) illustrates how children's relationships with online environments and mobile technologies are far from simplistic. From a social constructivist approach (as suggested by Sikes, 2004), a complicated and complex network of people, relationships, practices and technologies, functions and performances in children's everyday lives emerges. Through exchanging content (downloaded or user-generated) – texts, images and videos – amongst friends, in the form of gifting (see Maus, 2002; Berking, 1999), young people actively invest and sustain their relationships with one another. At the same time, however, mobile technologies can be negatively powerful tools for bullying (see Chapter 6 for further discussion) by the same sending of content in the form of text, images or videos. This notion of power is explored in some depth by Maus (2002) who suggests that gift-giving also facilitates status and rivalry in relationships, and there is much evidence from the extensive research carried out by Livingstone et al. (2011a) and my own study (see Bond, 2010, 2011, 2013) where children have described their feelings and expectations associated with not getting texted back, receiving nasty messages or using online and mobile content to bully others.

Friendships

The title of Ling's (2012) fifth chapter is ' "If I Didn't Have a Mobile Phone then I Would Be Stuck": The Diffusion of Mobile Communication'. In it, he states: 'the mobile phone has become increasingly common. People often cannot think of leaving home without their purse or wallet, their keys, and their mobile phone. Many teens feel excluded from social life if they do not have a mobile phone' (Ling, 2012, p. 102). In my study, many of the children I spoke to talked about mobile technologies, namely mobile phones, in these terms. For example:

> *Cathy [aged 17]*: You can't have friends without one.

Without a mobile you would have no friends. Cathy's example above, taken from a discussion about the importance of mobile phones to friendships, demonstrates the centrality of the mobile mediation technologies in children's everyday social lives and to their friendships and social relationships. This online participation was explored by Mascheroni and Ólafsson's (2013, p. 25), who found that:

> Given that these activities are far more popular among children who are also smartphones or tablets users, then we can assume a correlation – though not a causal relationship – between mobile convergent media and online participatory activities.

Buunk (2001, p. 385) considers friendships as a relationship proposing that 'individuals involved in such relationships are motivated to invest in their relationship, to coordinate their behaviours, and to take the interests of the other into account'. The mobile phone and other mobile internet technologies, such as iPads and tablets, have become essential in the formation and management of young people's friendships and relationships.

Local friendship groups are often the focus of mobile technology interaction (Smoreda and Thomas, 2001) and children actively use mobile technologies to manage and then maintain relationships with both friends and family members. These relationships are complex and often complicated, but the data from the EU Kids Online survey echoes the importance of friendship to young people in late modernity. These findings confirm Pahl's (2000) analysis of friendship, drawing on Aristotle, amongst others, to emphasise the fundamental aspects of friendship associated with contemporary Western society to highlight how friends form the basic structure of lives, and are important in the private and public spheres relating to self-identity.

> Friendship is a relationship built upon the whole person and aims at a psychological intimacy, which in this limited form makes it, in practice, a rare phenomenon, even though it may be more widely desired. It is a relationship based on freedom and is, at the same time, a guarantor of freedom. A society in which this kind of relationship is growing and flourishing is qualitatively different from a society based on the culturally reinforced norms of kinship and institutional roles and behaviour.
>
> (Pahl, 2000, pp. 63–64)

In my qualitative study, the young people talked about the importance of using mobile technologies to maintain their friendship group, and this was especially important for those living in a rural area where they were often a considerable distance from their friends geographically.

> *Cathy [aged 17]*: Yeah and like that's going to be like really important when school's finished because like our real connection is school so to be out of school it's like texting or calling.
> *Megan [aged 17]*: Yeah our connection is school so if we want to meet up then it has to be like texting or calling and texting is cheaper so if like we want to talk and it's after like 4.30 then it has to be like your mobile.

Uzelac (2008) suggests that often academic discussions on the internet society tend to focus on ICT and internet potentials rather than on wider changes to the cultural and media ecology but this is important as we need to consider what is happening in the new context that new technologies have brought to our attention. Fischer (2008, p. 145) defines media ecology as 'a human science dedicated to the study of media environments' Ling (2012, p. 33) uses the concept of social ecology to describe how 'a new technology will rearrange interrelationships between elements in a social context' and mobile internet technologies have transformed how children communicate with each other. 'Interaction within cyberspace offers new possibilities for connecting people' (Čopič, 2008, p. 114). Using social network sites, text, apps and social media platforms through a mobile device everyday friendships are constantly managed, maintained and performed in virtual spaces. Ling

(2004) suggests that the mobile phone is associated with both constructive and potentially negative effects (as discussed later in Chapter 6), and discusses the implications of its adoption and use, highlighting both advantages and disadvantages. This paradox is discussed in more detail later; however, it is important to note here that the negative aspects of mobile technology use are not limited to explicit examples of bullying by or of others, but are often also depicted as feelings of insecurity and anxiety associated with their use or indeed lack of use. The notion of *perpetual contact* (see Katz and Aakhus, 2002) is helpful here as children and young people worry about not getting texted back or missing a call, and want to be in, what Agar (2003) describes as, *constant touch*. This subjective experience of uncertainty, a symptom of individualisation in late modernity, appears alongside the positive contribution that mobile technologies play in terms of providing security, reassurance and increased cohesion in relationships. This is especially important when consideration is given to the children talking about their phones not working or not having credit, as they are anxious about not having contact or limited/reduced contact, which may impact on their friendships. Becky (aged 14), for example, described how using a mobile phone is both important for maintaining friendships but how it can also incite worry, anxiety and uncertainty:

> *Pip [aged 14]*: I think that they are important though 'cos we like text each other all the time.
> *Becky [aged 14]*: Yeah and if we didn't like text each other also they are a way of ruining friendships.
> *Laura [aged 14]*: They are.
> *Becky [aged 14]*: Because you can use mobile phones to like ... it's like they can ruin friendships because if you don't text back or if someone doesn't like text you back that really annoys me.
> *Laura [aged 14]*: And you can get arguments on your mobile phone a lot.
> *Becky [aged 14]*: Yeah I think we use our phones a lot for that.
> *Pip [aged 14]*: Yeah it creates a lot of worry as well – 'cos you are like ...
> *Laura [aged 14]*: Yeah paranoia, paranoia.

For the girls in this group, communication practices through mobile technologies were fundamental to their communication as friends and to facilitating cohesion as a cultural group, and in minimising the risk of isolation characteristic of late modernity, but also in inciting potentially increased anxiety and uncertainty within those relationships simultaneously. The notions of risk versus trust so prominent in Giddens (1990) and the individualisation emphasised by Giddens (1990, 1991) and Beck (1992) are evident. 'Today's virtual spaces drastically change users' behaviours and positioning online: from consumers of information and an "information-receiving" attitude, users become active participants and collaborators' (Varbanova, 2008, p. 169). Berking's (1999) notion of gift-giving is also of conceptual use in understanding this secure/insecure paradox, as he suggests that failure to reciprocate can lead to the other's uncertainty as everyday consciousness is imbued with feelings of mutual trust and norms of reciprocity. Ling (2012, p. 23) suggests that 'the complex of the "reciprocal typifications" eventually becomes a system of interactions'. In these systems of interactions, the risk of paranoia that the girls above describe is an example of the increased anxiety and uncertainty associated with the prominence of individuality and the rise in feelings of isolation conceptually linked to the postmodern exercise (as outlined by Wilkinson, 2001).

Mobile technologies have a reciprocal characteristic in children's everyday lives echoing Berking's (1999, p. 8) suggestion that:

> The ritual context requires some attention. It would be impolite simply to push the present to one side. The compulsion to act passes from the giver to the recipient, whose task it now is to consummate the ritual of staged uncertainty.

This *ritual of staged uncertainty* resonates in the literature on children and mobile technologies, as they are often concerned and anxious about both reciprocating appropriately and the other person's perceptions of both the timing and the nature of the responding message, and also about the timing and the nature of the response that they themselves received. Taylor and Harper (2002, p. 3) observe the obligation to reciprocate 'through such phone-mediated gift-giving, relationships are expressed in tangible ways and the moral commitment to these relationships are demonstrated and preserved'. Ling (2012) also observes there are moral dimensions in the use and non-use of systems of interaction and, in considering the seemingly mundane communication practices more closely, Goffman's (1959) notion of *arranging face*, is helpful as it highlights practices of social reflexivity in everyday communications. Whilst Goffman (1959) is referring to face-to-face interaction, mobile technologies provide links to the networked platforms and virtual spaces to maintain physical and emotional contact between friends and to support both family and intimate relationships in late modernity.

The swapping or sharing of both mobile technologies as artefacts themselves and mobile media content can be seen as an important part of achieving an identity as a gendered, preferably popular, being, and also as maintaining part of a cultural friendship group. The role of routines in the performances and how individuals attach more importance to some, rather than others, is also important to understanding children's everyday experiences. Butler's (1990, p. 25) discussion of performance is helpful here as she suggests that it is 'performatively constituted by the very "expressions" that are said to be its results'. Young people's relationships are not homogenised and they differentiate close friendships and those not so close; romantic relationships; parental relationships and between in-groups and out-groups.

The nature of the mobile phone as personal (Plant, 2002; Ling, 2012) provides a further dynamic and the sharing of content is fundamental to an understanding of children's everyday relationships. Drawing on the insights from material culture which has 'established a detailed understanding of the symbolic properties that adhere to objects of human manufacture' and that individuals 'use inanimate objects to claim, to legitimate, and compete for status meaning' (McCracken, 1990, p. 31), the allowing of others access to and the viewing and sharing of personal mobile content is, for young people, often an act of closeness and intimacy. 'Culture and communication are two closely related concepts' (Uzelac, 2008, p. 9). Gillies (2003, p. 3) claims that 'the phrase "intimate relationship" is a broad and fluid term, in that it can encompass numerous different associations between friends, sexual partners, family and kin'. Although some material is quite openly shared, even distributed, young people segregate their audiences as to whom they share particular types of content with according to intimacy and whom they share intimate content with, allowing only those closest to them to view and share the more personal content. This exemplifies Goffman's (1959) proposal about individuals segregating their audience so that some people may see the individual in a particular role that others may not and this facilitates members of a shared friendship-group identity in relationships. McLuhan (1964) discusses the personal and social consequences of the introduction of a new technology as an extension of ourselves. Popović and Hromadžić (2008, p. 47) suggest that 'new electronic media created a need for an extension of the commonly understood concept of "audience" defined as a "group of people before whom a performance of one kind or another takes place"' Thus, the affordances (see Hutchby, 2001b) and interoperability of mobile communication technologies are very much linked to sociality and intimacy in children's everyday relationships. Ling and Yttri (2002) suggest that certain affordances of mobile phone technologies are especially attractive to children and teenagers, and they highlight the importance of being constantly accessible to friends.

It has also been argued that non-ownership of a mobile telephone may limit children's experience and understanding of other communication technologies (Charlton et al., 2002), and may lead to social exclusion (Leung and Wei, 1999). Most research has concentrated on the growth of mobile phone ownership and use; however, Selwyn (2005) helpfully undertook a study of a group of non-users of mobile telephony. Selwyn (2005, p. 19) describes the explanation of non-users in his study as 'an occasional line of resistance against the restructuring of society and the social'. In my research, the child non-users who were the youngest group, however, gave the explanation that they simply had not been given a mobile phone yet, but were 'getting one very soon' (Bond, 2008), reflecting Vincent's (2004) observation that mobile phone ownership has become a right of passage for most 10–11-year-olds.

Mobile media content acts as gifts of mutual disclosure between close friends, and selective sharing may be viewed as part of maintaining close relationships and as a symbolic mechanism for creating and sustaining a shared group or paired identity. The theory of reciprocal altruism (see Trivers, 1971 cited in Bierhoff, 2001) is helpful to the analysis here as it offers an explanation of prosocial behaviour on the basis of reciprocity between individuals. Whilst mobile technology may be viewed as an object or a device, it is the content and material associated with it that provides a vehicle for intimacy and closeness amongst young people. In the exchange relationship, there are prosocial transformations which are mutually desirable for the interdependent persons involved, which contribute to the communal relationship (see Kelly and Thibaut, 1978; Clark and Mills, 1993 cited in Bierhoff, 2001). Goffman (1959) outlines the importance of reciprocal dependence and familiarity, and Giddens (1992) suggests that trust, mobilised by mutual shared disclosure, is one of the key sustaining dynamics of a pure relationship (as outlined by Jamieson, 1999). Thus, identifying patterns of reciprocal effects in using mobile content to maintain friendships and relationships through gifting (see Maus, 2002; Berking, 1999) is important to gain an understanding of the complex interrelationship between mobile technologies and young people's relationships based on trust and intimacy.

Family

This section discusses the relationship between young people, mobile technologies and family relationships, and highlights the centrality of risk anxiety to children's mobile technology ownership and use. 'Traditional values have been challenged and the conceptualization of "family" has changed in response to increasing options in post-modern society' (McKenry and Price, 2005, p. 2) and there is a well-acknowledged increase in family diversity and pluralistic families (Allen, 2005). Zelizer (1985) argues that the late-modern child has become emotionally priceless in fulfilling the parent's need for intimacy, and Furedi's (2002) observations on the role of anxiety in late modernity in parent/child relationships and the notion that children should be constantly monitored and supervised are especially relevant here. Furedi (2002, p. 12) observes the rise in, what he terms 'parental paranoia' in late modernity and he comments: 'many parents issue phones as a safety measure in case a child is stranded and needs a lift home'. Furthermore, Ribbens McCarthy et al. (2008, p. 2) propose:

> The idea of 'family' is thus very powerful, at least in the contemporary cultures of Europe and the new World. At the same time, family lives have been under constant scrutiny from all sides – from family members themselves, politicians, professionals, and media pundits. And this scrutiny does not seem to be abating, as people and governments struggle to deal with anxieties about the complexities and uncertainties of changing and diverse communities in a globalising world.

Bell's (2006, p. 44) ethnographic study identifies the different ways which mobile technologies function as cultural, rather than technological objects – 'as objects for communication, as manifestations of information, as a form of identity politic, and as sites of anxiety and control'. In the globalising world, risks and uncertainties associated with online environments impact on family relationships. Dürager and Livingstone (2012) found that many parents consider it important to participate in their child's internet use, and adopt a variety of strategies, depending on age and sometimes gender of the child, although some parents, even of young children, do not. Livingstone et al. (2011a) found that whilst the actual incidence of online risk affects a minority of children comparatively there is substantial parental underestimation. As discussed in Chapter 2, contemporary social and cultural constructions of childhood are framed around children remaining vulnerable in public space. Ling (2000) and Williams and Williams (2005) note how mobile phones are bought by parents to keep in touch with their children, so that children can contact parents if they get into difficulty. The mobile phone has changed practices in family functioning and the management of children's space. Morrow (2009, p. 66) observes how 'parents, especially mothers, provide physical and emotional care', which is explicitly acknowledged by children, and Bell (2006) found that mothers use mobile technologies to coordinate and navigate everyday commitments, childcare arrangements and to communicate with family members.

Mobile phones are often bought and used by parents to ameliorate perceived risk, especially in relation to physical, outside space, but the analysis of the data in my research also revealed how children themselves use mobile technologies to manage their parents' anxiety; for example, texting parents 'not sure when netball finishing' or 'I am going to be 10 mins late'. My research found that although mobile technologies appeared to be of less importance to the younger children's friendships initially, they appear to have rapidly assumed an essential position to the children's communication with friends as they got older and in the management of their relationships generally whilst maintaining a functional role with other family members, especially mothers (agreeing with Ling, 2004). Mothers are far more closely associated with mobile communications than fathers, probably due to mothers being more active in family functioning/management generally. The phone was used by the older children to reassure parents that they were safe. The children in my research were well aware of parental, especially mothers', anxiety and used the mobile phone to ameliorate this anxiety in their everyday lives. Ling (2004, p. 62) discusses the coordination in common everyday activities and notes how this 'effective coordination minimizes uncertainty regarding interdependent activity', which he terms *micro-coordination*, and suggests that mobile phones allow mothers as caregivers to remain accessible. This also reflects Jordon's (2000, p. 1) notion of designing for disorganisation and the 'idea that new technologies support us in remaining, or becoming, disorganised'. In minimising the uncertainty through such micro-coordination, mobile technologies are important, therefore, in reducing risk anxiety in children's everyday lives, facilitating effective family functioning and easing concerns. This reflects contemporary sociological theory on family relationships and on individualisation characteristic of late modernity, as discussed by Giddens (1999). Hood et al.'s (1996a) study found that parents view their role as loving, protecting and nurturing their children, who are the recipients of love, attention and aspirations. However, the child is positioned as a passive receiver of love and attention, reinforcing the notion that childhood remains constructed as a time of innocence, vulnerability and dependence (Jenks, 2005), yet children actively manage risk (Green, 1997a) and use mobile technologies to do so.

Ideas from social geography are relevant to understanding the desire to keep children safe and give rise to risk anxiety, which can, according to Scott et al. (1998), result in children's activities being limited and curtailed. Sibley (1995, p. 4) outlines the shaping of social and spatial exclusion, the control and regulation of individuals and groups by dominant others to outline how individual identity relates to 'social, cultural and spatial contexts'. Jenks (2005) develops Foucault's ideas of spatial control to suggest that the exercise and manipulation of space is a primary example of adults controlling the child's world. Furedi's (2002, p. 5) commentary on the redefinition of parenting suggests that the close monitoring of children's activities by parents is due to the 'inflated sense of risk', and he illustrates how mobile technologies have extended the spaces of parenting and their increasingly important role in notions of children's security and well-being in late modernity. Accident-prevention strategies adopted by parents signify the responsibility of a good parent, knowledge about risk is used in everyday conversation to construct sociological variables and, for women, risk consideration may be an important factor in their construction of an identity as a proper mother (Green, 1997b). The mobile phone thus emerges as a significant tool in facilitating identities in relation to parenthood or motherhood. In late modernity, there is an increasing importance of the notion of independent space (as opposed to specific space – office, house etc.) in the individualisation process (García-Montes et al., 2006). Children's independence in public space has, according to Ling (2004, p. 86), been enhanced thanks to mobile phone technology in that it 'is a midwife to the eventual emancipation of the children'. Similarly, Pain et al. (2005), Ling (2000) and Williams and Williams (2005) also concur that mobile phones can expand the space available to young people and offer more freedom away from home. Thus, mobile mediation technologies offer security and reassurance in family relationships as well as providing an emotional bond and have extended the boundaries of parenting. As Ling (2012, p. 144) argues:

> It [the mobile phone] is changing the way parenting is done, and it is changing the conditions of its practice. Because of the mobile phone, the radius of action for both the parent and the child is somewhat larger and more robust. The link can be abused by overly nosey parents and/or overly secretive children, but both know that, if needed, the other is only a phone call away.

Intimate relationships

García-Montes et al. (2006, p. 78) propose that 'the mobile phone promotes the development of an individual uncoupled from traditional institutional forms'. The modern world is cluttered with all kinds of sexual stories (Plummer, 1995, p. 49). I have argued (Bond, 2011) that the children's accounts in my study illustrated how mobile technologies have become a fundamental part of their public and private selves, including, for the older children, their sexual selves. Buunk (2001, p. 389) discusses how many aspects of romantic relationships are based on similar characteristics to friendship but how 'propinquity makes the beginning of romantic attraction more likely, and similarly is also important for love relationships'. The affordances (see Hutchby, 2001b) of mobile technologies facilitate such propinquity (nearness) and play an increasingly important yet ubiquitous role in young people's romantic relationships in late modernity. Children are reaching sexual maturity earlier than previous generations (Mercer, 2010) and, although a problematic area to undertake research in, the topic of sexuality in childhood has recently become the subject of much debate. Renolds' (2005) feminist post-structural analysis of children's sexual and gender relationships emphasises how children are simultaneously 'sexual beings' and also 'sexual becomings', and how adults have tended to fear and avoid recognising children's sexuality and seeing them as sexual beings. According to Scraton (1997, p. xi) 'one of the most volatile debates concerning young people, bringing with it significant changes in legislation and policy, has centred on sex, sexuality and access to reliable information'. Foucault [1979] (1990, p. 104) explains how this came about through what he terms the *pedagogisation of children's sex*:

> a double assertion that practically all children indulge or are prone to indulge in sexual activity; and that, being unwarranted, at the

same time 'natural' and 'contrary to nature', this sexual activity posed physical and moral, individual and collective dangers; children were defined as 'preliminary' sexual beings, on this side of sex, yet within it, astride a dangerous dividing line. Parents, families, educators, doctors and eventually psychologists would take charge, in a continuous way, of this precious and perilous, dangerous and endangered sexual potential: this pedagogization was especially evident in the war against onanism, which in the West lasted nearly two centuries.

Children are using mobile technologies in their everyday lives to explore each other's bodies and for intimate and sexual purposes in their everyday relationships (Bond, 2011), and Garca-Montes et al. (2006, p. 76) suggest that the mobile phone is 'becoming the fetish of our century'. The link between mobile phones, other mobile technologies and sex is evident in the public sphere, academic debate and media discourse. However, 'sex and its associations with "new" and "novel" inventions and technology is nothing new', and the relationship between sex and technology is fundamental to understanding complex everyday lives (Barber, 2004, p. 142). The 'traditional portrayal of technological innovation fails to address the complexity of the interaction between technology, personal consumption and the construction of identity' and we need to know how ordinary people appropriate ordinary technologies (Green, 2001, p. 174). Further careful consideration needs to be given to mobile technologies, young people's consumption practices and their construction of identity in late modernity as gendered, sexual beings.

It has already been emphasised that it is important to consider the context of the children's everyday lives, and analyses of the debates on social change, the media and sexuality suggest that a liberational discourse dominates both everyday and media representations of sexuality (Jackson and Scott, 2004). Sexuality is, however, often neglected in academic literature on childhood (Clarke, 2004), and the debate surrounding childhood, sexuality and media is fraught with contradictions and anxieties associated with protecting children's sexual innocence (Jackson and Scott, 2004). Few commentators see the increased sexualisation of the media as a positive development for children (Buckingham and Bragg, 2004; Renolds, 2005).

The impression of a sexually freer, more diverse society is reflected in representations of sexuality and intimate relations in popular culture and reinforced by the everyday knowledge gained from living in a social environment increasingly saturated with sexual imagery.

(Jackson and Scott, 2004, p. 234)

The prominence of sex and sexuality in contemporary Western culture is discussed by Cover (2003) to illustrate how pervasive both are and how easily sexuality encroaches into areas previously considered non-sexual and, according to Attwood (2005, p. 91), 'pornography now signifies a cool form of representation'. Green (2001) argues for interdisciplinary perspectives to consider Giddens' (1991) proposal that the appropriation, acquisition and use of ICTs are part of the wider pursuit of self- and personal identity that characterises late modernity. Attwood (2006) suggests that there is a preoccupation with sexual values, practices and identities, and there is a proliferation of sexual texts in contemporary society. McNair (1996) comments on how the iconography of pornography is increasingly common and Kent (2005, p. 430) suggests that 'post-modern culture arguably has enabled taboos to be transgressed through pleasing erotic imagery packaged as fashion not pornography' but, as Jackson and Scott (2004) point out, changes in societal attitudes simply cannot capture the complex and context-specific aspects of everyday thought and practice.

There is a more detailed discussion in the following chapter on pornography and sexting in relation to risk but understanding the debates on 'pornification' (see Dines, 2010) and that contemporary childhoods are being played out in an increasingly sexualised society are also important here. It is, however, essential to bear in mind in the following discussion the point made by Hasinoff (2012, p. 2) that 'a teenager who chooses to send sexually explicit images to a peer is engaging in a very different activity than someone who distributes a private image with malicious intent or coerces another person to produce an explicit image'.

The children in my research talked about their everyday use of mobile technologies in relation to sexuality, sexual acts and intimate relationships, and the recent study by Ringrose et al. (2012) highlights the diversity of children's experiences.

Sexting practices are culturally specific. New technologies enable public displays of identity, which bring with them pleasures but also pressures to perform particular idealised forms of femininities and masculinities which are culturally, class and 'race' specific. Young people are also, however, managing globalised consumer oriented cultures of consumption, which present challenges and pressures to have the 'right' types of embodiment, commodities, and status symbols.

(Ringrose et al., 2012, p. 8)

Constructions of self-identity are apparent in young people's talk as sexual and gendered individuals, and in their use of mobile technologies in their everyday relationships and in the sharing of sexual content, both user-generated and downloaded. In the following excerpt, for example, the boys discussed a recent incident when Josh had called Kev on his mobile phone. Again, the importance of context was highlighted. Kev had just had sex with his girlfriend and the boys' discourse again emphasises the significance of the geography and context of use, and Josh stresses that this was one time for Kev not to have his mobile switched on. Further analysis, however, again reveals the multifunctional use of the phone as Kev was using his phone at the time to see what the time was, not to communicate with others when Josh had called him. Verifying Plummer (1995, p. 72) that 'people tell sexual stories to assemble a sense of self and self identity', what is important to observe here is that the boys' talk demonstrates Kev's construction of self-identity as a (hetero)sexual, gendered being and the acceptability of having sex (under the legal age), but the unacceptability of having your mobile phone switched on highlighting the associated social norms.

Josh [aged 15]: And now it's on all the time isn't it Kev? [laughter] Yes in awkward situations when you don't want your friend to answer their phone [laughter] but they do.

Andy [aged 15]: Oh no! I don't want to know.

Josh [aged 15]: Oh God, whilst you are actually on the job?

Kev [aged 15]: Yeah well it was like 'Oh no! Hi Josh. How are you? I'm great'.

Josh [aged 15]: Yeah disgusting child! See that's when you switch your phone off!

Kev [aged 15]: Yeah I did but I turned it back on just to see what time it was.

Josh [aged 15]: What half way through?

Kev [aged 15]: No it wasn't half way through that was the thing it was like . . . after . . .

Andy [aged 15]: And your [indicating Josh] typical timing.

Kev [aged 15]: Yeah I had just switched my phone on – 'ring ring Josh! Oh for Christ's sake!'

The data from my research confirms Adams' (1995) assertion on the social construction of individuals' perceptions of risk associated with different types of behaviour influenced by the norms and experiences of social groups. Social influence, 'a change in the judgements, opinions and attitudes of an individual as a result of being exposed to the views of others' (Van Avermat, 2001, p. 404) is also important to the debates presented here. Furthermore, home, school and peers are all fundamental factors in forming sociocultural conceptions of sexuality, as considered by Rapoport (1992), and some of the girls in my study were keen to establish their identity as being part of a relationship by talking about their boyfriends and of the importance of mobile technologies in their relationships. Mobile technologies are central to contemporary intimate relationships from initiating contact with someone and 'asking them out' to 'dumping' someone, and the sharing of sexual content either downloaded or user-generated is frequently part of intimate relationships (Bond, 2011, p. 593). 'The boundaries of public and private are critical to understanding microblogging as well as its predecessor technologies' (Murthy, 2012, p. 1062). What is very apparent is, therefore, the blurring of the boundaries between the public and the private, and this is highly significant in children's perceptions of mobile technology use in intimate relationships. Mascheroni and Ólafsson's (2013) study found that social networking was the most popular activity done by children on a daily basis. Other virtual spaces are also significant here in that they are used to share and publish intimate content and, as Popović and Hromadžić (2008) suggest Facebook use includes diffused user engagement and in the increasing diversity of media more individualised and intimate practices emerge. What is conceptualised as 'private', the naked body or sexual act in certain contexts, is transformed into being public by the mobile technology. It is the sharing (usually within the context of an intimate relationship) that makes it public, especially when it is further shared with a wider, non-intimate and sometimes hostile audience online that transforms the trusting intimate act into a risky one (discussed in more detail in Chapter 6). In the following excerpt, Tilly, John and Sid discuss a boy masturbating in front of a webcam and the images were sent to girls that he knew at school. The girls had saved the images to their mobile phones and had subsequently sent the images to others at school.

Sid [aged 16]: Oh yeah he has webcam on and he was wanking over the webcam.

Tilly [aged 16]: Oh yeah to these girls and they saved it on their phone and sent to everyone.

Sid [aged 16]: Yeah but he's a bit of a freak though.

John [aged 16]: Yeah he took a picture of himself naked and sent to someone and they sent it to everyone – things like that – you heard about that.

Sid [aged 16]: I've heard of stuff like that more in the year below.

Although children experience conversations of a sexual nature online, the extent of cyberflirting or the degree of cybersex involved is unclear (O'Connell et al., 2004). Hasinoff (2012, p. 6) highlights the importance of further consideration being needed in relation to issues of 'privacy and consent for all authors of social media content'. Thorogood (2000) highlights the socially symbolic nature of sex, and Began and Allison (2003, p. 321) claim that more 'scholarly effort should be geared toward considering the possible positive effects of sexually explicit material on human social interaction'. Baudrillard (1988) suggests that in the development of ecstasy of communication, the subject comes into close proximity to instantaneous images and information in an overexposed and transparent world. Kehily (1999) discusses the well-established role of teen magazines as media in demystifying sex and Peter and Valkenburg's (2004) research that suggests that males with younger friends are more likely to use sexual content with other media. Bourdieu (1991, p. 245) argues that 'social space is a multi-dimensional space, an open set of relatively autonomous fields, fields which are more or less strongly and directly subordinate, in their functioning and transformations'. Davis (2011) suggests that young people balance the risks and opportunities associated with self-multiplicity in their experiences of identity in a networked era. From the EU Kids Online data, Ólafsson et al. (2013) suggest that the viewing of sexual images and receiving sexual messages was reported by one in eight children, but they were not generally viewed as harmful. It was the younger groups of 14–15-year-olds in my study who discussed having sexual content on their phones either downloaded or user-generated and the ease of availability in obtaining sexual material was apparent even a few years ago, and all the groups of children I spoke to mentioned sexual images in relation to their use of mobile technologies.

Jackson and Scott (2004) note the increasing public disclosure of private sexual lives and Plummer (1995) argues that, in the late-modern period, the media break down previously defined boundaries and enable people to tell their own sexual stories and read others. Cybersex within an online context is defined by O'Connell et al. (2004, p. 16) as 'flirting or talking about sex with other chatters'. Applied to mobile technology use, in the flirting and sharing of photographs of a sexual nature, the mobile technologies provide a platform for this to happen more easily with greater accessibility to previously privatised spaces and bodies, thus reflecting Barber's (2004, p. 150) argument that cybersex is part of self-expression and our evolutionary process. Mobile technologies provide a space in contemporary children's lives for developing their sexuality, the sharing of and exploration of sexual material, and, indeed, each other's bodies, largely concealed from the adult world. A valuable example of sexuality, self-identity, changing notions of acceptability and late modernity is provided by Plummer's (1995, p. 91) discussion on homosexuality, suggesting that 'gay worlds came into being through a number of coinciding conditions brought about by modernity', including capitalism and the previous medicalisation of homosexuality. However, heteronormative social relations remain and Charles (2000) observes that in theorising institutionalised heterosexuality, heterosexual relations are institutionalised within marriage and the family, within education and wider society, whereas homosexuality is not. Butler's (1990) work on the constructionist theories and her notion of gender performativity is important to understanding the analysis presented here and importance of the consideration given to the context of the wider heterosexual ideologies in relation to children's performativity. Similarities can, arguably, be drawn between Plummer's argument on homosexuality and the development of the sociology of childhood, as a critique of the traditional developmental view of children, which demonstrates the low status of children within society and the dominance of adult knowledges and the medialisation of childhood, especially in the early years, as important in understanding the silencing of children's sexuality. Ling (2012, p. 33) contends that 'technologies can alter the niche into which they move' but I would argue that the actual extent to which and in what ways children's behaviour in exploring their developing sexual selves has changed from a generation ago when 'behind the bike shed' offered physical space for such activities and practices to take place is open to further debate (Bond, 2011).

Self-identity

'One of the central interests of sociology is the relationship between self and society' (May, V., 2011, p. 363). It is through relationships with others – friends, family and intimate relationships – that self-identity is constructed and it is 'through belonging to different communities and our membership of other groups that reflect, construct and sustain our identity' (Stainton Rogers, 2011, p. 280). 'Questions of "identity" have attained a remarkable centrality within human and social sciences' (du Gay et al., 2000, p. 1) and the 'endless performative self' is associated with postmodernism and the production of the self (Hall, [1996], 2000). According to McLuhan and Fiore (1967, p. 26), 'all media are extensions of some human faculty – psychic or physical'. The day-to-day interactions in various relationships in children's everyday lives are interwoven in the complex construction of self-identity. Individuals have one self but many different identities depending on the nature of the relationship with others and 'the self and its identities participate in social life through self-presentation' (Valkenburg et al., 2005, p. 384). In late modernity, self-identity has become, according to Giddens (1991), a reflexively organised behaviour in which individuals make choices about lifestyle and life plans. The presentation of the self and the construction of self-identity through mobile technologies in everyday life has only recently begun to be considered, and Primorac and Jurlin (2008, p. 71) suggest that 'in order to be present in the virtual sphere, one needs to have access to digital technology and thus, to the content it holds'. Valentine and Holloway (2001) argue that children are interested in the social relationships within which they have to manage their own identities, and notions of privacy, risk and trust are also particularly important in the relationship between childhood, mobile technologies and children's self-identity.

Lindholm et al. (2003, p. 94) suggest that a mobile phone user is 'a consumer with a lifestyle'. In order to understand the social implications of technology, Fischer (1992) suggests that it is beneficial to adopt a social constructivist approach and focus on the consumer. Children have become consumers from a very early age (Selwyn, 2000) and there is increasing recognition of children as consumers (Lee, 2001a), and that there is a complex interaction between children and their consumption of mobile technologies. Consumption practices (including the consumption of mobile technologies and media content) and 'lifestyles have become central to the process of identity construction' (Furlong and Cartmel, 1997, p. 9). 'Postmodern adolescence is a phase where new codes and implied understandings are acquired, where the self is placed in social context and where individual meaning is created' (Söderström, 2009, p. 711). Valkenburg et al. (2005, p. 388) observe that 'research on people's motives for media use falls traditionally within the uses and gratifications paradigm' (see Chapter 3 for earlier discussion), but there is now a growing body of research which has focused on people's motives for using the internet. Valkenburg et al.'s (2005) study investigated how often adolescents engaged in internet-based identity experiments and found that early adolescents experimented with their identities significantly more often than older adolescents. In their consideration of self-presentational strategies, they concluded that the most important motives to engage in internet-based identity experiments were self-exploration, social compensation and social facilitation, and that the internet plays an important role in adolescents' identity exploration. The popularity associated with mobile phone content – downloads, images, screensavers and so on has been linked to individualisation by Ling (2004, p. 55) and he draws on Goffman's (1971) notion of possessional territory to argue that 'the mobile phone is an object that can be identified with the self and that, in turn, helps others to identify and perhaps characterise the individual'. Facebook opens up possibilities to establish new contacts, which enriches to social capital of users (Vitak and Ellsion, 2012; Popović and Hromadžić, 2008). Furthermore, Garca-Montes et al. (2006) suggest that mobile internet technologies are influential in both performing and understanding self-identity. Social media is about self-presentation (Murthy, 2012). Davis (2010, p. 1113) observes that the adoption and use of new technologies influence how people interact and communicate, and they also impact on both self-presentation and identity formation and that 'self construction is understood as a process of negotiation between actor and audience'. Young people construct a variety of complex and often fluid identities online that differ according to the relationship/audience and the digital platform which is comprised of a complex array of images, videos, text, audio and links to other online content and mobile technology platforms. With quasi-broadcast features, mobile technologies, as social mediation technologies (Ling, 2012), allow constant access to identity information, construction and reconstruction.

McLuhan (1964, p. 25) differentiates between hot and cool media to suggest that 'hot media are low in participation' and that 'cool media are high in participation by the audience'. Silverstone (1994) suggests that objects present themselves for consumption both as material and symbolic goods, and McCracken (1990) highlights how the field of material culture has established a detailed understanding of the symbolic properties that attach themselves to objects of human manufacture. 'Consumption has been one of the leading indicators to discuss the relationship between issues of identity and the changing character of society in a modern/postmodern world' (Hetherington, 1998,

p. 2). 'Audiences respond selectively to the media by drawing upon the social discourses of their everyday world' (Popović and Hromadžić, 2008, p. 50). Conspicuous consumption proposed by Veblen (1994), whilst criticised (Trigg, 2001), has been developed by Baudrillard to extend to consumer society as a whole. Medak (2008, p. 59) proposes using the term 'prosumers' as people both consume and produce digital artefacts within a community of users and creators in 'using the networked production tools and exchange of cultural goods'. Contemporary young people's use of mobile technologies reinforce Baudrillard's (1968) concept of sign-value and how objects are not just characterised for their usefulness or exchange value but for their expression of style, importance, popularity and wealth. Drotner (2011, p. 360) argues that such signs are now digitised and children's media cultures are made up of 'signs such as text, images, numbers and sound'.

For Bourdieu (1997), in his account of the relation between the social and the cultural, consumption is about distinction and his concept of habitus – defined by a set of distinguishing values through which people distinguish their own culture (Silverstone, 1994) – is also useful here. Identity construction is, however, far from straightforward and not always positive, as choice and anxiety are interrelated (Bauman, 1988). As Warde et al. (1999, p. 120) comment:

> To the extent that individuals are free in the sphere of consumption, and identity is no longer guaranteed by or even closely associated with social position, then misconceived aesthetic decisions will convey regrettable and damaging messages about the self.

Mobile technologies are a vehicle for the continual construction and reconstruction of self-identity in late modernity, confirming Bourdieu's (1984) modes of consumption argument that consumption is motivated by the need for social groups to achieve status and young people's use of mobile technologies is rich in social meaning. This relates to class, but Buckingham and Bragg (2009) suggest that, in relation to children, we should consider how they use mobile phones; for example, as markers of status and authority in a group. Social identity theory is also important to my discussion in this chapter as it 'assumes that there is not one "personal self" but a more complex and flexible self that works in different ways' (Stainton Rogers, 2011, p. 292). Agger (2004) draws on Marcuse's claim that people develop false needs in the acquisition of status symbols that attain, what Baudrillard terms, *sign value*. Consumption is involved with constructing identity and, just as identities can change rapidly, so do mobile technologies and content. My own research reflects Ling's (2004) suggestion that the mobile phone, and I would argue other mobile technologies also, are fashionable items linked to self-identity. Thus, the design and branding of mobile technologies as well as the digital content is important to children's self-identity, and Ólafsson et al.'s (2013) report also notes that the influence of peers (e.g. on mobile phone brands) is important and that children use them to enhance social status (e.g. to differentiate themselves from younger children). Ling (2004) argues that functions and the appearance of mobile phones indicate something about the owner and the young people in my research talked at great length about which technologies were 'cool'. As Silverstone (1994, p. 107) notes: 'we speak through our commodities, about ourselves and to each other, making claims for status and for difference, and actively and creatively marking out a map for the negotiation of everyday life'. Thus, goods and commodities are symbolic objects in a system of meanings (Silverstone, 1994) and it is not just handset design or the affordances of mobile technologies that are important to young people. Kellner (1992, p. 153) suggests that in late modernity 'identity revolves around leisure, centred on looks, images and consumption', and Buckingham and Bragg (2004) discuss understandings of the self. They highlight how consumption shapes identities 'through choices in a world of self-referenced objects and images' and suggest that the notion of self-creation through consumption is important to understanding young people's self-identity (Buckingham and Bragg, 2004, p. 81). Furthermore, there are cultural constructions of mobile and digital media linked to age, gender and membership of different cultural and social groups, and possession of certain types of mobile content is important to children's self-identity, as well as being popular and accepted by a particular group. Thornton (1995) develops Bourdieu's idea of cultural capital to present the development of subcultural capital in that popular culture is a space in which cultural differences are formed as groups create distinctions between themselves and others on the basis of subcultural capital. Mobile digital content is, therefore, understood as both cultural and social capital for young people and central to self-identity. Goffman (1959) discusses the role of sign vehicles and artefacts in presenting the image of self and wanting to portray certain desired characteristics, and, thus, the sharing of content is a vehicle through which self-identities are formed and an essential part of belonging to a cultural, social or gendered group. According to Baudrillard (1994), identities are constructed by the appropriation of images that determine how individuals perceive themselves and how they relate to each other in everyday life. The boys in my study, for example, often observed that the role of pornographic imagery was not necessarily for sexual interest but for popularity and presenting a certain image of oneself in public. Goffman (1959) uses performance to refer to activities of an individual before a set of observers. He suggests that everyone is playing a role and defines interaction as 'the reciprocal influence of individuals upon one another's actions in performance, and may be defined as all the activity of a given participant on a given occasion which serves to influence in any way any of the other participants' (Goffman, 1959, p. 26). Ling (2012) observes how individuals construct expectations of others in relation to the use of mediation artefacts and mobile media technologies, and that mobile communication is dynamic. 'Feelings about and connections to others are crucial to reflexive practices, even within a climate of individualization' (Holmes, 2010, p. 143). Participatory platforms present powerful, networked spaces for the (progressive) reconstruction of social life (Uzelac, 2008) and children's consumption of mobile technologies and digitised content is integral to their continual construction and reconstruction of self-identity in an individualised society.

Reflecting Barns' (1999) suggestions that technologies are part of the process of the construction of self and that technologies, as a central focus for cultural analysis are a powerful factor in shaping postmodern identities and the ongoing construction of subjectivity, I have argued (Bond, 2013) that children are reflexive in their construction of self-identity through their everyday interaction with mobile technologies. Reflexivity and multiplicity (as emphasised in Chapter 2) underpins my argument here, together with Mol's (1999, p. 79) notion of perspectivism to illustrate how reality is not only viewed in many different ways but that how it is also 'manipulated by means of various tools in the course of a diversity of practices and it is these different performances, different versions, different realities that co-exist in the present'. The children in my research certainly did not discuss mobile technologies as separate entities but as components in a broad spectrum of media in general, comprising both human and non-human elements in their everyday lives. These complex interrelationships have powerful associations between the mobile technologies (objects) and the young people (humans) that can be understood in term of Latour's concept of *actants* as quasi-subjects and quasi-objects, especially in relation to self-identity and confirming Baudrillard (1988) on the ecstasy of communication. The girls, in the excerpt below, for example, describe how they associate the phone as being part of them:

> *Debbie [aged 15]*: I'd die without it.
> *Sarah [aged 14]*: Terrible.
> *Sally [aged 15]*: Vulnerable.
> *Debbie [aged 15]*: It is like a part of me.
> *Sarah [aged 14]*: I'd feel lonely.
> *Sally [aged 15]*: Yeah I'd feel like I had no friends.

Conclusion

As everyday life is entwined with various technologies which are fundamental to the contemporary human condition (MacKenzie and Wajcman, 1999), the importance of recognising the contemporary technological context is central to the debates presented in this chapter and in the discussion of mobile technologies in relation to children's everyday relationships with each other, their families and in their intimate relationships. Uzelac (2008, p. 11) observes how

> when communication and multimedial dimensions joined in, networked us, and when convergence processes started being more visible and affecting the changes mot only in the technical sphere but also in our social institutions it became obvious that the changes taking place were happening on the level of the social eco-system.

As Law (1999, p. 10) suggests, 'what appears to be social is partly technical. What we usually call technical is partly social'. Mobile internet technologies, as opposed to stand-alone artefacts, have become social mediation technologies which, according to Ling (2012, p. 9), are understood as a 'technological intermediary which facilitates our social dealings'. Such social dealings form the basis on our interactions in everyday relationships. As exemplified by Pip below:

> *Pip [aged 14]*: I would feel really unloved, unpopular and lonely without my mobile.

Gillis (2011, p. 122) suggests 'this virtual landscape of childhood is created and sustained by a unique set of rituals and narratives which have developed in the modern era'. Mobile technologies are part of the warp and weft of contemporary social and cultural constructions of childhood and central to the continual construction and reconstruction of children's self-identity in late modernity. Mobile technologies are becoming increasingly essential, yet simultaneously more taken for granted, in children's day-to-day interactions and communication practices in their relationships.

> Thus belonging plays a role in connecting individuals to the social. This is important because our sense of self is constructed in a relational process in our interactions with other people as well as in relation to more abstract notions of collectively held social norms, values and customs. These social origins of the self have been the particular focus of the symbolic interactionist school of thought.
>
> (May, V., 2011, p. 368)

Parents and children are enrolled into ongoing interaction in which technologies and people mutually constitute each other, and my discussion here has intended to highlight and expose some of the consequences and complexities in understanding mobile technologies, contemporary childhoods and children's everyday relationships. Ling (2012, pp. ix–x) asserts that 'having access to our nearest sphere of friends and family helps in the larger project of sustaining social cohesion' but whilst mobile technologies provide *perpetual contact* (see Katz and Aakus, 2002) in family relationships and friendships, they can also incite insecurities and anxieties. Digital media serves as a catalyst for change in children's everyday lives, and in social relations 'digital media intensify meaning-making practices as forms of action, participation, collaboration and reflexivity' (Drotner, 2011, p. 368). 'Digital culture changes the relationships between actors' (Cvjetičanin, 2008, p. 195). I suggest here that children are active social co-constructors of their relationships through mobile technologies and mobile media content.

Strathern (1999) points out that people are always negotiating their relationships with others; relations also achieve divisions as relationships separate out capabilities for action and difference is constantly being created in the conduct of social life. Young people are reflexive in their consumption of mobile technologies, and they manage and maintain their everyday relationships through mobile technology practices and actively control many aspects of their relationships through the mobile technologies. Drawing on both Goffman's concepts of performance; role-playing; scripts and audiences, and Giddens' reflexive self in late modernity, Frost (2005, p. 71) offers a theoretical framework in considering 'the nature of the subject in late consumer capitalism as fundamentally and increasingly tied into appearance construction' and emphasises the importance of how understanding the nature of multifaceted relationships is made even more complex by the socially constructed nature of both childhood and technology in late modernity.

Ling (2012), in relation to the mobile phone, argues that it is important to understand how it has become embedded in everyday lives and how it is restructuring social interaction. Garca-Montes et al. (2006, p. 73) claim that 'it is understandable, then, that dilemma of identity (and trust in others) can be exacerbated by the use of the mobile phone'. The children in my research viewed mobile technologies as fulfilling both emotional and functional needs, and it appears that the family is more closely associated with the functional, and relationships, especially intimate ones, with the emotional. It is important, however, to avoid homogenous assumptions (Selwyn, 2004) and these associations are far from straightforward. Context is important to understanding Ling's (2012) point on restructuring social interaction and through my analysis presented here a complicated and complex network of people, relationships, practices and technologies emerges. Trust is an important concept and young people share mobile mediation technologies and mobile digital content in order to demonstrate closeness and intimacy in a relationship. Gift-giving, through mobile content, is pertinent to conceptualising children's everyday relationships and failure to reciprocate increases uncertainty and insecurity. Children use mobile technologies to form and communicate in friendships with text, images and mobile content to reinforce their emotional ties within their friendships and family relationships, and especially to ameliorate parental risk anxiety. However, as Scott et al. (1998) point out, children's participation in constructing their own everyday world takes place within the constraints set by their subordinate location in relation to adults, as children's understanding of what it means to be a child has been shaped by their interaction with more powerful, adult social actors with pre-existing, albeit negotiable, ideas about childhood and children.

6
Risk

Introduction

It is the blurring of boundaries characteristic of the rapidly changing media environments that have led to a wide variety of paradoxes in relation to children, childhood and mobile technologies in late modernity. The concept of *interaction* is important to understanding users' paradigms within new media-digitised technologies (Popović and Hromadžić, 2008). 'Virtual space has fewer boundaries and different characteristics than the real one. Digitization has enabled the process of media convergence to take place' (Uzelac, 2008, p. 14). 'McLuhan famously thought that the media are extensions of the human senses' (Siapera, 2012, p. 7). The use of smartphones, tablets and handheld devices by children is an often taken-for-granted part of their day-to-day lives.

> A cyborg is a cybernetic organism, a hybrid of machine and organism, a creature of social reality as well as a creature of fiction. Social reality is lived social relations, our most important political construction, a world-changing fiction.
>
> (Haraway, 1991, p. 149)

Using games and apps and the mobile internet for entertainment, social networks to communicate, to find information and extend knowledge, the mobile device has transformed modern childhoods reflecting Haraway's (1991) notion of 'cyborg' above. 'This is an example of a new type of interactive networked media user, who actively participates and co-creates media content around these internet social networks' (Popović and Hromadžić, 2008, p. 54). Whilst recent research demonstrates the many positive, and indeed creative, uses of mobile technologies, it also highlights how, in ameliorating risk and uncertainty in everyday life, they simultaneously facilitate risk and risk anxiety. The concept of risk has recently dominated media discourse and mobile technology – namely the Blackberry – was, for example, held responsible by the media for communication between young people in the riots in London in 2011. Halliday (2011), writing in the *Guardian*, suggests:

> ...the most powerful and up-to-the-minute rallying appears to have taken place on a more covert social network: BlackBerry Messenger (BBM). Using BlackBerry handsets – the smartphone of choice for the majority (37%) of British teens, according to last week's Ofcom study – BBM allows users to send one-to-many messages to their network of contacts, who are connected by 'BBM PINs'. For many teens armed with a BlackBerry, BBM has replaced text messaging because it is free, instant and more part of a much larger community than regular SMS. And unlike Twitter or Facebook, many BBM messages are untraceable by the authorities (which is why, in large part, BBM is so favoured by Emirati teens to spread illicit gossip about officialdom). One BBM broadcast sent on Sunday, which has been shown to the Guardian by multiple sources, calls on 'everyone from all sides of London' to vandalise shops on Oxford street.

Whilst such reporting reflects technological determinism, explanations for the more negative side to mobile technology use in young people's social worlds, including sexual and violent content and bullying behaviours, have received considerable recent media attention, and are the focus of this chapter. The findings from recent literature, however, challenge the homogenous assumptions of children's use of mobile technologies and demonstrate that the associations between the childhood, risk and mobile technologies are far from straightforward. In relation to the riots, one youth worker quoted by a reporter offers an alternative explanation to blaming mobile technologies for the riots:

> Youths are frustrated, they want all the nice clothes. They ain't got no money, they don't have jobs...Couple this with the growing police harassment, the shutting down of social services, rising rents

and gentrification and an ideologically bankrupt – in many cases just plain bankrupt – economic system that rewards only the most avaricious, competitive individualism and nobody should still be surprised that a generation born of futility and resentment, wholly unheard and bereft of any sense of consequence or accountability, has seized upon an opportunity to reclaim some small and fleeting handful of power.

(Eloff, 2011 cited in Dorling, 2012, pp. 3–4)

Savirimuthu (2011, p. 548) suggests that 'child safety issues are now being transformed into legal and social obligations that adhere to the standards and principles of the UNCRC' and this chapter explores the interrelatedness of objects and humans in everyday experiences with mobile mediation technologies, risk and wider political developments. Furthermore, as Mascheroni and Ólafsson (2013, p. 11) point out, daily internet access varies with older children having more access everywhere:

home is still the main context of internet use. In terms of policy recommendations, therefore, empirical evidence confirms the need to focus on promoting awareness among parents as a means to reaching wider populations of children. However, as we have seen, teenagers use the internet at home in the privacy of their own bedroom more than in a public room. Additionally, a further challenge to parental mediation comes from portable, personal devices through which children can create new spaces of privacy within the domestic context, shared rooms included.

This chapter critically examines the risk discourses and argues that children are reflexive in their individualised landscapes of risk associated with mobile technologies; it considers the paradoxical conceptualisations of childhood and of children – as innocent victims and as demonised threats – to suggest that the homogenised assumptions in the debates on risk in the mobile networked society required further consideration.

Ling (2012, p. 116) asserts that it is 'the desire for safety and security has become one of the ways that we justify ownership of the [mobile] device'. Perceptions of risk connect individuals, communities and the larger social structure (Hart, 1997), and risk is central to the social construction of childhood (as discussed in Chapter 2). Risk-profiling, a central part of modernity (Giddens, 1991), is certainly apparent in children's conversations about mobile technologies, especially in relation to their use of mobile phones. Goffman (1971) suggests that the related increased vulnerability associated with public life undermines *Umwelt* – 'a core of accomplished normalcy with which individuals surround themselves' (Hood et al., 1996a, p. 18). Giddens (1991, p. 129) views *Umwelt* as sustained by a skilled watchfulness and suggests that 'trust here incorporates actual and potential events in the physical world as well as encounters and activities in the sphere of social life'. For a group of girls in my study, this was especially pertinent and the network of security provided by a working mobile phone and having someone to contact provided them with, what could be argued to be, a viable *Umwelt* when feeling vulnerable in public space. The girls discuss the action that they took when feeling in potential danger and how they would have their finger resting on the phone just in case. This sort of discussion was common during the focus-group talks and what is interesting is that they took steps to be responsible for their own safety in public space by using their mobile phone as a tool but also discuss how, without it, Beth (16), for example, 'would not know what to do', thus increasing their insecurity.

> *Cathy [aged 17]*: Does your mobile phone make you feel safer?
> *Beth [aged 16]*: Oh yeah.
> *Emily [aged 16]*: Definitely.
> *Mega*: Oh yeah 'cos like you can call someone.
> *Emily [aged 16]*: If anything happens then you can like just call somebody.
> *Beth [aged 16]*: We were in [name of town] once and someone was like following us.
> *Megan [aged 17]*: Oh yeah...
> *Beth [aged 16]*: And like I had my hand on my mobile in case we like needed to like ring someone.
> *Emily [aged 16]*: 'Cos like if you didn't have your phone then you'd be like lost and you couldn't call someone.
> *Beth [aged 16]*: Yeah you could be like in trouble and I wouldn't know what to do but if I've got my phone I just hold it in my pocket and like I can just ring someone.

However, as depicted above, mobile technologies are not only associated with ameliorating risk, but also they simultaneously incite risk. ICT and mobile technologies are central to the social construction of risk and childhood in late modernity and, thus, to the risk society.

ICT and digital networks are a necessary infrastructure that supports globalization processes and they are used to support global markets and production processes, enabling central control and coordination over dispersed production units. On the other hand, the Internet is a communication tool that is intensely used by citizens, activists and NGOs, as it facilitates efficient and far-reaching communication. On the Internet, as in the real world, not everyone is equal, as possibilities depend on the resources available.

(Uzelac, 2008, p. 14)

Beck's (1992) risk society thesis is based on two interrelated issues – reflexive modernisation and risk – and he contrasts it with traditional analyses and discusses the political implications on science and technology. Beck (1992) claims that the new paradigm of risk society, based on how risks produced by modernisation can be prevented and distributed in an acceptable way, overlap with the concepts of an industrial, class-based society, which aim to distribute socially produced wealth in a legitimate way. In striving to overcome poverty, hazardous side effects previously went unnoticed, but there is growing critique of modernisation that influences public discussions. Modernisation has become reflexive and, as such, reflexive modernisation becomes increasingly individualised, and this structural change results in further uncertainty and individuals reflexively constructing their own life biographies. The concept of risk is, therefore, directly bound to reflexive modernisation. Beck's theoretical idea of reflexive modernisation is worked out on two lines of argument: the basis of the logic of risk distribution and the basis of the individualisation theorem.

This form of individualization is related to contemporary understanding of media users. We are witnessing parallel trends in the analysis of new media users which seems to be in opposition at first glance; on the one hand we are face with an ever so obvious fragmentation of the audiences, consisting of small niches useful for market players. This trend of fragmentation is to a large extent the result of technological features of new media which prompt individual usage. On the other hand, we can spot new forms of social integration (networking) of media users, created and supported by interactive digital computer technology, visible in virtual social communities connected by a network of various relationships between their members.

(Popović and Hromadžić, 2008, p. 56)

Reflexivity is, according to Holmes (2010), a sort of mediatory process through which people make sense of and react to the various situations they find themselves in. The term reflexivity is central to Beck's thesis, yet, as Benton and Craib (2001) point out, his risk society theory is essentially derived from a realist perspective, and other work, including that of feminist approaches, have taken anti-realist perspectives towards a more reflexive standpoint in order to overcome previous dichotomies. According to Holmes (2010, p. 143), 'reflexive processes involve relational struggles' and Wynne (1996) argues that the risk society work underestimates the extent to which scientific knowledge is, in itself, contextualised and that lay subjective perceptions of risk have their own rationality, not just, as Giddens suggests, one taken from expert systems. According to Wynne (1996), lay perceptions are relational in nature and defined according to risk in relation to familiar social relationships. In *Runaway World*, for example, Giddens (1999) describes the impact of global change on aspects of everyday life and how its accompanying risks result from man's intervention in the environment. Although science and technology are involved in reducing risks, they contributed to creating them initially. Giddens (1999) distinguishes two types of risk: external risk (for example, nature); and manufactured risk, which includes risks of marriage and family, which he claims concern society now. Both Beck (1992) and Giddens (1990, 1991, 1999) suggest that modernity is a risk culture and contrast traditional with modern societies in terms of the hazards to which they are vulnerable. However, Giddens differs from Beck in his analysis on two issues: he is more hopeful of risk resolution and offers a different history of risk (Culpitt, 1999). Giddens (1991, p. 116) discusses risk and basic life security and states: 'the risk-reducing elements seem substantially to outweigh the new array of risks'. The heightened focus on risk 'in modern life has nothing directly to do with the actual prevalence of life-threatening dangers' (Giddens, 1991, p. 115). Giddens views the concept of risk as replacing that of fate and fortune (Culpitt, 1999). This is in contrast to Beck (1992), who argues that the fundamental nature of risk has changed from the environmental problems experienced at the beginning of the century. Risks emerging today are distinguished from earlier ones by their society-changing scope and by their scientific and technical construction.

Online risks are a prime example of the risk society thesis. Concern over identity theft, financial scams, fear of being 'stalked' and viruses influence how we use the internet and why we in invest in software to protect ourselves, our children and our finances online. However, legal control and regulation of the internet and digital content is also problematic as Kohl (2007, p. 4) points out: 'although regulators have for years struggled with rising transnationality, in the forms of global trade and transnational corporations, the Internet presents an entirely new dimension to the problems of squeezing transnational activity into the national legal straightjacket'.

Risks, in relation to children also include cyberbullying, online grooming, exposure to pornographic and violent content, and include risks from children themselves and what boyd et al. (2010) highlight as a new area of concern: *youth-generated problematic content*. Children and adults perceive risk differently (Livingstone et al., 2011a). The debates on researching children and technology (as set out in Chapter 4) are essential to understanding approaches to and responding to risk, and we need to have a sound understanding of children's experiences and their perceptions of risk in their use of mobile technologies. In their report, 'In their own words: What bothers children online?', Livingstone et al.'s (2013) research in Europe with 9,636 9–16-year-olds found that over half identified one risk, a third identified two risks and 15 per cent identified three or more risks in relation to online environments, and that content risks concern children most especially in relation to pornographic and violent content.

The classification of online risks by Hasebrink et al. (2009, p. 8) helpfully set out the range and nature of the risks identified in the EU Kids online research previously as *Content* (the child as recipient), *Contact* (the child as participant) and *Conduct* (the child as actor). It is important to remember, however, that there are both opportunities and risks associated with the internet (Livingstone, 2009), and the most comprehensive research to date in the EU Kids Online project offers a robust analysis of online risks encountered by European children (Ólafsson, 2013).

Along with the benefits, this access has brought exposure to a wide array of online risks, some of which are familiar in the offline world (e.g. bullying, pornography, sexual exploitation) and some of which are new, or at least substantially reconfigured in the lives of ordinary children (e.g. grooming, abuse of personal data and privacy, geo-location tracking, unwelcome forms of sexual messaging and harassment, the facilitation of self-harm).

(Ólafsson, 2013, p. 6)

Young people have varying degrees of awareness of online risk depending on age, access to e-safety information and actual online experiences. Savirimuthu (2011, p. 558) suggests that:

> Children may not realise the potential exposure to peer victimisation or online sexual solicitation that may accompany the disclosure of personal information like lifestyle choices and contact details on social networking sites. A lack of awareness that digital information can easily be manipulated, accessed and even distributed to unintended recipients may lead a child to upload images to their social networking sites or send these to friends by SMS text or instant messages.

In the following extract, the girls are discussing the media and technological environments and their use of everyday technologies, in addition to their mobile phone. They compare the perceived risks associated with the various ICTs that they make use of in their everyday lives and discuss their understanding of the risks associated with them. Laura talks about Facebook and children putting their number onto their personal profile, and how she considers that to be an ill-advised thing to do. The uncertainty associated with unknown others, whether they will be reading your profile on a social network site or if you receive a call not knowing who is calling you, for example, highlights the lack of trust associated with late modernity and threatens the children's *Umwelt* in this case. However, as Laura goes on to mention, it is the active embrace of risk that for some children is an important component for engaging in certain activities with the technologies, and her observations are in acquiescence to Green (1997b) that risk-taking is an important part of the development of self-identity in late modernity and contributes to understanding the risk climate. The children in the research interact with the risk conditions and the various technologies in their lives by taking responsibility for themselves and trying to understand and manage risk by choosing (as opposed to naively) to take risks. The account below also reflects much of the media discourse associated with chat rooms and online identities, and risk in relation to online paedophile activities and people pretending to be someone else:

> *Laura [aged 14]*: But going back to like [name of social network] – you can put your number down and I think that that is like really stupid – a lots of kids like put their numbers out but they don't know like what they are getting themselves into yeah 'cos it's like well you

can choose to accept the call or not but you don't know who it is on the phone – it may be a paedophile on the phone do you? And on some of them it is like live texting so it could be anyone, you know? But kids take the risk like to talk and to get adrenaline and stuff but I think mobiles are safer than [social network sites] and chat rooms and stuff 'cos you get so many weirdos there that is what – everyone says that and that is where they all hang out if you know what I mean. That is where they pretend to be like a teenager and people get sucked in.

Pip [aged 14]: But if you think about it is not only like the technology that people slip up and you can get caught in these kind of situations where you can meet those kind of people but it is also you being stupid and being like oh I'm ... if you go on chat rooms what do you expect? People always say they are who they aren't, they always make things up and you get that with other people.

The new mobility of access to social networks and technological convergence means that young people can be constantly in touch and connected, and they can update their status and profile information instantly from wherever they are. 'Users are more and more becoming producers in the network environment and they also claim the right to use and re-use existing information and cultural expressions that are available in the digital environment and that form part of cultural memory and identities' (Uzelac, 2008, p. 18). Convergence, according to Uzelac (2008, p. 14), 'is more than simply a technological shift and it affects changes that shape relations in a society'. This *culture of real virtuality* (Castells, 2000, p. 358) has changed the performativity of self in late modernity (see Chapter 5). Pip's comprehension of the online environment here also reflects the lack of trust characteristic of late modernity discussed by Giddens (1991, p. 136), who suggests that 'abstract systems depend on trust, yet they provide none of the moral rewards which can be obtained from personalised trust, or were often available in traditional settings from the moral frameworks within which everyday life was undertaken'. Laura's talk exemplifies Gidden's notion of social reflexivity, which 'refers to the fact that we have constantly to think about, or reflect upon, the circumstances in which we live our lives' (Giddens, 2006, p. 123). Young people's everyday lives are being lived and experienced in cultures of real virtuality; there is 'no separation between "reality" and symbolic representation' (Castells, 2000, p. 403). Consideration of the audience (Goffman, 1959) – who can view information and personal, digitised artefacts online – alters the risk landscape, and is central to current risk-prevention strategies and educational campaigns promoted by organisations like CEOP, Childnet and Get Safe Online. CEOP's ThinkUKnow (online) advice is:

> Be careful what information you give out on your profile. Remember that you don't know who your friend's friends are...or your friend's friends' friends! And you don't know what they'll do with your picture or your phone number if you give it out by mistake. Once your picture is out there, it's out there forever and you won't be able to get it back.

> Be aware that information on your profile could potentially be viewed by anyone. So if you wouldn't be comfortable printing it off and handing it out on the street, maybe it shouldn't be on your profile

> (www.thinkuknow.co.uk)

Sexting

'The creative potentials of the audiences and the notion of "active audiences" have been put forward in the last few decades, with focus on the way meaning is created' (Popović and Hromadžić, 2008, p. 49). In relation to childhood, risk and mobile internet technologies, it is the sexual risk which dominates most public discussions. Concerns over the viewing of pornography and the sharing of sexualised self-generated images by children are also high on the political and policy agenda but, as highlighted in Chapter 4, this is a problematic area to research, both methodologically and ethically. Thus, symbolic representation and the performativity of self are essential to understanding the discourses on risk in relation to sexting and, according to Castells (2000, p. 404), in the networked society 'all realities are communicated through symbols'. Hasinoff (2012, p. 1) explains: 'sexting is often defined as the practice of sending sexually explicit images or text through mobile phones or via internet applications, and teenage girls who create and share images of themselves garner a great deal of anxiety – sexting is typically seen as a technological, sexual, and moral crisis'. This 'moral crisis' combined with the protectionist discourses played out in the debates on the sexualisation of childhood (see Bailey, 2011) is based on the social and cultural constructions of childhood which views children as innocent victims. Buckingham (2000) offers a comprehensive account of children and media, and discusses various alternative perspectives in considerable detail. He is critical of the many accounts of technology that take an essentialist view of childhood, arguing that they reflect a sentimentality about childhood that fails to recognise the diversity in children's lived experiences and in their relationships with media technologies. Buckingham's (2000) claim is apparent in Postman's (1983, p. 80) suggestion that:

> The new media environment that is emerging provides everyone, simultaneously, with the same information. Given the conditions I have described, electric media find it impossible to withhold any secrets. Without secrets, of course, there can be no such thing as childhood.

Whilst Postman's argument above is in relation to television it is very relevant here and highlights the importance of contextualising current debates and concerns in a historical context. The child is portrayed as technically competent but immature (Valentine and Holloway, 2001) – a biologically essentialist approach (see Jenks, 2005). Buckingham (2000) criticises many previous analyses, claiming that they fail to address how the technologies are designed, produced, marketed and actually used by children, and argues for moving beyond essentialism and conceptualising childhood as a homogenous category. It is the reality of the diversity of childhoods that is also too absent from these debates. Drawing on the central tenets of the social studies of childhood (as set out in Chapter 2), reconceptualising childhood towards the complexity and multiplicity of the diversities of childhoods (as proposed by Qvortrup, 2005) is essential if we are to avoid deterministic approaches to debates on protecting children. Furthermore, conceptualising children as persons with rights – rights to participate in the networked, information society – should be at the forefront of both social analyses and policy development (Savirimuthu, 2011).

Paradoxically, the conceptualisation of the child as an innocent victim is mirrored in simultaneous portrayals of the child as an evil threat; for example, in the dialogues on cyberbullying and the production of sexualised images using mobile technologies. Hanson (2011, p. 674) writes: 'children, especially the ones who happen also to be teenaged minors, often exchange gossip and images that sexually expose themselves and others for amusement, profit, or vengeance'. The sexual risks associated with new media are also associated with gender and, whilst for boys the risks are associated with pornography, for girls the risks are associated with the creation of sexual content (Hasinoff, 2012).

Livingstone et al. (2010, p. 9) found that in the UK 15 per cent of 11–16-year-old internet users have received sexual messages, although 3 per cent say they have sent them. In the UK, 'sexting' appears a little less common than across Europe. In the EU Kids Online survey, 15 per cent of 11–16-year-olds in Europe had received sexual messages and 3 per cent claimed that they have sent sexual messages to someone, but amongst those children who have received sexual messages, 52 per cent of their parents are unaware of this. However, this is more common amongst parents of girls and younger children (Livingstone et al., 2011a).

There was clear evidence of this happening when I undertook the research on mobile phones in 2007, when the term *sexting* was not such an issue of such debate in the public realm. Sexting is now, however, a topic of considerable academic, legal and public debate, and there is a growing body of published research on the topic. It is interesting to note from Ringrose et al. (2011, p. 6) that 'many teenagers do not even use the term "sexting" indicating a gap between adult discourse and young people's experiences'. When I started my research back in 2007, many of the children I spoke to did have a mobile phone with a camera but, at the time, an internet-enabled smartphone was still reasonably rare in children's ownership and use. However, even then, discussions of sexting behaviours dominated many of the focus groups and it was certainly already considered to be quite an everyday mundane behaviour amongst teenagers.

> *Megan [aged 17]:* Yeah I'm not going to mention any names right? But someone I know like this girl was starting like taking pictures of like themselves like of their bits right and someone else got into their phone and started sending the pictures round to everyone.
> *Beth [aged 16]:* That happened at our school.
> *Cathy [aged 17]:* What – a girl or a boy was sending the pictures?
> *Megan [aged 17]:* A girl was taking pictures of herself – revealing pictures, shall I say? And sent them to her boyfriend – they like split up and he sent them to like everyone, and everyone found out who it was and that, and everyone knew.

Ringrose et al.'s (2012) more recent research with 35 young people in London found similar themes and that it was not the threat from strangers in relation to sexual material but from peers that was more concerning for young people. This phenomenon though is challenging the traditional constructions of childhood and adulthood. Hanson

(2011, p. 673) writes in relation to the *Justin Berry* case in the US: 'the digital sexual revolution has encouraged a new breed of sexual offender who thrives particularly well online: the child a producer of child pornography, the child and exploiter of child prostitution, the child a self-employed child prostitute, and the child as the sexual abuser of other children'.

As outlined in Chapter 5, many of the concerns in relation to sexting are based around the blurring of the boundaries of private/public and child/adult. The image once sent can be published in more public forums and digitally altered. The subject of many educational awareness campaigns through organisations like CEOP, sexting has become the focus of public interest and adults' attempts to control children's behaviours. However, it is the sharing of and/or uploading of sexualised content on to a social networking service (SNS), for example, that can leave children vulnerable to bullying and exploitation from both their peers and adults. It is easy for children to take pictures, not only of themselves but also of their peers and partners, and the seamless intermeshing of virtual, physical, digital and embodied space exemplifies the cyborg notion. 'If we take the cyborg to represent the meshing of human with technological, then technologies, however rudimentary or complex (the bicycle, the ball point pen, the bow and arrow) – perfectly and elegantly make us cyborgs' (Stokes, 2010, p. 322). There are increasing concerns around the practice of sexting which are fuelling both the moral and the legal debate in relation to user-generated sexual content online, but it is often difficult to differentiate between young people sharing images peer-to-peer and more harmful adult activity. The Association of Chief Police Officers of England, Wales and Northern Ireland (ACPO) Child Protection and Abuse Investigation (CPAI) Lead's Position on Young People Who Post Self-Taken Indecent Images [online] states:

> The 2010 Strategic Overview from the Child Exploitation and Online Protection (CEOP) Centre also identifies a wider range of 'risk taking' behaviour by children, including making online contact with strangers. The report highlighted that it can be difficult to distinguish between self-taken indecent images resulting from grooming or facilitation by adult offenders who have a sexual interest in children, from the images that result from children and young people simply pushing boundaries and experimenting with their friends.

An image on the internet has no natural lifespan; once posted an image may be copied by many others including those who may be predatory abusers. CEOP is aware of cases where self-taken indecent images (which were not produced as a result of grooming or facilitation) have ended up on paedophile chat sites and forums.

Much of the discourse on sexting is dominated by concerns in relation to girls and current concerns in relation to sexting are underpinned by unwanted sexual and/or aggressive attention from predators, paedophiles and peers. Ringrose et al.'s (2012) research suggested that sexting is often coercive, that girls are more likely to be affected than boys, and often reveals wider sexual pressures and expectations, including media influences and pornography. They also found that, although the older children were more sexually aware and resilient, the children in year eight (12–13 years) were more concerned by the sexual pressures and sexting behaviours but received little support. The research concluded that more support and resources are vital:

> To overcome the culture of silence, adult embarrassment, and a paralysing uncertainty over changing sexual norms, the adults who variously provide for youth – teachers, parents, industry, commerce and others – should develop an explicit discourse that recognises, critiques and redresses the gendered sexual pressures on youth. Sexting many only reveal the tip of the iceberg in terms of these unequal and often coercive sexual pressures, but they also make such pressures visible, available for discussion and so potentially open to resolution.
> (Ringrose et al., 2012, p. 8)

Mobile, affordable digital technologies 'have opened up entirely new possibilities for amateur film making and video production' (Čopič, 2008, p. 114) as well as making digitised images easy and affordable. Whilst avoiding a determinist approach, it is important to consider the role of the changing affordances of mobile technologies in the sexting phenomena and, again, drawing on Buckingham's argument on the usefulness of the concept of generation, the rapidly changing technological developments are apparent. When I was a child, if I had wanted to take a sexualised picture of myself, I would have had to borrow my father's camera. I would have had to save up my pocket money to buy camera film and to work out how to get the film into the camera, and it would have been more likely that I exposed the film before myself! Once the film was loaded into the camera, I would have had to somehow balance the camera on furniture in the bedroom, remove my clothes and, using the timer, attempt to take some photographs. I would not have been able to see the images until I had removed the film and taken it to the local chemist for processing, at which point the person who worked in the chemist would probably have contacted my mother! This seems like a rather amusing scenario now, but in considering the complex network of the technology, people and societal context in that assemblage it is very clear that it would have been a more complicated process a few decades ago to the contemporary equivalent. Nowadays, children can easily take pictures of themselves, and others, in any space and publish and share the images taken immediately with potentially hundreds, if not thousands, of viewers. In the reflection above, the time taken to produce just a few paper-based images would have been considerable, and in that time there would have been ample opportunity for reflection on whether or not this was such a good idea. The images would have had limited distribution compared with contemporary digitised environments. Thanks to the interoperability of mobile technologies and media convergence, some images can be produced and distributed in a matter of seconds with often little or no time to think and self-moderate the behaviours or consider the potential consequences of these actions. Hanson (2011, p. 688) observes how 'these children have become the boldest producers of child pornography, ironically on the very gadgets that a parent may have given them to ensure their safety and further their education'. Thus, the importance of understanding the changing contexts within communication practices and the multimodal connectedness of mobile phone behaviours (see Schroeder, 2010) is essential to the discussion presented here. However, many questions remain unanswered, and both policy and educational responses to the sexting phenomenon require further consideration, as Stokes (2010, p. 322) suggests:

> Who can regulate these cyborg bodies that exist across this Technomediaself Scape and how can they do it? Can we deny adolescents a crucial component of their selves (their sexuality) in a growing arena of self-development and realization; the web. Perhaps we need to rethink abstinence as a workable model for technologically mediated adolescent 'sex'.

Pornography

The children in Livingstone et al.'s (2013) report were most worried about pornography. According to Dines (2010, p. xiii), the 'Internet caused a revolution in porn' and the average age that children access pornography is 11 years. She argues that in a hypersexualised culture, children have unlimited access to what she describes as 'gonzo' (violent, hard core) porn. Her discussion on the changes in pornography since the internet questions the effect of easily available, free hardcore pornography on the sexuality of boys and girls in contemporary society. Research is this area, however, is sketchy and highly problematic ethically. Hanson (2011, p. 690) suggests that 'in light of new statistics and media coverage on child-initiated violence, harassment, and sexual activity this past decade has witnessed a loss of faith in the embattled fantasy of children as innocents'. Within the protectionist discourses, adult anxieties about children viewing pornography are concerned with protecting children's innocence, but it is also the violent nature of pornographic content that is of concern. According to Dines (2010, p. xxi), 'in one of the few studies that have been conducted on the content of contemporary porn, it was found that the majority of scenes from fifty of the top-rented porn movies contained both physical and verbal abuse of the female performers'.

In July 2013, Prime Minister David Cameron stated that, within a year, all households in the UK would have their internet access filtered, so that if they wanted to access pornography they would have to opt in. According to the BBC (online), the other measures announced by the prime minister included new laws so that videos streamed online in the UK will be subject to the same restrictions as those sold in shops, search engines will have to introduce further measures to block illegal content, experts from the CEOP will be given more powers to examine secretive file-sharing networks and a secure database of banned child pornography images gathered by police across the country will be used to trace illegal content and the paedophiles viewing it. Whilst the BBC used the term *child pornography* in its reporting of the changes David Cameron was announcing, it is worth commenting here that organisations like the CEOP have been campaigning for many years against using terms like child pornography and urging the media to be clear that these are images of child abuse. Chief Executive of the CEOP Peter Davies, in the same article (BBC, online), stated: 'Let's not lose sight that every child abuse image is a crime scene and every time an image is accessed the child is being re-victimised. Also, those who access child abuse images often have a sexual interest in children which manifests itself in other even more harmful ways'.

It is important to differentiate clearly between pornography and images of child abuse. Nielssen et al. (2011, p. 216) highlight the role of the changing nature of technology in facilitating the availability of child-abuse images online and 'how it has allowed those with an interest in child pornography to view and disseminate this material without personal contact', and they suggest that researching 'child pornography offenders' is highly problematic, but that 'Internet surveillance has aided apprehension of sexual offenders who would not otherwise have been caught, especially those involved in making and disseminating child pornography'. Goggin (2006) highlights the role of the incorporation of the camera to the mobile phone in the panics surrounding their potential use by paedophiles to take photographs of children. One high-profile example of such use is discussed by Siapera (2012) in the case of Vanessa George, the 39-year-old nursery worker in Plymouth, UK, who used her mobile phone to take images of the sexual abuse of young children in her care, which she then uploaded and shared on Facebook.

> There is no doubt that the new media have created opportunities for child abusers, who can produce, distribute and download abusive images in mere minutes. Although the legal framework for this kind of activity exists, the internet's vast size and geographical spread makes difficult the control of either the production or the distribution of such images.
>
> (Siapera, 2012, p. 119)

As a result of George's conviction, most early years settings have banned to use of mobile phones on the premises. Current perceptions of constructions of risk in relation to child-abuse images online have, at the time of writing, recently been changed following the case of Mark Bridger, who was jailed in 2013 for the murder of five-year-old April Jones in Powys, Wales. After the trial, the media reported that Bridger searched the internet for child-abuse and rape images.

However, current constructions of risk in relation to child abuse images also include children themselves as perpetrators. Hanson (2011, p. 673) suggests that amongst the more prolific child pornographers now are children themselves: 'the digital sexual revolution has encouraged a new breed of sexual offender who thrives particularly well online: the child a producer of child pornography, the child and exploiter of child prostitution, the child a self-employed child prostitute, and the child as the sexual abuser of other children'.

Bullying

It is not just in relation to the child as a sexual abuser of other children that the risk discourses resonate. As discussed in the previous chapter, mobile mediation technologies play a fundamental role in positively maintaining and managing children's friendships and family relationships. However, they are also simultaneously facilitating negative roles in more risky relationships and in bullying. Bullying behaviour has been the subject of a considerable amount of research and is well documented by the media, appearing repeatedly in news headlines.

Briggs (2008, p. 120) defines bullying as such: 'bullying occurs when there is a reciprocal fit between the projection of murderousness into someone identified as vulnerable, with the victim of bullying projection aggression into the aggressor'. Mobile technologies are blamed for the reported increase in bullying, cyberstalking and social phenomena like *happy slapping* (when a physical assault is recorded, often videoed, on a mobile device and the material sent to others to further the humiliation). The children in my research held highly complex perceptions of the interwoven and complicated relationships between people and technologies, and it is hard to distinguish between the different roles played by the human actors and the object (technology) actors in the accounts of such performances. Some of the children actually admitted to bullying others, or sending nasty messages, exemplifying Berking's (1999) argument that aggression can be expressed as gift-giving. They commented on happy slapping and discussed the effects that such behaviours may have on others, such as humiliation and embarrassment, and their accounts revealed a detailed understanding of notions of power and control through mobile phone use. Withholding an anticipated text back or not responding to a text message, or not returning a call or failing to answer a call, was also viewed in terms of a punishment or weapon against another. In my research, the children's talk included incidents which ranged from outright personal threats delivered via a mobile device to concerns over how text could be misinterpreted and, therefore, seen to be offensive, even though that was not the intention. They also detailed peer pressure associated with mobile technology ownership and using mobile technologies as a device to get others into trouble (e.g. with teachers).

In relation to bullying, Mercer (2010, p. 191) states:

> There is no doubt that bullying in schools is highly undesirable. As its worst, bullying causes physical injury or even death. Long-term bullying and rejection are associated with suicide. In the short term, bullying affects school attendance because bullied children often avoid school as often as they can, resulting in missed academic work and fewer positive social interactions with other children.

Unfortunately, there is also no doubt that bullying and intimidation of children is widespread.

Previous issues regarding bullying behaviour in childhood have been, like the quote above, concerned with the development and educational outcomes of the *becoming* child. However, Savirimuthu (2011) advocates adopting a children's rights perspective in considering children's use of the internet, and in the analysis presented here it is apparent that there is a rapid blurring of traditional boundaries associated with bullying discourses and, therefore, also with child-protection advice and policy. Sibley (1995) discusses the zones of ambiguity between public and private, and suggests that uncertainty exists in marginal states. Buckingham (2000) argues that the concept of generation is important to understanding technologies and everyday lives, and his suggestion is certainly pertinent here. A generation ago, bullying behaviour was predominantly associated with school or with the physical spaces which children inhabited and shared with each other. If someone said or did something unpleasant in the playground, the victim would endeavour to keep away from them. The gendering of bullying behaviours and the construction of hegemonic masculinities, particularly as part of the playground culture and its role in bullying, has been well documented and children inhabit physical spaces to create a 'borderland', real and metaphorical, to keep away from aggressors (Newman et al., 2006). Children adopt strategies to try to keep themselves safe and ameliorate opportunities for the bullying to take place. Safety could be sought away from the playground and the physical spaces of bullying, for example, at home and, although anxiety may have remained, the bullying behaviours were subjected to boundaries. The idealisation of the private sphere of the home as a central feature of modernity (Slater, 1998) is compromised by mobile technologies and associated behaviours which have blurred boundaries between public and private further in late modernity. Contemporary childhoods are not neatly played out in such distinct spaces and through mobile mediation technologies bullying behaviour is viewed as no longer confined to the playground, street or other public space, but understood to be potentially possible at any time of day or night through what Stokes (2010) terms the 'geomorphic web'. This is important as 'the perception that there is a defined sphere or venue where risks originate and end is a misguided one' (Savirimuthu, 2011, p. 557). It no longer conforms to spatial or even virtual boundaries even within the previously private and protected sphere of the bedroom. Forty-nine per cent of children go online in their bedroom (Livingstone et al., 2011a) and this number continues to increase with the rapid adoption of mobile mediation technologies. Whilst Harden's (2000) research suggested that children viewed the home in terms of safety in their conceptualisations of risk, mobile media technologies have changed children's risk landscapes, and children are now vulnerable and feel insecure in the very spaces that were previously associated with certainty and security.

Six out of 30 children who took part in my study admitted either bullying other children by using a mobile device or sending nasty text messages to other children. Becky, for example, confessed to sending such messages and was reassured by the other members of her group that she was far from alone in this behaviour:

> *Becky [aged 14]*: I'll admit that I have sent nasty text messages off my phone to hurt people.
> *Laura [aged 14]*: I have.
> *Becky [aged 14]*: I think everyone does it.

Livingstone et al. (2013) suggest that children's concern about bullying in online environments increases with age and peaks at 13–14 years. Recent research by Cross et al. (2012, p. 4) studied primary-school-aged children and found that:

> 21% of eight–11-year-olds have been deliberately targeted, threatened or humiliated by an individual or group through the use of mobile phones or the internet. For nearly half of these (46%), this experience was ongoing, meaning that the individual described the bullying as continuous cyberbullying by the same person or group over a prolonged period of time. This would suggest that one-in-10 primary school-aged children have experienced persistent and intentional bullying inflicted via technology.

Across Europe, 6 per cent of 9–16-year-old internet users report having been bullied online, and 3 per cent confess to having bullied others and the EU Kids Online data suggests that half of online bullies claimed that they had also bullied people face-to-face and similarly half of online bullying victims have been bullied face-to-face (Livingstone et al., 2011a). The EU Kids Online research concluded that the more children used the internet, the more likely they were to experience risk. Mobile mediation technologies have transformed the accessibility of online environments and social media for children, thus the opportunities to bully and/or be bullied are increasing. The anonymity of the internet and social media has also been attributed to the increasing incidence of bullying behaviours experienced in childhood. Cross et al.'s (2012) study reflects the boundary blurring between the physical and virtual spaces of childhood in that, of the children who reported persistent and intentional bullying, 48 per cent were first victimised offline (e.g. at school) and then experienced the bullying continuing in online environments. This compares with 28 per cent of children in their study who reported that the bullying first started online, which suggests that many children who are persistently cyberbullied often experience the bullying in addition to offline bullying, which additionally would suggest that they may well know the identity of the aggressor(s).

The children's talk in my research reflected gender-stereotypical public discourses on bullying behaviours in childhood and upholds Smith et al.'s (2005) assertion that girls are more likely to both bully others and be involved in text-message bullying than boys. However, many more children had discussed being a victim of such behaviours and receiving spiteful text messages, sometimes in the form of either name-calling, a less-than-flattering photograph (girls) or an outright threat (boys). For Josh, the mobile phone had been significant in a prolonged period of threats, menace and intimidation from an older boy who was the boyfriend of Josh's female friend. The texting back and forth between the two boys is viewed not only in terms of a power struggle, but also in terms of a gendered power struggle and the dominance of hegemonic masculinities. This supports Frosh et al.'s (2002) findings on the performances of masculinities, constructed through everyday practices, which include emphasising their toughness. It is also notable that the text messages are seen by the boys as concurrently as both a threatening and lamentable behaviour on the part of the other boy, suggesting that 'the ways in which boys act as masculine, and their masculine identities, need to be seen as gendered practices which are relational, contradictory and multiple' (Frosh et al., 2002, p. 119).

Josh [aged 15]: I have had some threatening text messages off our friend's Hannah's boyfriend.
Kev [aged 15]: Ah yes our good friend the Dark Lord...
Andy [aged 15]: So he threatens you with a text message?!
Josh [aged 15]: I know it is pretty lame...
Kev [aged 15]: Very threatening!

> *Josh [aged 15]*: But then I ended up having a little text message dick-waving thing with [name of boy] like who can prove that they are hardest – it was lame really.

The children discussed incidences that were not personal to them in terms of bullying, but that they had either heard of or had happened to one of their friends. No one in the focus groups from this study either admitted happy slapping or being a victim of it at the time that the field work was carried out. However, the phenomenon was deliberated on by the children in all the groups to some extent and most of the children had either heard of someone close to them or within their school having some experience of it happening. It is not only the actual behaviour of happy slapping, but also the sharing of the material which causes additional humiliation and psychological harm.

> *Emily [aged 16]*: My friend like when he was in year 9 and got like into all drugs and that and he like got into a thing like 'happy slapping' and then he...not him...his friend...did it...like to this little boy like beating him and up and stuff like really badly and it went round the whole school and it was of this boy who was a lot younger...he didn't even go to that school but it went round the whole school and everyone in the school had it and I know that there are loads on problems with it in [name of town] schools and stuff.

The children's conversations, however, were not just based on their own experiences of bullying associated with mobile phone use and they were concerned with media coverage of the happy slapping phenomenon, outlining what the behaviour entailed and why people did it. Victimisation of young people is high and, according to the ONS (2013), there were an estimated 821,000 crimes experienced by children aged 10–15 in the previous year. What is remarkable from the children's accounts is that, whilst they reflect some of the concerns raised by the media attention given to the phenomenon of happy slapping, it also demonstrates the children's personal understanding of the consequences of the phenomenon on an individualised basis.

'Being bullied online is the risk that upsets children the most, even though it is among the least common' (Livingstone et al., 2011a, p. 30). Livingstone et al. (2013) found that from research with nearly 10,000 children across Europe that conduct-related risks come second in children's ranking of concerns is doubtless because of cyberbullying and sexting linked to the widespread use of personal and networked devices.

Harmful content – pro-anorexia, self-harm and pro-suicide

There is considerable concern currently in relation to the increasing proliferation of harmful 'pro-sites', which include pro-self-harm, pro-suicide and pro-anorexia (and other eating disorder) websites. Little is known, however, about why young people use the sites and what risk they actually pose to children's mental well-being. Greater accessibility to the increasingly mobile internet is often blamed for the rise in risk-related websites. boyd et al. (2010, p. 4) note in relation to self-harm sites:

> Although people participated in self-harm [behaviours] before the Internet, the Internet has made it easier for those engaged in self-harm to document and share self-harm techniques, build communities around self-harm practices, and promote self-harm lifestyles. Of course, those who practice deliberate self-harm techniques also use the Internet as a crucial tool for getting help. Whilst some sites are solely dedicated to the promotion or eradication of self-harm, content that promotes self-harm is often intertwined with content that enables support and recovery. Furthermore, what might be triggering content to one person – such as a personal account of self-injury – may encourage another person to seek help. This makes it difficult to categorise what constitutes problematic self-harm content.

My own research in 2012 investigated the increasing prevalence pro-eating disorder websites online. I analysed 126 pro-eating disorder (pro-ED) websites, which promote a disordered view of perfection in relation to body image and which offered extreme or dangerous dieting advice given which promote harmful behaviours. Previous estimates found 400–500 pro-ED websites available online (Giles, 2006) and, additionally, I found hundreds of individual blogs and social network sites also claiming to be pro-ana (Bond, 2012). A significant number of sites are actually created by girls under 18 years old (Norris et al. 2006) and there is increasing concern over the nature and potentially harmful content of these sites for children. According to Mind (the leading mental health charity for England and Wales), one in 100 women aged 15–30 in the UK suffer from anorexia and recent reports show some girls as young as five years of age have weight concerns and think about going on a diet. Anorexia nervosa is most likely to strike during the mid-teenage years and it affects approximately one in 150 15-year-old females, and one in 1,000 15-year-old males (the Royal College of Psychiatrists, online). According to BEAT (online), there are diagnosed cases of anorexia nervosa in children as young as six and anorexia has the highest mortality rate of any psychiatric disorder, as 20 per cent of anorexia sufferers will die prematurely from their illness. Young people with an eating disorder are also like to suffer from other mental health issues and frequently also suffer from depression or social anxiety (Juarascio et al., 2010). Csipke and Horne's (2007) study, for example, of users of a pro-ana site found that 84 per cent had an eating disorder; 46 per cent also experienced problems with self-harm; 37 per cent experienced anxiety and panic attacks; 24 per cent suffered from depression; and 24 per cent experienced another type of social difficulty.

According to Livingstone et al. (2011), approximately 10 per cent of children have visited a pro-ED website, yet little is known about why young people set them up, and whether or to what extent they are contributing to either the anorexic condition in childhood or the pro-ana phenomenon. The pro-ana community is substantial (Harshbarger et al., 2009) and the rise of the popularity of the internet, new media and mobile-mediated technologies has played a significant part in providing easier access to information on how to diet, stay thin and maintain the anorexic/eating-disordered condition. A

> pro-eating disorder Website is defined as a collection of Internet pages, all assessed through a domain name or IP address, that deliver content about eating disorders such as anorexia and bulimia. This content can be conveyed through text, images, or audio, and it encourages knowledge, attitudes, and behaviours to achieve terribly low body weights.
>
> (Borzekowski et al., 2010, p. 1526)

Whilst media discourse and public concern centred on the risk of the potentially harmful content, it is important to look at the wider content of young people's interactions with pro-ED sites. The effects model of explanation fails to adequately consider young people's everyday lives and, in our perception of why these sites are used, we need to remember that young people with eating disorders, or who self-harm or are depressed, often lack social support (Tiller et al., 1997). This need for social support, combined with technological developments (including mobility) which allow new online communities to develop quickly with little financial cost, has led to the plethora of pro-ED, pro-self-harm and pro-suicide websites, online forums and communities available online. In understanding these phenomena, it is important to remember that there are alternative approaches to understanding them (Bond, 2013). Whilst the medical model views eating disorders as an illness to be cured, young people who use pro-ana (and similarly pro-self-harm, see boyd, 2010) websites 'actually "want" their anorexia because of the positive perception that they have towards it' (Williams and Reid, 2010, p. 553). Additionally, Chandler (2012, p. 455) suggests that, in relation to self-harm, although the biomedical perspective emphasises rationality over emotions, considering 'self-injury as embodied emotion work' demonstrates the problematic nature of dualistic approaches. The right to participate in these environments is not unproblematic as Livingstone (2009) points out and is it questionable, in the case of pro-ED (and other risk-related environments e.g. pro-suicide and pro-self-harm) how far these rights should be upheld when there are potentially harmful consequences from such participation.

The more complex sites have hundreds of users worldwide with different pages for different functions and topics. They offer, for example, a new members forum; a forum to talk about different types of eating disorders; a chat room for members who are pro-recovery (which included clear text-based instructions requesting users did not post anything that could be considered triggering); and forums for discussions about family issues. Some sites offer tips and advice for hiding symptoms of the eating disorder from family and medical professionals and discussions on traumas; for example, relating to abuse. Opportunities to find an 'anabuddy' – an online friend, for support and advice is provided by many sites and users can also exchange email or contact details to communicate with each other away from the more public forum environments. A large proportion of these sites is dedicated to 'thinspiration' or 'thinspo' (see section below for further discussion) with photographs and images, competitions and dieting challenges. Easily accessible through mobile technology devices, young people can be constantly connected to the negative support network. Nearly 90 per cent of the sites I analysed contained thinspiration material and more than 80 per cent contained overt information on personally engaging in pro-eating-disordered behaviours. What is significant in relation to the pro-ana sites is that the audience viewing these images are eating-disordered young people who are already very vulnerable. These images can have a negative impact on the children viewing them, as Higbed and Fox's (2010) research suggests. Their participants reported feeling low when they visited sites and felt worse about their body image as a result, which overall discouraged them from seeking recovery. The risks from posting images are also closely related to the frequent incidences of cyberbullying, and as many of the images are of scantily clad, thin, young bodies; the sexualised nature of many of the images is also cause for concern. Young women have reported being targeted for 'skinny porn', with agencies hosting anorexia pornography on YouTube and advertising on anorexia-pornography forums (Hobbs, 2011).

In pursuit of perfection, many anorexics are prepared to starve themselves in order to carry on losing weight and the harsh regimes which include advice on purging, taking diet pills and laxatives are potentially dangerous. Twenty-seven per cent of the overall sample also contained images of self-harm, and images linked to depression and suicide. The age at which children visit pro-ED sites is, also, an increasing concern. The majority of users of pro-ana sites are young and female, but the sites are also visited by boys and young men (Csipke and Horne, 2000). Custers and Van den Bulck's (2009) study in Belgium of 711 secondary-school children found that 12.6 per cent of girls and 5.9 per cent of boys had visited pro-ana websites; they found that users of pro-ana websites scored higher on a desire for thinness, perfectionism and a lower BMI. Pro-ED websites are unlikely to disappear and research demonstrating the negative consequences of pro-ED websites argues for actions that might minimise damage (Bardone-Cone and Cass, 2006, p. 546). The findings of my study illustrate that risk in relation to these online spaces is a complex relationship between the accessibility and availability of these sites, the frequency of the visits, the nature and content of the site, and the vulnerability and/or resilience of the user. Mobile internet technologies make these sites constantly available and accessible, so for young people they can be constantly in touch with these communities and potentially harmful content. It is the paradoxical relationship between the negative aspects of the potentially harmful online content and the positive aspects of online support combined with the ambiguous nature of the individuals' feelings towards the disease that makes it so difficult to manage the risk in relation to these online environments.

Conclusion

'The digitalization processes during the 1990s have opened enthusiastic discussions on the egalitarian properties on the Internet and the Web. The last decade has shown the other side of digitization – the great digital divide, possible breaches of privacy and the issues of control'

(Primorac and Jurlin, 2008, p. 86). As a clear example of the risk society thesis, it is important to remember that how we understand risk influences how we respond to and attempt to manage risk. Livingstone (2009, p. 151) observes:

> With headlines full of paedophiles, internet sex beasts, cyber-bullies and online suicide pacts easily predominating positive stories of the educational, civic or expressive dimensions of internet use, it is perhaps unsurprising that public anxiety regarding risk in relation to children and the internet is considerable, at times resulting in disproportionate reactions to perceived threats.

What I have argued in this chapter is that the risk society thesis is helpful to understanding the socially constructed nature of risk and how perceptions of risk in relation to mobile technologies impact on social and cultural constructions of childhood. The dominant discourses on childhood, which underpin current social constructions, similarly influence the responses to the perceived risk from mobile technologies, and there is, therefore, a reciprocal intertwining between the social construction of risk, children and the social construction of mobile technologies in late-modern society.

> This new technology has had undoubted benefits within the spheres of, for example, work, education and leisure. However, it also entails negative or harmful consequences, especially for children. Chief among these are the risks children face in being made the subjects of, or exposed to pornography ... and the possibility of being groomed over the internet for child sexual abuse (CSA). These risks are, though, becoming more diverse, with increasing reports, in the media at least, of mobile phones being used to record images of children being physically or sexually assaulted or send texts to children for the purposes of bullying them.
>
> (Gallagher, 2005, p. 367)

Beck (1992) argues that modernisation must become reflexive in order for society to evolve, and issues of political and economic management of risks are overshadowing issues of employment and development of political, technical and societal responses to risk, illustrating Beck's notion of reflexive modernity. McLuhan argued that technology and media change and redirect human activity – 'be it social, political or economic' (Siapera, 2012, p. 7). It is the lack of trust that parents and educators have in regard to online interactions and communication technologies can create tensions in relation to children's privacy and autonomy; restrictions on internet use and surveillance are seen as a way of inculcating responsible and safe use of communication technologies (Ofsted, 2010). Evidence from Livingstone et al. (2011a) highlights that parents are often unaware of the risks that children and young people have encountered online, and Savirimuthu (2011) suggests that many parents and educators are unaware that in a media-networked environment children can access online content from mobile internet devices, such as portable media players, mobile phones and games consoles. As our comprehension of the risks change, so does the advice on responses to risk and previous safety advice to keep a PC in a public area in the house and install filters and monitoring software is no longer appropriate and is of little value when children and young people are gaining increasing access to online environments and digital content through personalised, mobile devices and sharing it through a plethora of interlinked social network platforms. As Mascheroni and Ólafsson (2013, p. 25) observe:

> ...the home is still a strategic site for raising awareness on online risks and promoting safer and responsible uses of the internet. However, as we have seen, smartphones and mobile devices in general are personal, portable media which are thoroughly and seamlessly integrated in children's and their parents' everyday life. Consequently, the increasingly privatised conditions of internet use are likely to inhibit or challenge established parental mediation strategies such as active mediation of children's online experiences.

Many analyses of risk fail to recognise that risk is a subjective experience open to changing opinions and media discourses, and one which adopts a technologically determinist approach. As such, they are too simplistic in their responses to risk and in their risk-management approach. In relation to pro-self-harm sites, for example, Boyd et al. (2010, p. 5) 'highlight the weaknesses of a content-centric approach, for even if a legal or technical intervention could curb problematic self-harm content, it would not address the underlying issues'. If we are to understand the complexity of the risk landscape and how it is viewed and understood by different children and in different contexts, we need to explore the complex interrelationships that exist between the young people, the mobile technologies, other people, wider society and the political, economic and media environments.

Mundane masses (the everyday and the humdrum that are frequently overlooked), assemblages (description of things holding
together), materiality (that which does or does not endure), heterogeneity (achieved diversity within an assemblage, and flows/fluidity
(movement without necessary stability).

(Neyland, 2006, p. 45)

According to Savirimuthu (2011, p. 551), 'current EU policymaking
and regulatory activity is directed at three groups of actors: (i) those
who *make* the technologies; (ii) those who *make* consumption of the
technologies and services available; and (iii) those who *consume* the
technologies and services' (emphasis in the original). Consideration of
the environment is also important, supporting McLuhan and Fiore's
(1967, p. 68) observation that 'environments are not passive wrappings,
but are, rather, active processes which are visible'; it is apparent from the
research available that children are reflexive in their conceptualisation
of risk and that many children actively take steps to keep themselves
safe, viewing themselves as having a degree of responsibility for risk
management. Harden (2000) argues that children reflexively construct
their landscapes of risk around the concepts of private, local and public.
From the debates outlined in this chapter concerning our comprehension of risk, I have argued that it is important to consider the complex
multifaceted and complicated perceptions derived from many different factors, including both human and non-human elements. Whilst
childhood is constructed as a time of innocence, vulnerability and
dependence (Jenks, 2005), risk anxiety, engendered by the desire to keep
children safe, frequently has negative consequences for children themselves and curtails children's activities in ways which may restrict their
autonomy and their opportunities to develop the necessary skills to cope
with the world (Scott et al., 1998). The context as well as the classification of the risks children encounter is also important to understanding
potential harm, as whilst there is a growing body of evidence in relation
to online risk, only a relatively small number of children say that they
have been upset by what they have seen (Hasebrink et al., 2009). Some
children are more vulnerable than others online (see Carrick-Davies,
2011 for a more extensive discussion on vulnerability), and it is often
difficult to separate risk from opportunities (Livingstone et al., 2011a).
Other online risks include upselling pressure (games that are free initially but then cost); age-restricted products (pornography, alcohol and
weapons); and online advertising, which is a growing market. Abstract
notions of risk came up against everyday realities in children's lives, and

this is significant in the light of Freudenburg's (1993) argument that traditional factors of risk-perception analysis, such as technical assessments of the actual risk posed or socio-demographic characteristics of the risk perceiver, are sterile debates on whether perceptions of risk are rational or not, and suggests that it may be more productive for research to consider how people perceive risk. Recent technologies are making the young generation more mobile, in terms of gaining access to online environments, than they have ever been before, and which they take for granted and consider as a right (Jensen, 2006). Confirming the difference in emphasis between objective knowledge and subjective perceptions about risk, the data from the EU Kids Online survey and the associated reports highlight Adams' (1995) suggestion that we all possess our own 'lay' definitions of risk, and for young people it is the social aspects of risk that are more salient than the scientific aspects, which accentuates the social shaping of technology. Daliot-Bul's (2007) work in Japan also illustrates how mobile phone content is an example of self-presentation, and that cameras and messaging lead to new and novel applications emphasising playful and emotional communication practices. Drotner (2000, p. 161) suggests that it is 'the combination of the "seamless" embeddedness of media into everyday culture and the increasingly complex interweaving of programmes, formats, genres and media types is, indeed, a challenging analytical cocktail'. Mobile internet technologies are, therefore, a space of intimacy (Ito et al., 2005).

Children's use of mobile internet technologies in their everyday lives has become a cause for increasing concern, developing policy initiatives and legal intervention, yet few reports on managing risk in online environments take account of children themselves and often fail to consider the diversity of children's lived experiences. Exemplified by the Baudrillard (2003) quote above and by Haraway's (1991) cyborg manifesto, any discussion of these risks needs to be underpinned by an awareness that the boundaries between offline and online behaviours are increasingly blurred, and they are often interrelated and intersect with other adolescent risk behaviours, such as sexual activity, alcohol and drug experimentation. In the last few years, there has been a growing body of knowledge which attempts to address this need. However, as Ólafsson et al. (2013, p. 4) point out:

> For almost half (45%) of the studies, the findings are reported online; however, this makes it difficult for research users to find much of the research, especially when it has been conducted in other countries. Increasingly, research is published in peer-reviewed academic

journals, resulting in a higher quality output overall. A fair proportion of research, however, is poorly conducted and poorly reported and disseminated.

In our growing understanding of risk in relation to mobile technologies and children's everyday experiences, we need to explore these relationships within the technical, social and natural worlds, and not view them as simplistic cause-and-effect relationships, but as complex, multifarious relationships in the heterogeneous networks that have evolved in postmodernity (see Stalder, 2006). This chapter has highlighted the blurring of the boundaries of what was previously traditionally understood as the core sociological dichotomies of public/private; human/object; adulthood/childhood; security/danger; belonging/individualisation and risk/trust. 'Individuals are forced to rely on trust, not just in the abstract capabilities of systems, but in the people making the knowledge claims' (Holmes, 2010, p. 146). Through risk-profiling, sometimes deferring in space and time, individuals deflect potentially hazardous consequences and maintain a viable *Umwelt* (Giddens, 1991); and through social reflexivity, young people reflexively construct and maintain a viable *Umwelt* (see Goffman, 1971) from both human and technical entities in managing risk. Whilst viewing children as the experts in their own lives, it is essential that all children are equipped with the skills they need to navigate the landscapes of risk in relation to mobile technologies and the networked publics, and in managing risk it is essential that we do not deny young people their right to participate in the mobile networked society.

7
Rhetoric and Realities

Introduction

In late-modern society, the restructuring of education to create a highly skilled and knowledgeable workforce has been at the centre of educational reform (France, 2007), but what of the children who do not have equal access to the internet or to mobile internet technologies recently promoted for engaging children with educational opportunities?

> There is little doubt that society's main ambition for children's use of the internet centres on learning – informally at home and through formal education at school. Today in Britain, nearly every child uses the internet and other online technologies, most of them at home and school, some only at school, some elsewhere also. Not just computers on desks, information and communication technologies (ICTs) are becoming embedded in the fabric of every activity, part of the infrastructure that supports learning, communication and participation. In schools, lesson plans and classroom arrangements are being redesigned. At home, the perceived educational benefits of domestic internet access have fuelled its rapid diffusion – indeed, in our aspirational culture, little else could have so effectively driven the domestic ICT market than the expectation that internet access gets one's child 'ahead' or at least stops them falling behind.
>
> (Livingstone, 2009, p. 63)

McLuhan and Fiore (1967, p. 67) suggest that 'the new electronic interdependence recreates the world in the image of a global village'. The school is promoted as a setting for the promotion of digital inclusion of young people in a globalised, networked society (Meneses and

Mominó, 2010), yet, in reality, many children remain digitally excluded to some extent. Carrington and Marsh (2005, p. 280) observe how 'rapid advances in technology, combined with the process of globalization and the failure of neo-liberal governmentality to manage the complex changes of late modernity, have led to social and cultural instabilities which have profound implications for literacy and literacy education'. Whilst there has been considerable financial investment in ICTs in schools, Livingstone's analysis above illustrates what Valentine and Holloway (2001) consider to be the *cybertopian* celebration or what Selwyn (2011a) refers to as the 'techno-romantic' manner which underlies investment in children's command and use of technologies that is assumed to be essential to both our and their future.

As already established in the preceding chapters, children and young people are increasingly accessing the internet through mobile internet technologies, including smartphones, post-PC tablets, netbooks and e-readers. Within this seemingly ubiquitous adoption of mobile internet technologies in many children's everyday experiences, it is important to remember that not all children have equal access to either mobile internet technologies or the internet generally. Dutton (2013) highlights the many social issues which have arisen in relation to the internet, which include inequalities in access, digital divides to infrastructures and information, and the impact that this has on social relationships, community, participation, citizenship and identity. This chapter explores such inequalities of access and considers the rhetoric of educational ideology in relation to mobile internet technologies against the realities of children's everyday lives. Using the examples of poverty and disability, the taken-for-grantedness of the embedding of mobile internet technologies (see Ling, 2012) in children's everyday lives is critically considered in this chapter to argue that we need to move beyond conceptualising childhood and children as a homogenous group, and endeavour to meaningfully examine the reality and diversity of children's lived experiences in our perceptions of childhood, mobile, internet technologies and children's everyday experiences.

Technologised learning

The EU Kids Online survey found that 92 per cent of children use the internet for school work (Livingstone et al., 2010), which highlights the role of the internet in contemporary children's learning experiences. Mobile internet and gaming technologies are increasingly seen as fertile ground for the development of resources to support learning (Facer et al., 2004), and Meneses and Mominó (2010) consider the role of the school as a setting for the promotion of digital inclusion of young people in late-modern society.

> Digital technologies represent a relatively recent addition to this 'media-saturated' environment and, as we shall see, they are far from equally available to all young people. Yet the internet, computer games and mobile communication technologies are often seen to present unique opportunities – an indeed dangers – for the young. In these debates, the distinction between 'new' media and 'old' media is often drawn in stark and absolutist terms. As in education, the talk is of a fundamental transformation – a revolution – in young people's cultural experiences. We are warned of a 'digital generation gap' (Papert, 1996). As children have grown up with digital media they are apparently living in a different world from their parents, who grew up with television. Both socially and psychologically, the 'digital generation' is seen to operate in quite different ways from the generations that preceded it.
>
> (Buckingham, 2007, p. 75)

Whilst the mobile phone was previously attributed to changing children's cultural world and social interactions, it is the post-PC tablet (Clark and Luckin, 2013) that has been afforded a similar role in children's learning experiences and educational discourses. What is interesting to note from Mascheroni and Ólafsson's (2013, p. 21) research is that 'though many schools across Europe are experimenting the use of tablets in class, the use of tablets to go online is associated with a smaller increase in the overall use of the internet for schoolwork than the use of smartphones'.

Clark and Luckin's (2013, p. 2) review of the recent literature on the iPad and post-PC tablets concludes that students are generally positive in their views on iPads: 'seeing them as essential for 21st Century Education', they have been used to 'support collaborative learning, to provide personalised learning experiences, iPads to augment and enhance deep learning, as ubiquitous, distributed and connected learning tools' and they can also contribute to 'Digitally Enhanced Monitoring and Assessment'.

More associated with the post-PC tablet than the mobile phone, educational initiatives and wider policy rhetoric is centred on improving children's learning through technology and, more recently, through mobile internet technology. Whilst much emphasis has been on

technology-enhanced learning opportunities in transforming education, I have, however, argued elsewhere the relationship between
technology and teaching and technology and learning is far from
straightforward (see, for example, Bond and Goodchild, 2012, 2013).

> We have now become aware of the possibility of arranging the entire
> human environment as a work of art, as a teaching machine designed
> to maximize perception and to make everyday learning a process of
> discovery. Application to this knowledge would be the equivalent of
> a thermostat controlling room temperature. It would seem only rea-
> sonable to extend such controls to all the sensory thresholds of our
> being. We have no reason to be grateful to those who juggle these
> thresholds in name of haphazard innovation.
>
> (McLuhan and Fiore, 1967, p. 68)

Furthermore, Buckingham (2007, p. 7) points out that 'despite massive
government funding for ITC in schools, the fear of policy makers and of
companies is that technology is not becoming sufficiently "embedded"
in classroom practice'. It is not, however, the technology itself *per se* that
is significant in influencing learning as such but more the engagement
between the learner, the learning experience and the technology with
the wider context that is important. Luckin et al. (2012, p. 9) conclude
that 'what is clear is that no technology has an impact on learning in
its own right; rather its impact depends upon the way in which it is
used'. According to Fenwick (2010, p. 119), we can 'share notions of
human/non-human symmetry, network not as metaphor but as sociomaterial performances that enact reality and translation in multiple and
shifting formulations'. Therefore, it is important to consider the broader
interactions and the wider political and economic context in debates on
mobile internet technologies and children's everyday learning experiences, and avoid adopting a simplistic cause-and-effect-type approach
in our analyses.

In relation to changing constructions of childhood, what is changing
are the boundaries of learning opportunities that are becoming more
fluid and dynamic with learning no longer understood as being located
mainly within the physical walls of the classroom or confined to a
school setting. As discussed in Chapter 2, from the late nineteenth and
early twentieth centuries onwards, childhood had increasingly become
confined to the private spaces of the home and the classroom, with
the latter being very much a site for learning and educating the child
(Heywood, 2005; Cunningham, 2005). Conversely, in the late-modern

age, mobile internet technologies are now envisioned as learning spaces in childhood (and beyond), but no longer confined to the walls of the classroom and the school boundaries. The term *flipped classroom* is often associated with the use of internet-related, and more recently, mobile technologies whereby learning resources and materials can be made available to students for them to engage with from outside the context of the classroom (Milman, 2012; Roehl et al., 2013). Avoiding deterministic approaches, Zurita and Nussbaum (2007) helpfully distinguish between the social and technological components of a network to highlight how there is face-to-face communication and interaction between people and mobile devices, as well as between the devices themselves. They suggest that mobile internet technologies support collaborative learning as the scaffold coordination, supporting the social network and thus facilitate individual learning tasks which comprise the group activity and, as such, can provide possibilities for changing pedagogical approaches. Similarly, mobile learning has attracted much attention from the educational community, especially internationally, and Kearney et al. (2012) propose a pedagogical theoretical framework in which they argue that three components – authenticity, collaboration and personalisation – are essential in considering mobile learning. Similarly, mobile internet technologies have been viewed as positive interventions in addressing educational inequalities elsewhere. Kim et al. (2011, p. 465), for example, note that 'mobile devices are highly portable, easily distributable, substantially affordable, and have the potential to be pedagogically complementary resources in education'. Their study in Mexico found that the mobile learning technology adoption was rapid, seamless and actively driven by the students rather than the teacher, and they found that 'mobile learning devices could be effective in supplementing education particularly in a community with a poor educational infrastructure'. Similarly, from their empirical study, which explored the learning effectiveness of a science curriculum transformed for delivery and for learning on mobile technologies, Looi et al. (2010, p. 27) concluded that students were more engaged as a result of using the devices and 'through our observations of the enacted lessons and our analysis of student-created artefacts using their mobile devices, we detect a shift in the classroom behaviour after the introduction of the mobile devices'.

Fenwick and Edwards (2010, p. 79) promote the use of ANT in understanding the of ICT in education, and they suggest 'the point is that one particular ANT approach was found to be useful, in these cases, the method of tracing highly particular, moment-to-moment "translations" occurring among the heterogeneous materials, as a way to understand technological innovation and large scale implementation'. Thus, the importance of considering the wider social and educational context is highlighted as Meneses and Mominó (2010, p. 203) found in their research:

> compared with other contexts in the everyday life of children and young people, the school is found to be the second most important place for initial Internet training and, particularly for class time, a relatively common context in which to access and use the Internet. However, informal settings outside the school still represent more widespread contexts of online activity, where both initial training is provided and higher levels of Internet access and use are observed. In other words, with respect to children's and young people's reported appropriation of the Internet, in-school contexts matter, but other settings outside the school appear to be even more important.

What is important to remember here is that is it not the mobile internet technology as a device, *per se*, which influences children's learning opportunities, but the content, or the educational material, they are consuming through the device. Carrington and Marsh (2005, p. 279) highlight the role of text and consider the 'production and use of texts in an age of digital communications and changing perceptions of childhood and youth'. Another example is proffered by Larson (2010, p. 22), who considers the e-reader and suggests that 'the rapidly changing nature of e-books and digital reading devices demands a progressive research agenda that examines the use of new technologies in authentic school settings. It is recognised that e-book readers may support comprehension and children's involvement with and response to digital readers is interesting'. Larson (2010) observes how new literacies and extended connections between readers and text are possible through the engagement with and manipulation of text that is made possible through the electronic tools and features available with e-readers. Concerned with the relationship between media and children's cognitive, intellectual and academic skills, Strasburger et al. (2014) suggest that much of childhood learning occurs on-screen and that educationally beneficial media characters, curricula, games and stories can supplement teaching. In interactions of learning, Čopič (2008, p. 114) suggests that 'ICT can contribute to the democratization of culture, making better access to the means for cultural production and dissemination' The role of the material artefact and culture in the digitalised society is also changing as cultural artefacts previously hidden within buildings in specific, fixed locations, such as museums, libraries, art galleries and theatres, have become part of the digital revolution, and a new culture of interactivity and convergence is characterising the digitisation of heritage in a digital future (Cvjetičanin, 2008).

Meneses and Mominó (2010, p. 205) consider 'digital literacy as diverse and socially mediated opportunities to learn the rudiments of the internet as a prosaic object of our culture'. In relation to digital literacy, Sonck et al. (2011) found differences by socio-economic status (SES), as children from higher SES households have a wider online repertoire (7.6 activities), compared with those from middle- (7.3) and low-status groups (6.7). 'Literacy practices are inextricably woven into other social, cultural, economic, political, and institutional practices and contexts' (Carrington and Marsh, 2005, p. 279) and we need to consider the diversity of children's experiences and literacy practices. As Brown and Czerniewicz (2010, p. 366) note:

> it is crucial that we as educators, as academics and as educational technologists reject deterministic and exclusionary labels and actively change this discourse. Our research makes it clear that students who are classified as outsiders because of age or lack of computer experience are not without digital skills in various shapes and forms. That the world is increasingly shaped by digital technologies is not in doubt. Everyone engages somehow, everyone makes their own meaning; everyone mediates those technologies in one way or another. The challenge is therefore to situate our responses in that rich diversity, rather than in exclusionary dichotomies.

Recently, a more positive aspect of the relationship between children and technology has begun to emerge and, rather than passive victims, the notion of children possessing media literacy has received much attention. 'While there is burgeoning research around the role that participatory media play in improving learning, educators are identifying challenges toward implementation' (Garcia and Morrell, 2013, p. 125) and, although much more positive about the impact of the media and digital technology than Postman (1993), these more optimistic accounts, such as Tapscott (1998), are also technologically deterministic as technology remains perceived as instrumental in bringing about changes in many aspects of children's lives (Buckingham, 1998).

Buckingham (2000) criticises many analyses, claiming that they fail to address how the technologies are designed, produced, marketed and actually used by children, and argues for moving beyond essentialism and conceptualising childhood as a homogenous category. Furthermore, 'the framing of children, adults and technology within these deterministic discourses tends to hide the key shaping actors, the values and power relations behind the increasing use of ICT in society' (Selwyn, 2003, p. 368). Hughes and Hans (2001) propose that work is needed which is based on a social constructive approach, in order to provide a useful theoretical framework, which studies the actual ways people use technology. The social constructionist position 'begins from the viewpoint that precisely what the characteristics of any given technology are, as well as their relationship with social structures, are both socially constructed: the outcome of a whole range of social factors and processes' (Hutchby and Moran-Ellis, 2001, p. 2). Ling (1999) further argues that both the social definition of technology and the social understanding of childhood need to be examined. Livingstone (1998) stresses the importance of contextualising new media in relation to the contexts of young people's lives, including pre-existing media; theorising media use in relation to modernity and both being informed by and informing the academic study of childhood. Children's use of technologies and media is diverse and they use and do not use them in many different ways (Selwyn, 2003). Judge et al. (2004, p. 387) emphasise the importance of staff training and technological support in introducing technology in the classroom, suggesting that 'digital equity for young children, therefore, includes access to computer resources that are used in developmentally appropriate ways with teachers who have the knowledge and skills to integrate technology into meaningful activities of interest and relevance to children'. Garcia and Morrell (2013, p. 123) further suggest that 'as educators and educational researchers continue to grapple with how uses of new communications technologies can increase educational equity, the challenges of adjusting pedagogy to meet these needs are often being disregarded'.

Just as Ling (2012) suggests that the mobile phone is taken for granted in contemporary society, Selwyn (2011b) comments that the benefits of technology are often taken for granted in education. He questions, however, whether we conceptualise learning as a product or as a process, and how we understand education as either formal or informal. 'As a whole, then, the term "education" can be best understood as the conditions and arrangements where learning takes place' (Selwyn, 2011a,

p. 5). Aspects of social theory have been drawn upon throughout this book to examine the associations of children and mobile technologies, and Fenwick and Edwards (2010, p. 3) propose that ANT can offer valuable insights into education reform and policy, as well as educational technologies:

> Actor-network theory examines the associations of human and non-human entities in the performance of the social, the economic, the natural, the educational etc. the objective is to understand precisely how these things come together – and manage to hold together, however, temporarily – to form associations that produce agency and other effects: for example, ideas, identities, rules, routines, policies, instruments and reforms. In educational discourse, such an approach leads us to question common categories and distinctions, such as teacher and learner, curriculum and pedagogy, formal and informal learning.

Digital divides?

Concerns over the digital divide at the beginning of the previous decade led to considerable investment in ICT in schools (Judge et al., 2004), but the notion of 'digital divide' is, in itself, far from simple (Siapera, 2012). The debates initially set out in Chapter 2 are also pertinent to the discussion here as predominantly children are conceptualised in educational discourses as the *becoming* rather than the *being* child.

> Wherever children are identified as primarily as pupils, their levels of consciousness and cognitive performance are readily identified as sites of potential intervention. In the last decade, the UK Government has approached the treatment of pupils as a key mechanism for addressing concerns for the future economy.
>
> (Lee, 2008, p. 71)

What is interesting in the debates which surround children and the internet is that, whilst it was previously the notions of innocence and ignorance – the incompetent child (James et al., 2010) – that dominated conceptions of childhood, more recently in their interactions with the online world children are viewed as natural experts and highly competent in digital worlds. Livingstone (2009, p. 181) sums this assumption up:

Yet a certain complacency has arisen regarding children in the regard, for they are widely heralded as 'the digital' or 'internet generation', supposedly natural 'experts' in using the internet and so, for once, a source of wisdom rather than innocence or ignorance.

Yet, this assumption is problematic as there is considerable diversity in children's ability to use, and their knowledge of, the internet, and their opportunities to access and interact online. Mobile internet technologies have transformed children's access to virtual environments as individualised and, therefore, privatised and digital convergence has made it far easier (as argued in the previous chapter) to produce and share content online, but not all children have the same opportunities or even motivations to experience the internet in the same way. It is the diversity of use that, Buckingham (2003) argues, is central to understanding children's and young people's relationships with technology. In examining the differences and divides, however, it is still important to avoid simplistic assumptions of categorising childhood and children's lived experiences. Often, conceptualised as 'information haves and have-nots, of people who are either connected to the internet and have access to other new media or not', digital divides have underpinned recent policy developments in order to ameliorate problems of access and encourage as many people as possible to use new media (Siapera, 2012, p. 69). However, as argued earlier, such dualisms are unhelpful to our understanding of the complexity of children's diverse experiences, and Law (1991) distinguishes between the previous sociological approaches to society and technology as technological determinism (technical acts as explanation) or social reductionism (expression of social relations), arguing that it is a mistake in sociological practice to ignore the networks of heterogeneous materials that constitute the social.

Yet, 'the question of access to digital technologies' remains and 'is the core underlying issue for the increasing digital divide in the world, whereby the term "digital divide" denotes the gap between those who have access to digital and information technologies, and those who do not' (Primorac and Jurlin, 2008, p. 74). Notions of the digital divide have gained the attention of politicians and philanthropists in both the US (Attewell, 2001) and the UK (Buckingham, 2004; Livingstone and Bober, 2004). This recognition, Attewell (2001, p. 257) argues, 'is the latest effort to encourage our reluctant social and political leaders to ameliorate inequality and social exclusion'. However, Meneses and

Mominó (2010, p. 198) are critical of simplistic solutions to the concerns in relation to the digital divide and argue that:

> consistent with empirical research developed to test the knowledge gap hypothesis, there is no proven gain in retaining the binary and access-based operationalization underlying the 'digital divide', where a purely technological solution – that is, in access policies, providing computers of Internet subscriptions – appear to be deterministic, limited, and wasteful answer for the wrong sociological question.

In thinking about social exclusion in terms of access to mobile internet technologies, the importance of the way that technologies and people mutually develop is highlighted by Holloway and Valentine (2003). Meneses and Mominó (2010) propose adopting a multidimensional approach to digital exclusion, and Selwyn (2003, p. 353) claims that political and economic influences also need to be considered, as the child computer-user remains politically contentious, and explores how notions of 'children and technology have long been used to "sell" technology to a society sometimes resistant to such change'. The use of digital technologies in education has been surrounded by a considerable amount of inflated rhetoric, according to Buckingham (2007). It is interesting, in the light of these arguments, therefore, that there is more research on risks and harm than the opportunities and benefits of the internet (Ólafsson et al., 2013). Buckingham (2007) challenges the dominance of technological determinism in educational discourses and the significant government drive for ICT investment in schools, suggesting that recent discourses have constructed a 'digital generation' as a consequence of these technological developments. Furthermore, Brown and Czerniewicz (2010, p. 357) argue that:

> a serious problem with the idea of the 'digital native' is that it is an 'othering' concept. It sets up a binary opposition between those who are 'natives' and those who are not, the so-called 'digital immigrants'. This polarization makes the concept less flexible and more determinist in that it implies that if a person falls into one category, they cannot exhibit characteristics of the other category.

The idea of a digital generation is problematic, as Livingstone et al.'s (2011a) findings suggest that not all children have the same levels of digital literacy and skills, and that it should not be assumed that children are competent or confident in using and interacting with online environments. Brown and Czerniewicz (2010, p. 359) propose that 'age is a determining feature of the concept of the "digital native" in the net generation', and Cooper (2005, p. 286) argues that 'cognitive, physical, social and emotional development impact a child's ability to interact successfully with a digital environment'. Furthermore, the importance of supporting the development of media and digital literacy skills is essential for both ameliorating risk in online environments – digital protection – but also for enabling children to exploit the many opportunities to learn, interact and socialise online – digital participation. Livingstone (2009, pp. 206–07) stresses the importance of media literacy in understanding the relationship between mobile media technologies and children's learning:

> In future research and policy, a satisfactory analysis of media or internet literacy will require – similar to that long been argued for theories of print literacy – recognition of the historically and culturally conditioned relationship among three processes, no one of which is sufficient alone (i) the symbolic and material (textual, technological) representation of knowledge, culture and values – especially as there are now being rewritten for a convergent, multimodal, globalizing digital age; (ii) the distribution of socially situated practices across a (stratified) population – in which socially situated practices that actively sustain symbolic distinctions and privilege in everyday contexts are thoroughly integrated into an account of online literacy skills and practices; and (iii) the institutional (state, regulatory, educational) management of the power that skilled access to knowledge brings to the 'literate' – including a critical analysis of the public and private sector interests at stake in promoting or undermining mass media literacy.

Meneses and Mominó (2010, p. 201) also note that 'even in the most optimistic discourse concerning the relationship between technology and children and young people, deterministic conceptions can be found that consider them as having effortless ability to use ICT, thus making them be the very vanguard of the digital revolution'. Yet, as Carrington and Marsh (2005, p. 279) point out, 'it is the literate habitus of children and early adolescents that has caused the most unease and political manoeuvring amongst educators, policy makers and parents'. Gender is also significant to these debates as 'technology is believed to motivate learners in and of itself – particularly disaffected learners, who in contemporary debates are almost always implicitly identified as boys'

(Buckingham, 2007, p. 7). Thus, the relationship between childhood, mobile internet technologies and children's everyday experiences is constructed around adult concerns based on an essentialist ideas and an often-sentimentalised view of childhood. In relation to education, this is especially apparent. As childhood is itself constructed as a time for learning, it has been targeted as a site for considerable technological investment to improve educational outcomes, but Buckingham (2007) urges that a more balanced approach is needed and stresses the importance of considering the milieu of educational technologies, including the more traditional media of books, chalk and blackboard, and pen and paper, as well as mobile technologies, and that consideration needs to be given to their different affordances. Fenwick and Edwards (2010) additionally point out that education has always been intertwined with material technologies, with Fenwick (2010, p. 120) proposing that:

> ANT traces the ways in which human and non-human elements are enacted as they become assembled into collectives of activity. These complex, interwoven 'networks' can spread across space and time, and produce policies, knowledge, and practices. ANT-inspired studies trace the micro-interactions through which diverse elements or 'actants' are performed into being: how they come together – and manage to *hold* together – in 'networks' that can act. These networks produce force and other effects: knowledge, identities, rules, routines, behaviours, new technologies and instruments, regulatory regimes, reforms, illnesses, and so forth.

In consideration of the debates on mobilised and technologised learning, the complex interrelationships and the hybrid nature of the interplay between young people and mobile technologies is revealed, and how, in the constantly changing associations in the networks of the human, material and digital, learning takes place. Mobile technologies do not simply transform learning but are an actor or *actant* (see Latour, 1999) in a complex network of quasi-subjects and quasi-objects, which include politics, economics, attitudes and educational policy. Thus, within a network of interdependencies, each actant plays a role in the production of reality (Lee and Stanner, 1999). Uzelac (2008) argues that, in contrasting the expectations of widespread communication with reality, digital divides cannot be overlooked. Siapera (2012) suggests that it is more helpful to think in terms of digital inequalities rather than digital divides, as the differences in people's use are more complex than simply issues of access. Whilst the debates on and rhetoric of technology and mobile technologies often focus on the 'silver bullet' (see Selwyn, 2011a), in reality children's everyday experiences are very different. Certainly, the EU Kids Online study reveals the diversity in children's experiences in online environments as, although nearly all children use the internet, mainly for school work and playing games, some children (14 per cent) do not use the internet for anything other than this (Livingstone et al., 2011a). Eighty-six per cent of children across Europe also use the internet as a mass medium (see Chapter 3 for the similarities with the discussion of the development of the television), whilst 75 per cent of children also use it interactively for communication via social network sites, instant messaging and email. More than half of the children they surveyed (56 per cent) also used the internet to play interactively with others online (as opposed to alone or against the computer) and could share content peer-to-peer and download music files and films, but only 23 per cent of the children in the EU Kids Online research reached the top level of creative use, using chatrooms, blogging and spending time in virtual worlds (Livingstone et al., 2011a).

Children's everyday experiences online and, more recently, their use of mobile internet technologies have become the focus for political debate and policy initiatives at international, national and local (school) levels. This is important to the discussion here, as consideration of the wider context reveals how, although there has been considerable political emphasis on spending on ICTs and investment in technologies for education, in the UK more money is spent on the smallest group of pupils who achieve the highest grades educationally, who enter the most prestigious universities, and as such the UK has incredibly uneven social outcomes and a polarisation between those with degrees and those with hardly any qualifications (Dorling, 2013). Buckingham (2000) has argued for an understanding of diversity in our perception of childhood – a multiplicity of childhoods (Qvortrup, 2011) – and Priestley (2003, p. 63) suggests that this approach 'allows us to look more closely at the situated experiences of children in different social contexts, and at children's agency in shaping those contexts'. Like Livingstone (2009), Selwyn (2011a, p. 6) also stresses the importance of considering context and how learning is also intertwined with other factors like family SES, gender, race and class, and as such 'the study of education and technology would therefore, be seen in "social scientific" terms – moving beyond making sense of the "technical" aspects of learning and also paying close attention to the social world of education'.

There is a considerable body of research that documents social, economic and demographic differences with respect to mobile internet technologies, which also includes educational attainment, gender, ethnicity and age (Meneses and Mominó, 2010, p. 197). With increasing digitisation, the democratisation of mobile mediation technologies has been associated with recent transformations in the social and cultural constructions of childhood(s), but childhood should not be understood as a homogenous category. Across Europe, there are differences in access to digital and information technologies (Primorac and Jurlin, 2008), and as individuals, children vary in age, gender, SES and according to their psychological strengths, resilience and vulnerabilities (Livingstone et al., 2011b). As such, the diversity of childhood(s) and the reality of children's lived experiences must be both acknowledged and interrogated in order to avoid the oversimplification of the key issues pertinent to current debates.

Inequality

As technological availability improves, it is important to consider digital equity (Judge et al., 2004). Fenwick (2010) proposes that the concept of *assemblage* is helpful in wider policy analysis, especially if we consider how often-conflicting values like economics, issues of equality and social justice are all continually assembling and disassembling as a constantly changing entity. In Europe, for example, children of higher SES tend to have more private access to the internet and SES differences in going online via a handheld device are more marked in the UK than across Europe (Livingstone et al., 2010). In households where income is less than £200 per week, 6 per cent of adults have never used the internet, but it has reached full coverage for those households where income is in excess of £500 a week – with more than 98 per cent of adults online (ONS, 2013). However, it is important not to consider the role of socio-economic factors from a simplistic perspective (Meneses and Mominó, 2010). The children in my research were highly knowledgeable about the cost of mobile internet technologies and reflexive in their consumption practices, comparing and discussing tariffs and prices for digital content. They were largely critical of what they saw as excessive mobile technology consumption practices and also questioned ownership of expensive technologies. However, they weighed up the cost with the need to be constantly in touch and connected to their friends, family and social networks, but also saw the convergence of mobile internet technologies as giving them value for money.

> *Debbie [aged 15]*: Yeah 'cos I think that most teenagers spend a lot of money on their phone.

Sarah [aged 14]: Yeah too much.

Sally [aged 15]: Yeah but I think that the prices of phones are ridiculous and you can spend your money on so much more – like 250 quid?

Debbie [aged 15]: Yeah but like there's a lot of things on mine that I got with it like the video, camera, internet – that's a lot of technology.

They were also well aware that other children could not afford mobile internet technologies and that often they also lacked internet access at home. According to Ofcom (2012c) in 2011, households spent an average of £65.04 a month on telecoms services, but the recent data from the Department for Work and Pensions (Alzubaidi et al., 2013) shows that in 2011/2012, 17 per cent of children in the UK were living in a household with relatively low income (27 per cent if measured after housing costs are paid) and children in single-parent families or where one member of the family is disabled are far more like to live in poverty. A minimum standard of living in Britain today includes more than just food, clothes and shelter. Hirsch (2013) found that for families with children who are in receipt of out-of-work benefits, they provide only slightly more than half of the minimum income needed for what the public thinks is an adequate standard of living, and for families who are working the increasing costs of childcare, rent, transport, food and energy means that their disposable incomes are falling far short of the family's actual needs. Dorling (2013) considers inequalities in the UK as critical outcomes between different groups defined geographically. He suggests that as inequalities continue to rise an increasing number of people in Britain are going hungry again and how 'rising economic inequality has negative effects, and these effects are negative for everyone in our society, even those who are becoming richer' (Dorling, 2013, p. 102).

'It is about having what you need in order to have the opportunities and choices necessary to participate in society' (Hirsch, 2013, p. 9). Opportunities and choices to participate in society for children and young people are unequal and limited for those children living in low-income households. It is not only the lack of access to the information society and developing digital literacy skills, but also opportunities to socialise and access community support networks are compromised. 'Social capital comprises two aspects, the first being social networks and connection and the second being how these networks are sustained' (Montgomery, 2009, p. 170), and access to social networks sites and being part of virtual communities enhances bridging social capital (Steinfield et al., 2008). 'Educational technology tends to be viewed as a somewhat lesser endeavour – a peripheral distraction from the more pressing "real" issues of education and society' (Selwyn, 2011a, p. 174) and it is questionable just how meaningful the debates on digitalised learning and the mobilised, networked society are to those children who do not have enough food to eat, let alone engage in social networks or access information. 'For socially marginalised children and young people, poverty is not simply that they lack education, go to poorer schools or do not have the books at home to help them, it is also the internal construction of self that makes certain choices unthinkable' (Montgomery, 2009, p. 169).

Dorling (2012, p. 2), writing on inequality, comments on the relative poverty of many young people in the UK, proposing that they are 'excluded from the game of consumerism'. Selwyn (2011b, p. 717) suggests that 'an acceptance that there is no technical formula for overcoming the entrenched social, political, economic and cultural issues that underpin educational "problems"'. According to France (2007), educational policy disadvantages children from poorer backgrounds and fails to ameliorate the clear difference in attainment between class, gender and ethnicity. When exploring the multiple enactments that comprise any one object such as a policy, it is important to provoke questions about the politics that constrain, obscure or enable certain enactments to be most easily performed and recognised (Fenwick, 2010, p. 119). Buckingham (2000, p. 45) argues that both current discourse and academic debate on children and technology are dominated by technological determinism:

> From this perspective, technology is seen to emerge from a neutral process of scientific research and development, rather than from the interplay of complex social, economic and political forces – forces which play a crucial role in determining which technologies are developed and marketed in the first place. Technology is then seen to have effects to bring about social and psychological changes, irrespective of the ways in which it is used and of the social contexts and processes in which it enters.

Thus the debates on mobile internet technologies in relation to children's educational experiences and learning become diluted in the stark realities of child poverty and social inequality, and access to educational opportunities generally. Drawing on Bourdieu and Passeron's (1990) concept of cultural capital, children growing up without access to learning opportunities mediated through mobile internet technologies (*objectified cultural capital*) will not have the same opportunities to interact online and, therefore, for developing *embodied cultural capital*, which, in turn, comprise their *habitus* in everyday life. Medak (2008, p. 61) discusses the 'deeper transformation that culture and media as forms of communication are undergoing: from consumptive to productive, from mono-directional to multi-directional' but it does not necessarily extend equality to all childhoods and not to all children's everyday experiences. Thus, the dominant discourses on mobile internet technologies as being democratising, offering children and young people equity of access to information and social belonging as equal citizens, is a falsehood.

Disability

In addressing what Buckingham (2007) and James et al. (2010) claim is a need in social science to understand the diversity of children's lived experiences, this section considers disabled childhood and mobile internet technologies. Vicente and López's (2010) analysis of the disability digital divide found that people with a disability are less likely to use the internet as a result of accessibility and affordability issues, bearing in mind that assistive technologies are expensive and children with disabilities may lack digital skills. Goggin (2006, p. 102) observes that 'there is still little discussion of disability to be found in telecommunications, new media, or Internet studies literature, and there are even fewer scholarly discussions of social and cultural aspects of mobile communications technologies'. Disability, however, has, according to Galis (2011), recently become the subject of increasing attention amongst science and technology studies. 'The effects of the interaction between disability and experiences in the social world are extremely entangled' (Briggs, 2008, p. 130). There are marked digital divides in relation to disability and internet technologies. Individuals with a disability are just over three times more likely never to have used the internet than individuals with no disability (ONS, 2013). Yet, there is very little research on how people with a disability are using virtual worlds (Stendal et al., 2011) and 'people with disabilities are mostly overlooked as users, consumers, and audiences, when they could be profitably credited as everyday, do-it-yourself consumer producers of cell phones and media' (Goggin, 2006, p. 102). In the history of mobile phone culture, for example, disability has played a significant yet overlooked role, with disability and technology being generally under-theorised (Goggin, 2006). 'Disability does not reside solely in the body or in society. Disability is an effect that emerges when impaired bodies interact with disabling infrastructures/culture' (Galis, 2011, p. 385). The majority of the research that has been undertaken in this area is in relation to enabling rather than disabling technologies, known as assistive technologies (ATs), which Lindstand and Brodin (2004, p. 179) propose is 'a common metaphor [that] refers to ICT as a normalising tool and a tool for possibilities' and ICTs are often viewed as a 'communication bridge' for disabled children and their families and friends. The role of assistive and restorative technologies in disabled children's everyday lives is often seen as a way to improve their interaction with their environment (Weightman et al., 2010), as in the separation often characteristic of disabled childhoods there can be communication difficulties in everyday interaction with family, siblings, peers and the wider community. Lindstand and Brodin (2004) draw on Vygotsky's notion of scaffolding as helpful in understanding the relationship between disabled childhoods, mobile technologies and children's everyday lives. Mavrou (2011, p. 42) highlights the role that AT can play in inclusion and improving the quality of life for children with a disability and suggests that 'providing ICT to children with disabilities is a way of using the power of technology to remove barriers for accessing learning and increasing achievement'. However, Goggin and Newell (2007) point out that mobile internet technologies are rarely designed with accessibility or inclusivity in mind. Gillette and DePompei (2004, p. 233) suggest that mobile technologies can and do support 'inclusion and independence that are long sought-after goals of families and advocates for people with disabilities', but that AT programmes for disabled young people are not yet meeting their needs for memory and organisation systems to facilitate independence.

The concept of agency in childhood is often viewed dichotomously with structure but they should not be viewed in binary opposition to each other (Prout, 2005). Lee and Brown (1994) highlight the importance of considering both the theoretical limitations and political implications, claiming that, like Heidegger, humanistic determinations of agency should not be assumed. The more agency and independence a person appears to have, the more dependent they are on a network for their power and identity (Lee, 1998), and similar to Law's (1994, p. 384) view on agency, he argues that it is not something that people possess but an effect generated by a 'network of heterogeneous, interacting materials'. One example of facilitating independence is mobile geo-enabled technologies and services. According to Kamel Boulos et al. (2011), they can significantly contribute to converting complex urban areas that are problematic for persons with disabilities into more accessible and user-friendly environments for those with special needs and, if well designed, these technologies and services can have many positive benefits for people with a disability, helping them to live more independently and even saving their lives in an emergency. Mobile technologies can improve opportunities for people to have a greater degree of independence and they can contribute to social inclusion (Mavrou, 2011). But as Lindstand and Brodin (2004) point out, children with severe disabilities are rarely given the time that they need to participate in interaction. Boggis (2011) explores disabled children's views and experiences of using *high-tech augmentative and alternative communication systems* (AACS) in their everyday lives and suggests that, although young people are 'lent' voices by their AACS which do enable them to communicate certain words and phrases, it is adults who actually programme the aids often with vocabulary deemed appropriate for general use or curriculum purpose and, as such, she questions the authenticity of disabled children having a voice.

'One subgroup of vulnerable and marginalised young people is disabled youth' Söderström (2009, p. 710). Priestley (2003, p. 3) draws on the social studies of childhood (as set out in Chapter 2, this book) to examine the cultural constructions of disabled childhoods and to argue that both children and disabled people have historically been 'denied attributions of agency, competence and civil rights'. 'Disabled childhoods are not simply biologically determined, but also culturally constructed and socially produced' (Priestley, 2003, p. 68). I use the terms 'disabled children' and 'children with disabilities' interchangeably and intentionally, as Boggis (2011) suggests that such intentional use of the word 'disability' placed either before or after 'children' emphasises both the social barriers and individual impairment. Galis (2011, p. 831) notes:

> Thus, the attribution of agency cannot be detached from the surrounding material semiotic entities; disability cannot be detached from the existence or not of accessibility provisions. To be disabled is not only determined by the physical impairments of an individual's body but also by the interaction of the body with material and semiotic entities.

Plummer (2001, p. 255), in *An Invitation to Critical Humanism*, writes:

> a view which takes the human as being embodied, emotional, interactive self, striving for meaning in wider historically specific social

worlds and an even wider universe, is not a bad, even humbling, starting place for the 'human sciences'.

The embodied, interactive self that Plummer refers to above is important to the debates set out in this section on disabled children's everyday experiences of mobile technologies. 'Bodies are sites in themselves but are also locations where social identities are marked out and practiced, and so bodies are key locations in understanding the complexities of young people, place and identity' (Hopkins, 2010, p. 73). However, Priestley (2003, p. 67) argues that 'the experiences of disabled children themselves may easily be overshadowed by the needs of adults' and, as considered in Chapter 5, children have until relatively recently been ignored in social science research and disabled children are, as Boggis (2011) suggests above, doubly marginalised.

> The ways in which bodies are read, interpreted and responded to are therefore related to the ways in which different bodies are associated with power, authority and control or with weakness, marginality and submission; there are emotional geographies.
>
> (Hopkins, 2010, p. 76)

As embodied social beings, disabled children are located and situated in environments of artefacts and objects, of text and of meaning, and their bodies are sites of action and interaction. Artefacts and objects are significant in cultural meaning and identity, and this section considers the disabled body and how children with a disability experience mobile technologies and manage a disabled identity. Bloomfield et al. (2010, p. 420) suggest that we need to carefully consider the concept of affordance in relation to how 'dis-abled bodies engage with, and are engaged by, technological artefacts' and that 'affordances' rather than fixed properties are about the ongoing exchanges of characteristics between human bodies and objects.

However, it should also be noted that, as Priestley (2003, p. 64) suggests, 'the construction of disabled children as a homogenous group within institutions often overlooks the diversity and richness of their everyday lives' and people with different abilities will face different challenges in using mobile technologies – not as a homogenous group. 'People with different types of disabilities face different types of barriers when trying to use ICT' (Vicente and López, 2010, p. 62) and this is especially pertinent in consideration of young people with a disability, as they can find peer relationships difficult as well. 'Such challenges are barriers connected to physical accessibility, individual attitudes or social interactions toward people with disabilities. Often, people with disabilities are perceived as different and, therefore, at risk of being stigmatised' (Söderström, 2009, p. 711). Thus, ICT developments influence changes in life patterns and our opportunities in many situations (Lindstand and Brodin, 2004), yet there is very little research on how young people with a disability experience and use mobile technologies in their everyday lives. For people with disabilities, the research available suggests that online experiences have both positive and negative consequences that are often not taken into consideration (Cole et al., 2011, p. 1162). In his analysis of the relationship between disability and childhood, Priestley (2003) highlights the concept of *vulnerability*. Livingstone et al. (2011b) found that the incidence of online risk is raised by 15 per cent amongst children with a disability. Additionally, data from the Suffolk Cybersurvey suggested that children with a disability were twice as likely to by cyberbullied than children without a disability (Bond and Carter, 2013) and, similarly, Diddon et al.'s (2009) research on young people with intellectual disabilities in the Netherlands found that cyberbullying was prevalent. Their study 'found significant associations between cyberbullying and IQ, type of disorder (AHD, ASD), self-esteem and depressive feelings and frequency of computer use' (Diddon et al., 2009, p. 150).

Touch-screen technology, for example, has transformed online accessibility for young people with low levels of literacy, but Wong and Tan (2012) note that touch-screen technology can be problematic for blind people as there is no tactile feedback and thus can present significant accessibility barriers. There is an increasing number of apps designed for people with visual impairments, and Goggin (2006, p. 96) observes that 'as a new textual media, the cell phone and associated technologies, are deeply involved in significant and hotly debated transformations in Deaf identity and community'. Since mobile communication has rapidly become one of the main channels of communication in the world, texting is now a standard feature of the adolescent social sphere. The use of texting is a popular method of peer-to-peer communication amongst deaf high-school students (Okuyama, 2013), yet mobile technologies are not just used for text in communication practices as new apps to facilitate and support interaction are also becoming more common for young deaf people. The free Bio-Aid app, for example, which works as a hearing aid on mobile platforms, was developed by a team of researchers at the University of Essex (Clark et al., 2012 online) and works simply with normal headphones:

> While doing this we were stimulated to generate ideas of what would be required in a hearing aid to compensate for the different patterns of impairment that we had modelled. Our thinking led us to some design principles that were different in important respects from hearing aids that are currently available.

For young people with a hearing disability, the BioAid app offers a free alternative to the traditional and often thought of as 'ugly' hearing aid, which makes their deafness a visible disability. Thus, in the *assemblage*, an iPhone, a free app and 'cool' headphones contribute to a young person having a 'normalised' identity in public rather than a 'deaf' one. Kline and Pinch (1999) highlight the importance of the social construction of technology and argue that it is important to consider not only how social groups shape technology, but also how the identities of social groups are constituted in the process. Stendal et al. (2011, p. 81) point out that 'individuals with a lifelong disability may experience physical, financial, and transport difficulties with community access in real life; a virtual environment promises the possibility to establish and experience social interaction from the safe environment of a person's own home'. Also of note are the findings from Bowker and Tuffin's (2003) study with disabled adults, which suggested that visual anonymity afforded by online interaction allows participation in social interactions free from the stigma of a disabled identity. 'Both friendship and social acceptance are relationships where children with disabilities sometimes are at risk of being avoided or socially excluded' (Asbjørnslett et al., 2012, p. 481). From their research with 15 children in Norway with a physical disability, mobile technologies and the internet enabled young people to keep in touch with other children both with and without disabilities and to partake in shared interest groups online as well as Facebook to maintain their friendships (Asbjørnslett et al., 2012). 'The intimate link between technology and disability is found in a wide range of technologies adopted, consumed, and used by people with disabilities, who do so in unexpected and innovative ways, often unforeseen by the designers and promoters of such technologies' (Goggin and Newell, 2007, p. 159). People with disabilities often experience challenges with inclusion in their community (Stendal et al., 2011) but mobile internet technologies can provide young people with opportunities to socialise and interact with peers.

The majority of the current disabled youth use ICT to nourish online relationships to long-distance disabled friends. These online relationships provide the disabled youths with experiences of recognition, fellowship and understanding; even though disability is not a topic, the youths share an implicit understanding of one another's social experiences and context. Thus, these solid online relationships hold the same qualities as strong social ties and the youths experience them as supportive and important social ties. Their long-distance friendships promote online mediated networks which strengthen their identity projects.

(Söderström, 2009, p. 721)

Söderström's findings above are of real importance, especially in light of Vitak and Ellsion's (2012) work on how the use of social network sites is linked to social capital. Goggin (2006) draws on Latour's configuration of agency as not just being exercised by human actors, but also including non-human (technological) actors. As 'technology exists in networks of things, actors, actants, institutions, investments and, relationships' (Goggin, 2006, p. 11) we should be mindful of the multifarious associations that combine in assemblages of mobile internet technology use. In supporting families with a disabled child, Lindstand and Brodin (2004, p. 182) suggest that 'if we consider these standpoints ICT could be considered a mediating artefact that creates possibilities for interaction but families with children with severe disabilities must be allowed to express their needs, thoughts, and interests and make take part in ICT planning'. According to Moser (2000), the interconnected networks through which both human and non-human entitles evolve, interact and produce affects such a disability, and Galis (2011, p. 830) suggests that 'in an ANT framework, the study of disability involves identifying and addressing interactions between human bodies (including the disability experience) and non-humans, no ton top of impairment but an intermixing phenomenon'. A clear example of these complex network relationships is offered by Moser and Law (1999) in their case study considering the continuities and discontinuities of subjectivity. They discuss both technology and dis/ability in terms of a set of specificities, which are specific because they come in the form of networks of heterogeneous material, and they claim that if the networks are in place ability is achieved, but if the networks are not in place then disability arises. It is the character of the materials that Moser and Law (1999) argue enable passages and ways which secure or do not secure them. Technology use becomes an embodied skill and 'the competent subject is indeed one that can count, can calculate, can plan, can exercise discretion and so take responsibility for the decisions it has taken' within a paradigm of subjectivity (Moser and Law, 1999, p. 213).

Goodley (2011) draws on Lash (2001) to argue that technological forms of life and the speed at which information can be passed on and shared allows us to think not only about the past, but also the present and the future. Thus, 'technology can be regarded as an extension of our bodies and our senses. When it comes to children with disabilities this is of importance' (Lindstand and Brodin, 2004, p. 18), and Goodley (2011, p. 172) argues that 'for disabled people, this is crucial, in terms of configuring a place in the new technological age'. However, 'although the emergence of disability activism and disability studies has challenged such perceptions in the relation to disabled adults, there has been surprisingly little critical attention to disability issues in childhood' (Priestley, 2003, p. 85). This is, however, 'an important research agenda, not only as a matter of human rights and justice but also because these narratives unsettle our taken-for-granted – theories of technology' (Goggin, 2006, p. 102). As Oliver (2009, p. 117) also argues:

> Indeed, one could go further and suggest that the production of all knowledge needs itself to become increasingly a socially distributed process by taking much more seriously the experiential knowledge that oppressed groups produce about themselves and research based upon the discourse of production will have an increasingly important role to play in this. And, who knows, this may eventually lead to the fusion of knowledge and research production into a single coherent activity in which we produce ourselves and our worlds in ways that will make us all truly human.

Conclusion

It is apparent that there is considerable academic and political interest in mobile internet technologies and children's learning experiences, and whilst there is significant financial investment in mobile devices and educational software, it is unequally distributed across the educational landscape. However, as Mascheroni and Ólafsson (2013, p. 13) found:

> The use of a device and ownership do not necessarily coincide, with children having access to a wider range of devices than those they actually possess or have for private use. However, ownership and

private use shape the quality of online experience, with children possessing a certain device being more likely to use it intensively throughout the day.

However, many of the discourses and, indeed, current debates remain heavily influenced by a technologically deterministic approach that technology will magically transform children's learning. Whilst there is a considerable body of evidence to support the use of mobile technologies, it should be remembered that other elements are also essential for children's learning, which include teachers, other material artefacts like pens and paper, digital content and wider social and economic factors. However, is does appear that, overall, post-PC tablets are being used to facilitate and potentially enhance children's learning experiences and engage children with their education in the twenty-first century:

> For learners iPads are easy to use and attractive. The research on iPad use and adoptions overwhelmingly reports that tablet devices have a positive impact on student engagement with learning. Findings report increased motivation, enthusiasm, interest, engagement, interdependence and self-regulation, creativity and improved productivity.
>
> (Clark and Luckin, 2013, p. 4)

Childhood is still conceptualised as a site of investment, which remains the focus for current concerns centred on children developing sufficient literacy skills, which now include both digital and media literacies, promoting participation in the knowledge economy and the information society. More and more students will be using personal digital devices in the classroom and the increased use of digital technologies in the classroom has, for many children, transformed everyday educational activities (Liang et al., 2005). Unlike traditional approaches to education, contemporary technologies use a combination of visual, textual and aural forms of communication of which children are familiar with having grown up in an increasingly digitised popular culture. Children also develop skills and expertise learnt from informal settings that are different from what has previously been expected in schools. 'Educational technology is an essentially "positive project". Most people working in this area are driven by an underlying belief that digital technologies are – in some way – capable of improving education' (Selwyn, 2011b, p. 713). Whilst some schools have embraced mobile internet technologies as an element to support, develop and challenge children's learning, other schools have been less enthusiastic (often due to cost implications) in investing in individual learning devices and, as such, children's experiences could become more diverse and arguably more unequal. Not only can children access resources that the teacher has provided or signposted, but also children are viewing YouTube videos to understand maths and science problems outside the teacher's influence in the classroom. Educational provision online is changing how children access and engage with information with dedicated sites like BBC Bitesize and social network sites, like Facebook, which are used to discuss homework, discuss solutions to learning tasks and share learning/ educational resources peer-to-peer. Thus, the role of the teacher is being challenged due to the accessibility and availability of knowledge and information, and the medium by which children can both access and share it. Learning is moving towards a shared model of practice and is becoming more interactive, collaborative and globalised, but not all children have equal opportunities to access or engage in the changing educational paradigms of the twenty-first century.

> Because messages are interpreted and 'read' differently, depending on the social context and the individual, personal experience of the 'reader', the media audience could no longer be comprehended in a singular form, but in the plural. In addition, the analysis of particular media practices showed diverse modes of media usage in the context of everyday practice.
>
> Popović and Hromadžić (2008, p. 50)

Thus, it is the diversity of children's lived experiences and their relationship with mobile internet technologies and learning experiences which require further understanding. Often, the *impact* of a technology on learning is measured in the form of educational outcomes and this is normally in the form of assessment and school league tables. Yet, whilst learning experiences may be changing to be more interactive and empowering for increasing numbers of children, how their learning is assessed has not changed and remains very much along traditional methods. Selwyn's (2011a) point about whether we view education as a product or a process is important to the analysis here and if we are considering the child as an investment, a *becoming* or as an active social agent – a *being* child (see James et al., 2010).

Whilst technology is a component of the current changing landscape of education, my argument here is that we need to understand the process of learning with mobile internet technologies and the wider relationships between the elements in the networks that facilitate the learning. Too often, these factors are ignored in the digital generation rhetoric and technologically deterministic discourses on technology-enhanced learning or debates on ICT in the classroom. 'Supportive social networks are of vital importance to young people's wellbeing, just as fragmented networks are particularly unfortunate, especially for marginalised young people' (Söderström, 2009, p. 712). Too many children still live in poverty and cannot take even basic necessities for granted in their everyday lives, and without these supportive wider economic and social networks in place their educational experiences will continue to be compromised. The opportunities offered by mobile internet technologies to engage with knowledge and information and to share and collaborate in learning are only available to some children, and inequalities, differences and divisions remain powerful barriers to learning for many children. It is, therefore, important to understand how both natural and social entities come into being as a result of the complex relations (or networks) that link them together and, in viewing the world through this 'prism of the (heterogeneous) network', as nature and society are 'outcomes rather than causes and these great and powerful categories emerge from a complex set of relations' (Murdoch, 2001, p. 120).

Furthermore, it is argued that 'ANT is interested in the symbolic, material, physical and cultural practices within which disability ensues' (Galis, 2011, p. 835). The dearth of disabled children's voices in research on childhood, mobile technologies and their everyday experiences is deafening. What literature is available considers the assistive role of technologies, but as Boggis (2011) exposed, it is often adult agendas and adult-led interventions that are heard. More research is desperately needed which genuinely seeks to address this silence and meaningfully engage in dialogue with children with a disability to ensure that the rich variety of their experiences, views and perspective are listened to and heard.

I am not claiming that this will be easy to achieve but 'ANTs key contribution is to suggest analytic methods that honour the mess, disorder and ambivalences that order phenomena, including education' (Fenwick and Edwards, 2010, p. 1). It has been suggested by Brown and Czerniewicz (2010, p. 357) that 'the possibility for digital democracy does exist in the form of a mobile society which is not age specific, and which is ubiquitous'; however, if we are going to make progress towards such a digital democracy, issues of inequality and social exclusion need to be addressed. Yet, Meneses and Mominó (2010, p. 199) point out that, to date, 'complex explanations involving specific appropriation of the Internet by children and young people as active agents in their everyday life are still not so common':

> There is a growing body of invaluable evidence that demonstrates how technology can be used effectively to support learning. However, if that evidence is going to be useful in practice it needs to address the contexts within which the technology is used, and it needs to be presented in ways that are accessible to industry, teachers and learners.
>
> (Luckin et al., 2012, p. 83)

Recent developments in childhood and youth studies which conceptualise young people as active constructors of their own lives have started to influence digital-divide research and 'the latest thinking in the field has started to define and understand children and young people as heterogeneous, nonpassive, autonomous, diverse, and versatile agents actively appropriating the Internet in meaningful contexts of their everyday lives' (Meneses and Mominó, 2010, p. 197). To this end, the EU Kids Online network has undoubtedly been the single-most comprehensive research initiative to date and is the most up-to-date and coordinated, multi-method approach to understanding children's experiences online (see Livingstone et al., 2011a). It is the diversity of these experiences which require further research and the development of detailed theoretical understanding. If all children are to have equal opportunities to learn, socialise and explore the information society, more needs to be done to ameliorate inequality, reduce poverty and ensure that all children have access to technology-enhanced learning opportunities effectively supported by up-to-date, knowledgeable, high-quality supportive networks, both human and technological, in the broader and more inclusive political and economic agendas.

8
Some Concluding Thoughts

'McLuhan's insistence on the primacy of the media is suggestive of the importance of the media for social, political, and economic life: so much so that McLuhan held that the media determine the kind of life we lead' (Siapera, 2012, p. 229). Children's everyday lives, their identities, communities and relationships between the self and other are interwoven to some degree with mobile internet technologies. The title of this book reflects the arguments I have attempted to set out in the previous chapters to critically examine the assumptions that recent and rapid technological advances in mobile internet technologies have changed childhood(s).

> Everyday life is the realm of experience. It is where lives are led, where bodies are born and die, where humanity is constructed: identity, community, connectivity, the relationships between self and other. The everyday is common ground. It is where the social emerges, where values are tested, and beliefs fought over. It is where action takes place. It is where the struggles for existence, both material and symbolic, are waged, where certainties are sought and securities protected. The everyday is suffused with memory and hope, both individual and collective. There is difference and there is sameness. Things to be shared and things to be refused. Stories to be told, images to be framed, words to be spoken and heard.
>
> (Silverstone, 2007, p. 108)

Silverstone's observations resonate throughout this book. Buckingham (2000) suggests that the concept of generation is important to understanding the relationship between childhood and technology, and clearly children's experiences of their childhoods are very different to a generation ago, as Carrington and Marsh (2005, p. 284) observe:

> Even though those of us who might wish to dispute the pervasiveness of digital culture would recognise ourselves and our daily lives in these mundane activities. Possibly without wishing it so, digital technologies have become part of the everyday for all of us who live in industrial and post-industrial societies. The naturalization and invisibility of digital culture must be more so for early adolescents and children who do not have a cultural or personal memory of a time preceding digital culture.

These changes though are not limited technological advances or developments – and it is the wider social changes which form the basis of my argument here. According to McLuhan and Fiore (1967, p. 41), 'media, by altering the environment, evoke in us unique ratios of sense perceptions. The extension of any sense alters the way we think and act – the way we perceive the world'. As explored in Chapter 2, childhood, as a social and cultural construction, is constantly constructed and reconstructed as a result of wider changing norms and values in society. Mobile internet technologies have very quickly become taken for granted in everyday life (Ling, 2012); yet, to propose that they have changed modern childhoods without considering the wider social, political and economic changes would be too simplistic. As McLuhan (1964, p. 3) observes:

> Rapidly, we approach the final phase of the extensions of man – the technological simulation of consciousness, when the creative process of knowing will be collectively and corporately extended to the whole of human society, much as we have extended our sense and our nerves by the various media.

As I proposed in Chapter 3, technological determinist approaches need to be avoided, as they are unhelpful in furthering a broader understanding of changing constructions of childhood in late modernity. Underpinning the dynamic and multifarious nature of childhoods in late modernity are children's rights discourses informed by the UNCRC. Although in relation to adulthood, discussions surrounding rights have become common, almost to the extent that rights for adults are seen as 'part of the norm', in relation to promoting and ensuring children's rights challenges certainly remain and 'within sociology, both the study of rights and of childhood are marginal' (Morrow and Pells, 2012, p. 906). My main point throughout this book has been to propose that, if we are to understand the relationship between childhood, mobile internet technologies and children's everyday lives, we need to consider the multiple and complex factors that combine to perform collectively in constructing late-modern childhoods. I have argued throughout for adopting theoretical pluralism whilst constructing a conceptual framework in an attempt to understand the multifarious and complex network of hybridity and the wider social, political and economic environment.

In Chapter 2, the brief journey through the history of childhood reveals how children's everyday experiences are structured through social expectations and notions of innocence and vulnerability. Children as *becomings* – incomplete persons in need of protecting, but also in need of educating – has been the dominant ideology of childhood in Western society, which still remains today. However, these constructions of childhood have been challenged by the social studies of childhood (James et al., 2010) which views children as active social agents and wider social changes, especially in relation to individualisation, have also impacted on childhood and the importance of the child in late modernity is rising (Beck, 1992; Zelizer, 1985). The increasing prominence of the children's rights agenda in policy developments cannot be ignored as it is also having an impact on how childhood is understood and how children are treated. Risk remains central to the social construction of childhood (Scott et al., 1998) and to children's everyday experiences with mobile internet technologies, as parents, concerned about their children's safety, often view technology, especially mobile phones, as important to children's security and safety in the outside realm. Yet, as so clearly demonstrated by Livingstone et al. (2011a), Ling (2004) and Bond (2010) that, whilst viewed in terms of security and connectivity, mobile internet technologies simultaneously are viewed as risky. Concerns over risk associated with mobile internet technologies are influencing many current debates on both the nature and future of childhood, as children, often seen as passive victims, are able to engage with online spaces and digital content which is deemed inappropriate and sometimes harmful. It is these discussions of the risks that have induced both public debate and policy responses to protecting children online. Article 3 of the UNCRC ensures the child such protection and care as is necessary for his or her well-being. But childhood, once removed from the physical spaces of the adult world to be confined to the seemingly more suitable and sanitised spaces of the school and home, is now no longer experienced within these fixed, traditional boundaries and children are engaging with 'adult' spaces once more but virtually. It is fluidity and the blurring of the boundaries that is fascinating childhood scholars and media and cultural studies currently. Stalder (2006, p. 21) suggests:

> Addressing this blurring of the boundaries, entire new domains of inquiry – the sociology of technology and the social studies of science – have been established. Their aim is to reconceptualise, to use Bruno Latour's terms, the relationship between 'humans' and 'non-humans,' their fusion into 'hybrids,' exploring the 'socio-technical world' created in the process. At stake is nothing less than the definition of a new ontology for the (social) sciences. Bitter battles, the 'science wars,' are being fought over how to think about the relationship between the social, technical and natural. Undoubtedly, this is a problem central to any attempt to come to grips with the particular character of contemporary, technology-intensive societies.

Gane (2004) argues that the social, technological and natural processes that characterise contemporary social life all intersect and hybridise profusely. One of the key characteristics of mobile internet technologies in contemporary society is the rapid diffusion and adoption rates. In looking at the relationship between these social, technical and natural processes, consideration needs to be given to both technological changes and patterns of adoption and use. Livingstone (1999) proposes that it is the social-shaping characteristics and contexts of use that are significant in technological success and adoption into everyday lives rather than the technological functions themselves. This is what I have aimed to do in the analysis presented here, rather than attempt to explore the technological functions of mobile internet technologies in depth. However, some consideration of different technologies is necessary to understand the contemporary context as well as the affordances of various technologies. My examples of the television, telephone and internet as three very different technologies highlight the diversity in patterns of adoption and use, but also the alternative approaches and theoretical perspectives that have been employed in academic approaches to studying them. Mobile internet technologies combine the affordances of all three together with a convergence of other functions and interactions, combining both hardware development (for example the inclusion of camera) with software developments (for example internet connectivity, app design and integration and SNS). The complexity of our perceptions of mobile internet technologies in society is further compounded by the human elements and behaviours in the network of mobile technologies and how they are considered. As discussed in Chapter 3, many previous approaches have conceptualised the user as *audience* and often as *passive* – a recipient of information; a consumer of media. In relation to mobile internet technologies, however, the users are understood to be both consumers and producers of digitised content, as Popović and Hromadžić (2008, p. 50) comment:

> in this mode of understanding of the complex nature of media and communication, the old paradigm – according to which media represent mere channels of dissemination of information and messages of information communication – is replaced by a new paradigm within which media play an important role in the construction of reality; however, with various modes of reception.

Thus, in our research it is more helpful to consider the various and many entities that combine in a network to perform the many interactions between the natural (human), technical and social. Entities are conceptualised by Latour (1993) as hybrids, as quasi-objects and quasi-subjects, and the distinction between human and non-human is constantly changing and being renegotiated. Latour's conceptualisations of the hybrid nature of the relationship between the human and the object resonate with the similar ideas underlying Haraway's (1991, p. 149) cyborg manifesto and viewing, as she terms it, 'the hybrid of machine and organism, a creature of social reality'. It is this hybridity that underlies the ubiquitous connectivity (van Kranenburg, 2008) and embedded nature of mobile internet technologies in children's everyday lives. As Tilly (16), in my study, observed, 'my phone is a part of me' and Debbie (16) stated, in even stronger terms, 'I'd die without it'. Thus, mobile internet technologies have become woven into the fabric of childhood and they are seamlessly entrenched into children's everyday lives. As Livingstone (2009, p. 232) concurs:

> Now that we live in a ubiquitous and complex media and communication environment, it is timely to recognise that this environment contributes significantly to shaping our identities, our culture and learning, our opportunities in relation to others and thus the conditions for participation in society. No one can live outside it, no child wants to.

There is a growing evidence base of research into children's experiences and the internet. In Europe, much of which is a result of the EU Kids Online network and there is additional evidence emerging from the US and Australia. Much of the available research, especially the larger studies, however, does not focus specifically on mobile internet access, and so many of the findings relate to either fixed internet access or do not distinguish between mobile and fixed. Cross-country comparisons using qualitative data also remain difficult (Barbovschi et al., 2013). There are a number of smaller-scale studies which focus on mobile internet technologies in a localised context and they highlight the increasing importance of mobile internet technologies in children's constructions of self-identity; their day-to-day lives within their community; and in connecting them to others, their friends and families. Methodological advances in undertaking research with children are providing new insights into children's everyday lives and children's experiences can, and are, beginning to be taken seriously. Barbovschi et al.'s (2013) report draws on examples of innovative qualitative studies to consider how methodological innovation can retain the robust, responsible and ethical characteristics of high-quality research demanded in social science, but these examples also highlight the difficulties of researching this topic.

> Children's rapid adoption of the internet and other online technologies, together with the constantly changing media landscape (e.g. more apps and tailored sites, more individualised media use, more mobile internet), pose challenges to researchers concerning the difficult task of adopting and renewing their inventory of researchers tools in order to identify the risks and opportunities presented by the internet and new media use.
>
> (Barbovschi et al., 2013, p. 4)

The evidence to date does reflect a high degree of individualisation associated with postmodern conditions and the analysis presented here identifies some key themes in relation to childhood, mobile internet technologies and everyday experiences, which are examined both theoretically and conceptually. Mobile internet technologies and the digitised platforms of spaces of interaction connect individuals in an increasingly individualised society which is altering our interactions with each other, our communication practices generally and our understandings of self-identity in late modernity.

'All sociology is a reconstruction that aspires to confer intelligibility on human existences which, like all human existences, are confused and obscure' (Aron, 1970, p. 207). My account here hopefully offers some insight into children's everyday existences through examining their relationships and the role played by mobile internet technologies in children's constructions of self-identity. Uzelac (2008, p. 11) suggests that 'if we take a closer look at the digital environment we live in today we can see that it is enveloping us all – digital technologies are present in all aspects of our lives. Today we use digital technologies without noticing them'. This point is clearly illustrated in Chapter 5 in the discussion of how children manage and maintain their everyday relationships with their family and their peers through mobile internet technologies. Whilst they may be going unnoticed, as Uzelac (2008) suggests above, mobile internet technologies are increasingly important in children's everyday relationships and simultaneously play both a positive and negative role in that, on the one hand, they offer connectivity and security, but on the other, they can facilitate insecurity and anxiety. In family relationships, mobile internet technologies are central to communication practices and allow, what Ling (2004) refers to as, the micro-coordination of everyday life, which is becoming more and more essential in day-to-day family functioning. The concept of *gifting* (Berking, 1999; Maus, 2002) offers helpful insight into how children use digitised content to maintain and manage their friendships in the sharing of images, videos and text. Using mobile internet technologies to access and interact on SNS is an everyday experience for many children and, thanks to mobile apps, SNS can be accessed from anywhere, allowing children to keep up to date with their friends and wider acquaintances. Users of SNS create online profiles, upload photos tagged with their names, comment on photos of their friends, and find and form friendships as well as using chat and text to communicate with their social network (Varbanova, 2008), thus facilitating social capital (Vitak and Ellsion, 2012). The development of SNS such as Facebook is also significant as 'social network sites reconfigured people's engagement with online communities because they signalled a shift from interest-driven to friendship driven spaces' (Ellsion and boyd, 2013, p. 161). Furthermore, the use of SNS and mobile internet technologies is increasingly important to the construction and reconstruction of self-identity in late modernity. Longhurst (2007) suggests that ideas of performance are significant in a media-drenched society, but that sociology has not paid enough attention to performance practices in relation to the everyday. Chapter 5 analysed Goffman's (1959) ideas of the presentation of self in everyday life to provide an understanding of how mobile internet technologies play a vital role in children's perceptions of the image of self and, as an object, mobile internet technologies are identified with the image of self to both children and others, as they are strongly associated with how children present themselves in public. Whilst 16 per cent of children pretend to be someone different online (Livingstone et al., 2011), for most children online identities are based on their offline identities. Again, drawing on Goffman (1959), I argue that children both construct and perform their self-identity increasingly online. Self-identity as a network of elements – online and offline – of the body, relationships, images and interactions is far from fixed and, as such, is understood as a dynamic and fluid construction and reconstruction of the self. Mobile digitised content is an example of self-presentation, and images and messaging lead to new and novel applications emphasising playful and emotional communication practices (Daliot-Bul, 2007). This highlights the intricate connections between the members of the network and the human and non-human elements, without necessarily assigning any particular priority to those elements, whose identity and importance is constituted by the network itself (Hutchby, 2001a).

An important part of self-identity is a gendered, sexual identity, but children's sexuality remains a relatively contentious topic. Previously hidden from the adult gaze, children's opportunities for sexual explorations with each others' bodies were confined to being in close proximity to each other, but virtual spaces and the affordances of mobile internet technologies allow for exchanges of sexual images, both downloaded and user-generated, to take place easily. The proliferation of these images, which once shared, often end up on unintended sites online and other virtual spaces, have made these practices not only visible but also a topic of concern for adults as well as children themselves. Ethically, however, researching children and sexual activity is problematic, but the study on sexting by Ringrose et al. (2013) and my own study (Bond, 2011) provided a much-needed glimpse into such practices. The importance of considering the concept of consent in these debates cannot be emphasised enough (see Hasinoff, 2012). Endorsing and furthering Barber's (2004) claim that the relationship between sex and technology is fundamental to understanding complex everyday lives, mobile internet technologies are important to children's constructions of self-identity as gendered sexual selves – they provide a space for intimacy (Ito et al., 2005). The empirical evidence to date illustrates Plummer's

(1995, p. 16) advocacy of sexual stories as 'socially produced in social contexts by embodied concrete people experiencing thoughts and feelings of everyday life'. Jackson and Scott (2004) argue that sexuality needs to be investigated like any other aspect of social life and further research in this area would bring more to the contemporary debate on sexuality in childhood, contributing to the consideration of the social and cultural constructions of childhood.

Mobile internet technologies are becoming imperative in the formation, maintenance and manipulation of children's close, intimate relationships, but it is the sharing of sexual material both downloaded from the internet and user-generated that illustrates how they offer an alternative space in human sensory experience. As Baudrillard so eloquently observes:

> With the mobile phone, word no longer passes from mouth to mouth, but from ear to ear. And the ear is no longer the ear of hearing and the voice, but a sensory terminal. A further phase of the electronic colonization of the senses: tactility and the digitality (of screens) substituting for touch; film substituting for the skin; the visual substituting for looking; voice command substituting for the voice, and all the virtual sensors (including the erotic ones) substituting for the body and sensuality. Only smell and taste, it seems, have not yet undergone this computer-based metastasis.
>
> (Baudrillard, 2003, p. 103)

Sexual content appears as an important theme in the construction of self-identity but it is also viewed and considered in terms of risk. Chapter 6 critically examined the risk discourses in relation to childhood, mobile internet technologies and children's everyday experiences. Scott et al. (1998, p. 690) have argued that more needs to be known about how risk anxiety, a 'constant and pervasive feature of everyday consciousness, managed through everyday practices', is woven into our quotidian social reality.

> Therefore, it is of vital importance that industries, governments, policy makers, NGOs, researchers and other stakeholders cooperate to build a better internet for children, and reach priority goals such as content classification, age-appropriate services and privacy settings, and easy and robust reporting mechanisms on mobile devices and services.
>
> (Mascheroni and Ólafsson, 2013, p. 25)

Considerable research attention has been focused on risk and the internet, and the work of Sonia Livingstone and others in the EU Kids Online network continues to inform not only our knowledge of risk online, but also our responses and policy initiatives to prevent harm. Giddens (1991) argues that the reflexive adoption and lifestyle changes by lay people of risk parameters depend on the individual's interpretation of risk based on their own subjective experiences. The extensive work by the EU Kids Online network has provided a detailed and up-to-date analysis of the risks children face online, and the research helpfully distinguishes between risk and harm.

Recently, there has been considerable media interest in the risks associated with children's experiences online, exemplified by the tragic death in 2013 of Hannah Smith (aged 14) after she was anonymously bullied on Ask.FM, which prompted calls for greater safeguarding measures for children. Sadly, Hannah Smith's experience of being cyberbullied is not uncommon and, as Cross et al.'s (2012, pp. 4–5) study found, cyberbullying is also a significant problem in primary-school-aged children:

> The emotional consequences of cyberbullying for primary school-aged pupils are significant. Overall, half (50%) said the cyberbullying made them feel 'upset', 46% said it made them feel 'angry', and over a quarter (28%) said it made them feel 'scared'. Furthermore, nearly a quarter (23%) said it made them feel embarrassed, and two-in-five (20%) reported feeling 'lonely' or isolated, highlighting the significant emotional impact on victims of this form of aggression. As expected, these feelings were amplified significantly among children who experienced persistent and intentional cyberbullying.

Article 3 of the UNCRC maintains that:

> States Parties undertake to ensure the child such protection and care as is necessary for his or her well-being, taking into account the rights and duties of his or her parents, legal guardians, or other individuals legally responsible for him or her, and, to this end, shall take all appropriate legislative and administrative measures.

Concerns over cyberbullying, inappropriate and harmful content, and online grooming have resulted in calls for the industry and government to take greater control and more actively place restrictions on children's access to/use of internet content. The essential role of the industry is consistently emphasised in the European Internet Safety Policy and expressed through self-regulatory codes developed to promote good practice in safer internet use (Livingstone et al., 2011a). Warnings on websites are an example of good practice and can be an effective strategy to some extent in protecting children from inappropriate content. In protecting children online, McGuire (2012, p. 219) distinguishes between technological regulation and regulation by technology, arguing:

> as the previous reflections have repeatedly suggested, it is not so much technology itself that has caused the problem, but our readiness to defer to the codes and regulatory practices around technology – its technomia. At present this is too fragmented and too uneven for it to offer the kinds of protections that we have come to expect from traditional law.

Whilst this book does not have the space for an extended discussion on internet regulation, some consideration is important here in understanding the legal complexities of children's use of mobile internet technologies in relation to child protection. Savirimuthu (2011, p. 547) proposes that 'child safety issues are now being transformed into legal and social obligations', yet the legal basis for children's use of mobile internet is often confusing and there is considerable uncertainty over how the law can be applied and enforced. Cyber industries do recognise the need to work cooperatively with law enforcement agencies (Joseph, 2003), but whilst there has been dramatic developments in mobile technical convergence over the past few years, there has yet to be such progress in relation to legal convergence. The introduction of the UNCRC presents an international benchmark for valuing children, setting out the needs and obligations on nation states regarding respecting children and their childhoods.

Savirimuthu (2011, pp. 564–65) observes:

> Online child safety policies and measures cohere with the *EU Agenda for the Rights of the Child* requirement that regulations which have an impact on children 'should be designed, implemented, and monitored taking into account the principle of the best interests of the child enshrined in the EU the Charter and in the UNCRC' (European Commission, 2011). This Communication reflects current EU jurisprudence which not only views children as independent

and autonomous individuals who have a legitimate entitlement to human rights but recognises that the State and its institutions have an obligation to promote the rights of children (Article 2(3) of the Treaty on European Union). Public authorities and private institutions are however under an obligation to make the child's best interests a primary consideration when implementing child safety policies.

Maurás (2011, p. 52) argues that, as a result of the UNCRC, 'the concept of children took a radical turn: girls and boys ceased to be regarded as objects of protection and became recognised a subjects of rights'. Article 3 also acknowledges that the best interest of the child must be seen as a primary consideration in all actions concerning children, demonstrating that even a rights-based approach recognises that the outcome of welfarism, and that the best interest of the child, are of fundamental importance. However, such welfarism suggests that children are vulnerable, disempowered and need protection, whereas a rights-based approach provides the protection through recognising children as sentient human beings that are able and entitled to actively participate in their own lives. Article 12 sets out that 'States Parties shall assure to the child who is capable of forming his or her own views the right to express those views freely in all matters affecting the child, the views of the child being given due weight in accordance with the age and maturity of the child'. In addition, Article 13 proposes that:

the child shall have the right to freedom of expression; this right shall include freedom to seek, receive and impart information and ideas of all kinds, regardless of frontiers, either orally, in writing or in print, in the form of art, or through any other media of the child's choice.

The relationship between rights to protection and rights to participation is, therefore, problematic.

Livingstone et al. (2011a, p. 31) discuss this relationship in responding to risk online and suggest:

Since risk increases as use increases, it might seem simple to call for restrictions on children's use of the internet. But online opportunities and digital literacy also increase with use, so there is no simple solution. Rather, ways must be found to manage risk without unduly restricting opportunities.

Furthermore, mediating children's use of the internet is even more difficult as mobile internet access proliferates providing more private, personal and individualised access. O'Neill and McLaughlin (2010) suggest that media literacy is emerging as an invaluable policy response for safeguarding children and young people in online environments. Hasinoff (2012, p. 6) highlights the 'the importance of privacy and consent for all authors of ephemeral social media content'. There is currently an expansive network of educational resources, awareness campaigns and e-safety initiatives (see Childnet International, the Safer Internet Centre, CEOP's ThinkUKnow programmes and Get Safe Online). E-safety programmes need to be developmentally appropriate, involving both media literacy and critical thinking, and they require participation between educators, parents and children if they are to be effective (Grey, 2011).

The adoption of the UNCRC may be viewed as an acceptance of children as human beings who should have rights and entitlements afforded to them not just because of their status as human beings, but also because of their position within society. However, many of the controls that are placed upon children in late modernity call into question the realistic opportunities that all children have in being able to fully participate within society and also to have their voice heard (Burr and Montgomery, 2003). This is further complicated when considering the diverse lived realities facing children and young people, in terms of socio-economic position in society, discrimination and geo-political instability. As such, many children experience considerable marginalisation, which highlights the inadequacies of many governments regarding the introduction of policies and practices that will enable children to be recognised as active social agents, who are able to provide an insight into their own self-determination and, whilst it is the protectionist discourses that inform the debates on risk online, it is children's rights to participation that warrant attention and consideration here.

Jensen, (2006) observes how recent technologies are allowing the younger generation an unprecedented access to the internet via a mobile device, which they take for granted, and consider as a right. However, as discussed in Chapter 7, this right does not extent equally to all children.

A focus on belonging allows us to examine who is allowed to take part in the reflexive arguments that contribute to changes in society, who is excluded from these and on which grounds, and the effects that such inclusion and exclusion have on people's sense of self.

(May, V., 2011, p. 374)

May's point above is key to understanding my argument in Chapter 7 that the notion of 'the digital generation' conceptualises children as a homogenous group which hides the very marked inequalities to mobile internet technologies and education opportunities to meaningfully participate in the information society, and for socialising and developing a sense of belonging online. Similarly, the concept of the 'digital divide' has been criticised for being too simplistic (Siapera, 2012), but it is clear that many inequalities remain.

> Globally, developing countries are modernising rapidly and unevenly, and a sociological analysis becomes more pertinent. Yet despite some progress, thinking about children, childhood and children's rights remains marginal in the face of the relentless emphasis on what are ultimately human capital approaches based on 'outcomes' and realising children's potential as productive adults in an imagined perfect labour market.
>
> (Morrow and Pells, 2012, p. 917)

ICTs and, more recently, mobile internet technologies such as iPads and post-PC tablets have been heralded in 'techno-romantic' approaches to be transforming children's educational experiences and changing learning practices in the twenty-first century (Selwyn, 2011a). Both Buckingham (2007) and Selwyn (2011a) are cautious to avoid essentialist understandings of the role of technologies in children's learning; the research to date suggests that mobile internet technologies are viewed as positive (Clark and Luckin, 2013).

> However, despite the importance of technologies, both psychologised framing of learning as largely individual and cognitive and the sociologised framing of education as an engine for social mobility and reproduction have seemingly passed over the 'hard stuff' of the material in their rush to explain.
>
> (Fenwick and Edwards, 2010, p. 71)

It is important, therefore, to recognise all the different elements in the network of learning to include both old and new technologies, teachers, learners, the curriculum priorities as well as wider political and economic agendas. Selwyn (2011a, p. 12) suggests that overall:

> Digital technologies are seen to allow process and activities to take place on a greater scale than before, in far quicker and more powerful

ways. Crucially, digital technologies and digital practices are seen to give more control and flexibility to the individuals that use them. Digital technologies are therefore associated with dramatically enhanced and improved ways of doing things. For many people, digital technologies are seen to have underpinned a new and improved era of living – the so called digital age.

However, these improved opportunities that Selwyn proposes are not available to all children equally and many children remain marginalised in both their access and opportunities to engage with mobile internet technologies. I argue in Chapter 7 for the importance of considering digital equity (Judge et al., 2004) and for not assuming that all children have the same experiences or opportunities to engage with and interact through mobile internet technologies. Hamilton (2012, p. 74) suggests that families on low incomes sometimes engage in conspicuous consumption to try to give their children access to the 'right' goods and brands in order to 'avoid the social effects of stigmatization and alleviate threats to social identity'. But mobile internet technologies remain expensive to both buy and consume on a day-to-day basis and rely on other technologies of consumption – for example, the networked spaces of broadband, Wi-Fi or 3G access, which have additional ongoing costs. For families struggling to feed, clothe and provide a warm environment for their children, the cost of mobile internet technology remains prohibitive. Livingstone et al. (2010) found that children of higher SES tend to have more private access to online environments and that there are SES differences in going online via a handheld device, which interestingly is more marked in the UK than across Europe. Morrow and Pells (2012) argue that a sociological approach can bridge both rights and child-poverty discourses. In consideration of inequality, poverty and children's everyday lives, it is clear that many children are excluded from the opportunities offered by interacting with mobile internet technologies and, therefore, have fewer opportunities to learn, socialise and develop key media and digital literacy skills. 'Perhaps the most important theme of all that comes out of recent child poverty studies is the importance of listening to children themselves and the need to make policies based on their own accounts of living in difficult circumstances' (Montgomery, 2009, p. 178), and the discourses on mobile internet technologies as democratising are idealistic, failing to acknowledge difference and disadvantages in children's everyday lives.

It is not only children who live in material disadvantage who have been excluded from analyses of mobile internet technologies and everyday experiences, but also those children with a disability. Bloomfield et al. (2010, p. 420) propose that 'within the fields of sociology and disability studies there is an extensive literature that identifies the ways in which abilities and *dis*abilities emerge and are located within specific sociomaterial arrangements, settings and situations' (see also Law, 1994; Moser and Law, 1999). Many studies take either a positive stance, in relation to disabled children's experiences with technologies situated in the field of investigating ATs in enabling children with a disability to communicate with their families and friends, or a negative one, in cases of cyberbullying or trolling. Unhelpfully, such accounts can polarise the debates and mask children's own viewpoints and experiences.

> The convention on the Rights of the Child establishes children's right to be consulted in making the decisions that affect their lives as well as the right to form their own views and express them during legal proceedings, to connect with each other, and to be active in arts and culture. The goal of participation rights as a whole is for children to become full citizens in their communities, countries, and globally as their abilities evolve.
>
> (Rutgers, 2011, p. 79)

Whilst research in this area is beginning to gain momentum as a body of knowledge, it still has, as yet, to meaningfully interrogate disabled children's experiences with mobile internet technologies, especially from a child-centred perspective, and research which addresses this silence is desperately needed to contribute to a more realistic and meaningful understanding of children's everyday experiences. Qvortrup (2011) has argued for childhood studies to move towards a greater understanding of the multiplicities of childhood – for understanding the heterogeneous nature of embodied, contemporary childhoods through understanding children's lived experiences.

> It is therefore a *process* through which the body comes to grant particular affordances to the (made) world and conversely, the world comes to be 'mirrored' in the effectivities or action capabilities of the body. 'Sociality' and 'materiality' appear irredeemably entangled with one another. Drawing on this we might argue that the relationship between 'sociality' and 'materiality' in technological artefacts is a Derridean (1976) one of mutual (in)determination and supplementarity.
>
> (Bloomfield et al., 2010, p. 429)

The introduction of the UNCRC is an international benchmark for valuing children and sets out the needs and obligation on nation states regarding respecting children and their childhoods (Bond and Agnew, 2013), but the relationship between children's rights to protection (Article 4) and their participation rights (Articles 12 and 13) is problematic. Buckingham (2000, p. 15) asserts that 'the dominant construction of children as pre-social individuals effectively prevents any consideration of them as social beings, or indeed citizens'. Popović and Hromadžić (2008, p. 52) argue that 'these expectations are based on a utopian model of new digital media as a model that allows for direct and participatory democracy'. However, we have a long way to go before the rhetoric surrounding idealised notions of digital citizenship becomes a lived reality for many children. What is important is that future debates surrounding children and mobile internet technologies move beyond the essentialist views of childhood and communications media that have previously dominated much recent discourse. The construction of the child in previous debates that view childhood as a time of innocence that should not be corrupted or exploited by media does not 'match the reality of many children's lives and fails to acknowledge that children are active participants' (Selwyn, 2000, p. 148). It is children's active participation and recent theoretical advances in childhood studies and in the increasing recognition of children's rights that are beginning to effectively challenge unhelpful and unrealistic constructions of childhood, and, therefore, move towards an understanding of the diversity of the social realities that form children's everyday experiences with mobile internet technologies.

> Young people's participation cannot be discussed without considering power relations and the struggle for equal rights. It is important that all young people have the opportunity to learn to participate in programmes which directly affect their lives. This is especially so for disadvantaged children for through participation with others such children learn that to struggle against discrimination and repression, and to fight for their equal rights in solidarity with others is itself a fundamental democratic right.
>
> (Hart, 2011, pp. 83–84)

To this end, Ito et al. (2005) argue for a techno-social framework for examining technologies and society, reflecting Drotner's (2000, p. 161) claim that:

> The combination of the 'seamless' embeddedness of media into everyday culture and the increasingly complex interweaving of

programmes, formats, genres and media types is, indeed, a challenging analytical cocktail.

Prout (2005, p. 11) argues that childhood studies must move away from 'modernist conception, if they are to become closer to the open-ended, interdisciplinary form of enquiry necessary to present-day conditions'. Callon (1999) discusses how different actor networks, which previously have no *a priori* reason to be compatible with others, are able to work together and align in a convergent network. The convergent nature of multifunctional devices is essential to understanding the arguments presented here:

> ...convergent multifunctional devices, which support an ever grow- ing repertoire of communication practices and online activities. These combine options already supported by previous generations of mobile phones (such as telephone calls, text messages, games, radio, music, photos) with activities usually performed on computers, the internet and social media (such as email, instant message services, social network sites, maps, video, television, blogging). They also enable new activities such as those related to location-based services, and those performed through apps (which can shape new online experiences).
>
> (Mascheroni and Ólafsson, 2014, P. 5)

The dynamic, reflexive nature of sociological knowledge and under- standing will thus continue to develop, change and hybridise further in line with the evolving complexity of actor-networks, and more in-depth ongoing research is required into many changing aspects of contempo- rary children's everyday lives. Baudrillard (2003, p. 64) has proposed that 'raising theory to its state of grace, where, without being impos- ture (in its relation to truth), it can pass for a stratagem (in its relation to the world)'. My attempt here has been to adopt a theoretical plu- ralism (as outlined by Matthewman, 2011) of the everyday to examine thematic explanations of childhood, mobile internet technologies and children's everyday experiences without deliberately giving priority to any particular perspectives. The arguments presented here suggest that mobile technologies are, indeed, 'empowering users by giving them the tools to make their lives more pleasurable, to express and distinguish themselves by combining knowledge, information, skill and creativity' (Daliot-Bul, 2007, p. 967), but that childhood is not a homogenous category of analysis.

My analysis of childhood, mobile technologies and everyday experiences hopefully offers some insights into the complexity and dynamic nature of the interrelationships between them, but as Livingstone et al. (2011a) suggest, there is still relatively little known about children's use of mobile internet technologies. The EU Kids Online project investigating the risks associated with mobile internet and smartphones had only published its initial findings at the time of this book going to print (see Mascheroni and Ólafsson, 2013). The debates set out in this book are not intended to be exhaustive or finite – they probably raise more questions and debates than they answer, but such is the nature of this fascinating area of ongoing research. New studies are currently being undertaken and, as their findings are published, so our understanding is being constantly reformed and reformulated as this body of literature expands. I hope that this book in some way contributes as an *actant* to offer a timely contribution to addressing the lack of children's voices in socio-technical research and to highlight the significance of mobile internet technologies in the continual construction and reconstructions of childhood, and in children's everyday lives and their diverse experiences of childhood. I conclude with Sonia Livingstone's (2009, p. 211) Children's Internet Charter – which I suggest is just as equally important to mobile internet technologies:

1) Children should have online contents and services of high quality which are made specifically for them, and which do not exploit them. In addition to entertaining, these should allow children to develop physically, mentally and socially to their fullest potential.

2) Children should hear, see and express themselves, their culture, their languages and their life experiences, through online contents and services which affirm their sense of self, community and place.

3) Children's online contents and services should promote an awareness and appreciation of other cultures in parallel with the child's own cultural background.

4) Children's online contents and services should be wide-ranging in genre and content, but should not include gratuitous scenes of violence and sex.

5) Children's online contents and services should be accessible when and where children are available to engage, and/or distributed via other widely accessible media or technologies.

6) Sufficient funds must be made available to make these online contents and services to the highest possible standards.

7) Governments, production, distribution and funding organisations should recognise both the importance and vulnerability of indigenous online contents and services, and take steps to support and protect it.

References

Adams, J. (1995) *Risk* (London: University College London Press).

Agar, J. (2003) *Constant Touch: A Global History of the Mobile Phone* (Cambridge: Icon Books).

Agger, B. (2004) *The Virtual Self: A Contemporary Sociology* (Oxford: Blackwell).

Aitken, S. C., Lund, R. and Trine Kjørholt, A. (2007) 'Why children? Why now?', *Children's Geographies Vol. 5 (2)*, pp. 3–14.

Alderson, P. (2008) *Young Children's Rights Exploring Beliefs, Principles and Practice*, 2nd edn (London: Jessica Kingsley Publishers).

Allan, A. (2012) 'Doing ethnography and using visual methods' in Bradford, S. and Cullen, F. (eds.) *Research and Research Methods for Youth Practitioners* (London: Routledge).

Allen, K. R. (2005) 'Families facing the challenges of diversity' in McKendry, P. C. and Price, S. J. (eds.) *Families and Change* (London: Sage).

Alzubaidi, H., Carr, J., Councell, R. and Johnson, G. (eds.) (2013) 'Households Below Average Income – An analysis of the income distribution 1994/95 – 2011/12' *Department of Work and Pensions*, available from: http://www.gov.uk/government/uploads/system/uploads/attachment_data/file/206778/full_hbai13.pdf.

Ang, I. (1992) 'Living room wars: New technologies, audience measurement and the tactics of television consumption' in Silverstone, R. and Hirsch, E. (eds.) *Consuming Technologies Media and Information in Domestic Spaces* (London: Routledge).

Appadurai, A. J. (1996) *Modernity at Large: Cultural Dimensions of Globalization* (Minneapolis: University of Minnesota Press).

Archard, D. and Macleod, C. M. (2002) 'Introduction' in Archard, D. and Macleod, C. M. (eds.) *The Moral and Political Status of Children* (Oxford: Oxford University Press).

Ariès, P. (1962a) *Centuries of Childhood* (New York: Vintage Books).

Ariès, P. (1962b) 'The discovery of childhood' in *Centuries of Childhood: A Social History of Family Life* translated by Baldick, R. (New York: Knoft, A. A.). Reproduced in Morrison, H. (ed.) (2012) *The Global History of Childhood Reader* (London: Routledge).

Arneil, B. (2002) 'Becoming versus being: a critical analysis of the child in liberal theory' in Archard, D. and Macleod, C. M. (eds.) *The Moral and Political Status of Children* (Oxford: Oxford University Press).

Aron, R. (1970) *Main Currents in Sociological Thought: Durkheim, Pareto, Weber* (Harmondsworth: Penguin).

Arthur, W. B. (2009) *The Nature of Technology* (London: Penguin).

Artle, R. and Averous, C. (1973) 'The telephone system as a public good: static and dynamic aspects', *The Bell Journal of Economics and Management Science, Vol. 4 (1)*, pp. 89–100.

Asbjørnslett, M., Engelsrud, G. H. and Helseth (2012) 'Friendship in all directions: Norwegian children with physical disabilities experiencing friendship', *Childhood, Vol. 19 (4)*, pp. 481–494.

Association of Chief Police Officers of England, Wales and Northern Ireland (ACPO) Child Protection and Abuse Investigation (CPAI) Group ACPO CPAI Lead's Position on Young People Who Post Self-Taken Indecent Images, available from: http://ceop.police.uk/Documents/ceopdocs/externaldocs/ACPO_Lead_position_on_Self_Taken_Images.pdf.

Atkinson, D. (1993) 'Relating' in Shakespeare, P., Atkinson, D. and French. S. (eds.) *Reflecting on Research Practice* (Buckingham: Open University Press).

Attewell, P. (2001) 'The first and second digital divides', *Sociology of Education, Vol. 74 (3)*, p. 2.

Attwood, F. (2005) 'Tits and ass and porn and fighting male heterosexuality in magazines for men', *International Journal of Cultural Studies, Vol. 8 (1)*, pp. 83–100.

Attwood, F. (2006) 'Sexed up: theorizing the sexualization of culture', *Sexualities, Vol. 9 (1)*, pp. 77–94.

Backett Milburn, K. and Harden, J. (2004) 'How children and their families construct and negotiate risk, safety and danger', *Childhood, Vol. 11 (4)*, pp. 429–447

Bailey, R. (2011) *Letting Children Be Children: Report of an Independent Review of the Commercialisation and Sexualisation of Childhood* available from: http://www.gov.uk/government/uploads/system/uploads/attachment_data/file/175418/Bailey_Review.pdf.

Barber, T. (2004) 'Deviation as a key to innovation: understanding a culture of the future', *Foresight, Vol. 6 (3)*, pp. 141–152.

Barbovschi, M., Green, L. and Vandoninck, S. (eds.) (2013) *Innovative Approaches for Investigating How Children Understand Risk in New Media. Dealing with Methodological and Ethical Challenges* (LSE, London: EU Kids Online).

Bardone-Cone, A. M. and Cass, K, M. (2006) 'Investigating the impact of pro-anorexia websites: a pilot study', *European Eating Disorders Review, Vol. 1 (4)*, pp. 256–262.

Barker, J. and Smith, F. (2012) 'What's in focus? A critical discussion of photography, children and young people', *International Journal of Social Research Methodology, Vol. 15 (2)*, pp. 9–103.

Barker, J. and Weller, S. (2003) ' "Is it fun?" Developing children-centred research methods', *International Journal of Sociology and Social Policy, Vol. 23 (1–2)*, pp. 33–58.

Barns, I. (1999) 'Technology and citizenship' in Peterson, A., Barns, I., Dudley, J. and Harris, P. (eds.) *Poststructuralism, Citizenship and Social Policy* (London: Routledge).

Basalla, G. (1988) *The Evolution of Technology* (Cambridge: Cambridge University Press).

Baudrillard, J. (1968) *The System of Objects* (New York: Verso).

Baudrillard, J. (1971) 'Requiem for the media' from *For a Critique of the Political Economy of the Sign* (St. Louis: Telos Press).

Baudrillard, J. (1988) *The Ecstasy of Communication* (New York: Semiotext(e)).

Baudrillard, J. (1994) *Simulacra and Simulation* (Ann Abor: University of Michigan Press).

Baudrillard, J. (2003) *Cool memories iv 1995–2000* (New York: Verso).

Bauman, Z. (1988) *Freedom* (Milton Keynes: Open University Press).

BBC News (2013, online) 'Online pornography to be blocked by default, PM announces', available from: http://www.bbc.co.uk/news/uk-23401076.

BEAT available from: http://www.b-eat.co.uk (accessed on 26 February 2012).

Beck, U. (1992) *Risk Society Towards a New Modernity* (London: Sage).

Beck, U. (2009) *World at Risk* (Cambridge: Polity Press).

Beck, U. and Beck-Gernsheim, E. (2002) *Individualization* (London: Sage).

Began, J. A. and Allison, S. T. (2003) 'Reflexivity in the pornographic films of Candida Royalle', *Sexualities, Vol. 6 (3–4)*, pp. 301–324.

Bell, G. (2006) 'The age of the thumb: a cultural reading of mobile technologies from Asia', *Knowledge, Technology, and Policy, Vol. 19 (20)*, pp. 41–57.

Benton, T. (1999) 'Radical politics – neither left nor right?' in O'Brien, M., Penna, S. and Hay, C. (eds.) *Theorising Modernity: Reflexivity, Environment and Identity in Giddens' Social Theory* (London: Longman).

Benton, T. and Craib, I. (2001) *Philosophy of Social Science* (Basingstoke: Palgrave Macmillan).

Berg, A. J. (1999) 'A gendered socio-technical construction: the smart house' in MacKenzie, D. and Wajcman, J. (eds.) *The Social Shaping of Technology*, 2nd edn (Maidenhead: Open University Press).

Berking, H. (1999) *Sociology of Gifting* (London: Sage).

Berners-Lee, T. (2000) *Weaving the Web* (London: Texere).

Bierhoff, H. W. (2001) 'Prosocial behaviour' in Hewstone, M. and Stroebe, W. (eds.) *Introduction to Social Psychology* (Oxford: Blackwell).

Bingham, N. (1996) 'Object-ions from technological determinism towards geographies of relations', *Environment and Planning D: Society and Space, Vol. 14*, pp. 635–657.

Bloomfield, B. P., Latham, Y. and Vurdubakis, T. (2010) 'Bodies, technologies and action possibilities: when is an affordance?', *Sociology, Vol. 44 (3)*, pp. 415–433.

Boggis, A. (2011) 'Deafening silences: researching with inarticulate children', *Disability Studies Quarterly, Vol. 31 (4)*.

Bond, E. (2008) *Children's Perceptions of Risk and Mobile Phones in their Everyday Lives* (unpublished PhD Thesis, University of Essex).

Bond, E. (2010) 'Managing mobile relationships – children's perceptions of the impact of the mobile phone on relationships in their everyday lives', *Childhood, Vol. 17 (4)*, pp. 514–529.

Bond, E. (2011) 'The mobile phone = bike shed? Children, sex and mobile phones', *New Media and Society, Vol. 13 (4)*, pp. 587–604.

Bond, E. (2012) *Virtually Anorexic – Where's the Harm?* Available from: http://www.ucs.ac.uk.

Bond, E. (2013) 'Mobile phones, risk and responsibility: understanding children's perceptions', *CyberPsychology: Journal of Psychosocial Research on Cyberspace, Vol. 7 (1)*.

Bond, E. and Agnew, S. (2013) 'Understanding children's rights: examining the rhetoric with reality' in Taylor, J., Bond, E. and Woods, M. (eds.) *Early Childhood Studies: A Multidisciplinary and Holistic Introduction* (London: Hodder).

Bond, E. and Carter, P. (2013) *The Suffolk CyberSurvey*, available from: http://www.ucs.ac.uk/SchoolsAndNetwork/UCSSchools/SchoolofAppliedSocialSciences/e-Safer-Suffolk-Cybersurvey-2012-13.pdf.

Bond, E. and Goodchild, T. (2012) 'Challenges of teaching with technology in HE – towards a new third space?' in Carpenter, R. G. (ed.) *Cases on Higher Education Spaces: Innovation, Collaboration and Technology* (Hershey, PA: IGI Publishing).

Bond, E. and Goodchild, T. (2013) 'Paradigms, paradoxes and professionalism: an exploration of lecturers' perspectives on technology enhanced learning', *Journal of Applied Research in Higher Education, Vol. 5 (1)*, pp. 72–83.

Borzekowski, D. L. G., Schenk, S., Wilson, J. L. and Peebles, R. (2010) 'e-Ana and e-Mia: a content analysis of pro-eating disorder websites', *American Journal of Public Health, Vol. 100 (8)*, pp. 1526–1534.

Bourdieu, P. (1984) *Distinction: A Social Critique of Judgement and Taste* (London: Routledge).

Bourdieu, P. (1991) *Language and Symbolic Power* (Cambridge, MA: Harvard University Press).

Bourdieu, P. (1997) 'The forms of capital' in Halsey, A. H., Lauder, H., Brown, P. and Wells, A. S. (eds.) *Education: Culture, Economy, Society* (Oxford: Oxford University Press).

Bourdieu, P. and Passeron, J. C. (1990) *Reproduction in Education, Society and Culture*, 2nd edn (London: Sage).

Bowker, N. and Tuffin, K. (2003) 'Dicing with deception: people with disabilities' stategies for managing safety and identity online', *Journal of Computer-Mediated Communication, Vol. 8 (2)*, available from: http://jcmc.indiana.edu.vol8/issue2/bowker.html.

Boyd, D. (2006) 'A blogger's blog: exploring the definition of a medium', *Reconstruction: Studies in Contemporary Culture, Vol. 6 (4)*, available from: http://reconstruction.eserver.org/064/boyd.shtml.

Boyd, D., Ryan, J. and Leavitt, A. (2010) 'Pro-self-harm and the visibility of youth-generated problematic content', *I/S: A Journal of Law and Policy, Vol. 7 (1)*, pp. 1–32, available from: http://www.danah.org/papers/2011/IS-ProSelfHarm.pdf.

Brannen, J. and O'Brien, M. (1995) 'Childhood and the sociological gaze: paradigms and paradoxes', *Sociology, Vol. 29 (4)*, pp. 729–737.

Bray, Z. (2008) 'Ethnographic approaches' in della Porta, D. and Keating, M. (eds.) *Approaches and Methodologies in the Social Sciences: A Pluralist Perspective* (Cambridge: Cambridge University Press).

Briggs, A. and Burke, P. (2001) *A Social History of the Media: From Gutenberg to the Internet* (Cambridge: Polity Press).

Briggs, S. (2008) *Working with Adolescents and Young Adults: A Contemporary Psychodynamic Approach* (Basingstoke: Palgrave Macmillan).

Brown, C., and Czerniewicz, L. (2010) 'Debunking the digital native: beyond digital apartheid, towards digital democracy', *Journal of Computer Assisted Learning, Vol. 2 (5)*, pp. 357–369.

Brown, S. D. and Capdevila, R. (1999) 'Perpetuum mobile: substance, force and the sociology of translation' in Law, J. and Hassard, J. (eds.) *Actor Network Theory and After* (Oxford: Blackwell).

Bruseberg, A. and McDonagh-Philp, D. (2002) 'Focus groups to support the industrial/product designer: a review based on current literature and designers' feedback', *Applied Ergonomics, Vol. 33 (1)*, pp. 27–38.

Bryman, A. (2012) *Social Research Methods*, 4th edn (Oxford: Oxford University Press).

Bucchi, M. (2004) *Science in Society: An Introduction to the Social Studies of Science* (London: Routledge).

Buchner, B. J. (1998) 'Social control and the diffusion of modern telecommunications technologies: a cross-national study', *American Sociological Review*, Vol. *53 (3)*, pp. 446–453.

Buckingham, D. (1998) 'Review essay: children of the electronic age? Digital media and the new generational rhetoric', *European Journal of Communication*, Vol. *13 (4)*, pp. 557–565.

Buckingham, D. (2000) *After the Death of Childhood: Growing Up in the Age of Electronic Media* (Cambridge: Polity Press).

Buckingham, D. (2003) 'Media education and the end of the critical consumer', *Harvard Educational Review, Vol. 73 (3)*, pp. 309–328.

Buckingham, D. (2004) Keynote opening address presented at Digital Generations: Children, Young People and New Media Conference (London: LSE July 2004).

Buckingham, D. (2007) *Beyond Technology: Children's Learning in the Age of Digital Culture* (Cambridge: Polity Press).

Buckingham, D. and Bragg, S. (2004) *Young People, Sex and the Media: The Facts of Life* (Basingstoke: Palgrave Macmillan).

Buckingham, D. and Bragg, S. (2009) 'Children and consumer culture in the UK' in Montgomery, H. and Kellet, M. (eds.) *Children and Young People's Worlds: Developing Frameworks for Integrated Practice* (Bristol: Polity Press, in association with the Open University).

Bucknall, S. (2012) *Children as Researchers in Primary School: Choice, Voice and Participation* (Abingdon: David Foulton).

Burnett, R. and Marshall, P. D. (2003) *Web Theory* (London: Routledge).

Burr, R. and Montgomery, H. (2003) 'Family, kinship and beyond' in Maybin, J. and Woodhead, M. (eds.) *Childhoods in Context* (Chichester: Wiley).

Bušnja, A. Z. and Jelinčić, D. A. (2008) 'Managing culture in virtual realms: policy provisions and issues – a European perspective' in Uzelac, A. and Cvjetičanin, B. (eds.) *Digital Culture: The Changing Dynamics* (Zagreb: Institute for International Relations).

Butler, J. (1990) *Gender Trouble: Feminism and the Subversion of Identity* (London: Routledge).

Buunk, B. P. (2001) 'Affiliation, attraction and close relationships' in Hewstone, M. and Stroebe, W. (eds.) *Introduction to Social Psychology*, 3rd edn (Oxford: Blackwell).

Buzzard, K. S. F. (2003) 'Net ratings defining a new medium by the old, measuring Internet audiences' in Everett, A. and Caldwell, J. T. (eds.) *New Media Theories and Practices of Digitextuality* (London: Routledge).

Callon, M. (1999) 'Actor-network theory – the market test' in Law, J. and Hassard, J. (eds.) *Actor Network Theory and After* (Oxford: Blackwell).

Campbell, P. H., Milbourne, S., Dugan, L. M., Jefferson, T. and Wilcox, M. J. (2006) 'A review of evidence on practices for teaching young children to use assistive technology devices', *Topics in Early Childhood Special Education, Vol. 26 (1)*, pp. 3–13.

Carney, T., Murphy, S., McClure, J., Bishop, E., Kerr, C., Parker, J., Scott, F., Shield, C. and Wilson, L. (2003) 'Children's views of hospitalization: an exploratory study of data collection', *Journal of Child Health Care, Vol. 7*, pp. 27–40.

Carrabine, E. (2008) *Crime, Culture and the Media* (Cambridge: Polity Press).

Carrick-Davies, S. (2011) *Munch Poke Ping! Vulnerable Young People, Social media and E-Safety*, available from: http://www.carrick-davies.com/downloads/Munch_Poke_Ping_-_E-Safety_and_Vulnerable_Young_People_FULL_REPORT.pdf.

Carrington, V. (2008) ' "I'm Dylan and I'm not going to say my last name": some thoughts on childhood, text and new technologies', *British Educational Research Journal, Vol. 34 (2)*, pp. 151–166.

Carrington, V. and Marsh, J. (eds.) (2005) *Digital Childhood and Youth: New Texts, New Literacies. Special Edition of Discourse: Studies in the Cultural Politics of Education* (London: Taylor and Francis).

Castells, M. (2000) *The Rise of the Network Society*, 2nd edn (Oxford: Blackwell).

Chandler, A. (2012) 'Self-injury as embodied emotion work: managing rationality, emotions and bodies', *Sociology, Vol. 46 (3)*, pp. 442–457.

Charles, N. (2000) *Gender in Modern Britain* (Oxford: Oxford University Press).

Charlton, T., Panting, C. and Hannan, A. (2002) 'Mobile telephone ownership and usage among 10- and 11-year-olds', *Emotional and Behavioural Difficulties, Vol. 7 (3)*, pp. 152–163.

Christensen, P., Mikkelsen, M. R., Nielsen, T. A. S. and Harder, H. (2011) 'Children, mobility, and space: using GPS and mobile phone technologies in ethnographic research', *Journal of Mixed Methods Research, Vol. 2011 (5)*, pp. 227–246.

Christensen, P. and Prout, A. (2005) 'Anthropological and sociological perspectives on the study of children' in Greene, S. and Hogan, D. (eds.) *Researching Children's Experience Approaches and Methods* (London: Sage).

Christensen, P. H. (2004) 'Children's participation in ethnographic research: issues of power and representation', *Children and Society, Vol. 18 (2)*, pp. 165–176.

Christensen, P. H. and James, A. (2008) 'Introduction: researching children and childhood cultures of communication' in Christensen, P. H. and James, A. (eds.) *Research with Children Perspectives and Practices*, 2nd edn (London: Routledge).

Clark, N. R., Lecluyse, W., Jurgens, T. and Meddis, R. (2012) *BioAid: The Biologically Inspired Hearing Aid. Apple App Store*, available from http://www.bioaid.org.uk.

Clark, W. and Luckin, R. (2013) *What the Research Says: iPads in the Classroom Report*, available from: http://digitalteachingandlearning.files.wordpress.com/2013/03/ipads-in-the-classroom-report-lkl.pdf.

Clarke, A. and Moss, P. (2001) *Listening to Young Children: The Mosaic Approach* (London: National Children's Bureau in association with JRF).

Clarke, J. (2004) 'Sexuality' in Wyse, D. (ed.) *Childhood Studies An Introduction* (Oxford: Blackwell).

Clarke, J. (2010) 'The origins of childhood' in Kassem, D., Murphy, L. and Taylor, E. (eds.) *Key Issues in Childhood and Youth Studies* (London: Routledge).

Cloke, P. and Jones, O. (2005) ' "Unclaimed territory": childhood and disordered space(s)', *Social and Cultural Geography, Vol. 6 (3)*, pp. 311–333.

Cole, J., Nolan, J., Seko, Y., Mancuso, K. and Ospina, A. (2011) 'GimpGirl grows up: women with disabilities rethinking, redefining, and reclaiming community', *New Media & Society, Vol. 13 (7)*, pp. 1161–1179.

Coolican, H. (2009) *Research Methods and Statistics in Psychology*, 5th edn (London: Hodder and Stroughton).

Coombs, S. (forthcoming) 'Death wears a T-shirt – listening to young people talk about death', *Mortality*.

Cooper, L. Z. (2005) 'Developmentally appropriate digital environments for young children', *Library Trends, Vol. 54 (92)*, pp. 286–302.

Čopič, V. (2008) 'Digital culture in policy documents: the national(istic) perception of cultural diversity – the case of Slovenia' in Uzelac, A. and Cvjetičanin, B. (eds.) *Digital Culture: The Changing Dynamics* (Zagreb: Institute for International Relations).

Cordella, A. and Shaikh, M. (2006) *From Epistemology to Ontology: Challenging the Constructed 'Truth' of ANT*, available from: http://is2.lse.ac.uk/WP/PDF/wp143.pdf.

Corsaro, W. (2011) *The Sociology of Childhood*, 3rd edn (California: Pine Forge Press).

Couldry, N. (2004) 'Actor network theory and media. Do they connect and on what terms?' in Hepp, A. (ed.) *Cultures of Connectivity*, available from: http://www.lse.ac.uk/collections/media@lse/pdf/Couldry_ActorNetwork TheoryMedia.pdf.

Cover, R. (2003) 'The naked subject: context and sexualization in contemporary culture', *Body and Society, Vol. 9 (3)*, pp. 53–72.

Crabb, P. B. (1999) 'The use of answering machines and caller ID to regulate home privacy', *Environment and Behaviour, Vol. 31 (5)*, pp. 657–670.

Craig, G. (2003) 'Children's participation through community development' in Hallett, C. and Prout, A. (eds.) *Hearing the Voices of Children Social Policy for a New Century* (London: RoutledgeFalmer).

Cresswell, T. (2004) *Place: A Short Introduction* (Oxford: Blackwell).

Creswell, J. W. (2003) *Research Design: Qualitative, Quantitative and Mixed Methods Approaches* (London: Sage).

Cross, E. J., Piggin, R., Douglas, T., Vonkaenel-Flatt, J. and O'Brien, J. (2012) *Virtual Violence II Part II: Primary-Aged Children's Experience of Cyberbullying, Beatbullying*, available from: http://archive.beatbullying.org/pdfs/Virtual-Violence-Report-II-FINAL.pdf.

Croteau, D. and Hoynes, W. (2003) *Media Society Industries, Images and Audiences*, 3rd edn (London: Pine Forge Press).

Crouch, D. (2010) *Flirting with Space Journeys and Creativity* (Farnham: Ashgate).

Crowe, N. (2012) 'Virtual and online research with young people' in Bradford, S. and Cullen, F. (eds.) *Research and Research Methods for Youth Practitioners* (London: Routledge).

Csipke, E. and Horne, O. (2007) 'Pro-eating disorder websites: users' opinions', *European Eating Disorders Review, Vol. 15 (3)*, pp. 196–206.

Culpitt, I. (1999) *Social Policy and Risk* (London: Sage).

Cunningham, H. (2003) 'Children's changing lives from 1800 to 2000' in Maybin, J. and Woodhead, M. (eds.) *Childhoods in Context* (Chichester: John Wiley, in association with Open University Press).

Cunningham, H. (2005) 'Saving the children, c 1830–c.1920' in *Children and Childhood in Western Society since 1500* (London: Pearson) reproduced in Morrison, H. (ed.) *The Global History of Childhood Reader* (London: Routledge).

Cunningham, H. (2006) *The Invention of Childhood* (London: BBC Books).

Curran, J. (2012) 'Rethinking Internet history' in Curran, J., Fenton, N. and Freedman, D. (eds.) *Misunderstanding the Internet* (London: Routledge).

Custers, K. and Van den Bulck, J. (2009) 'Viewership of pro-anorexia websites in seventh, ninth and eleventh graders', *European Eating Disorders Review*, Vol. 1 (3), pp. 214–219.

Cvjetičanin, B. (2008) 'Challenges for cultural polcies: the example of digital culture' in Uzelac, A. and Cvjetičanin, B. (eds.) *Digital Culture: The Changing Dynamics* (Zagreb: Institute for International Relations).

Daliot-Bul, M. (2007) 'Japan's mobile technoculture: the production of a cellular playscape and its cultural implications', *Media, Culture and Society*, Vol. 29 (6), pp. 954–971.

Dant, T. (1999) *Material Culture in the Social World: Values, Activities, Lifestyles* (Buckingham: Open University Press).

Davies, J. (2009) 'Keeping connected: textual cohesion and textual selves, how young people stay together online' in Thomas, N. (ed.) *Children, Politics and Communication Participation at the Margins* (Bristol: Polity Press).

Davis, J. (2010) 'Architecture of the personal interactive homepage: constructing the self through MySpace', *New Media and Society*, Vol. 12 (7), pp. 1103–1119.

Davis, K. (2011) 'Tensions of identity in a networked era: young people's perspectives on the risks and rewards of online self-expression', *New Media and Society*, Vol. 14 (4), pp. 634–651.

De Mause, L. (1974) *The History of Childhood* (New York: Harper and Row).

Delamont, S. (2003) *Feminist Sociology* (London: Sage).

della Porta, D. and Keating, M. (2008a) 'Introduction' in della Porta, D. and Keating, M. (eds.) *Approaches and Methodologies in the Social Sciences: A Pluralist Perspective* (Cambridge: Cambridge University Press).

della Porta, D. and Keating, M. (2008b) 'Comparing approaches, methodologies and methods. Some concluding remarks' in della Porta, D. and Keating, M. (eds.) *Approaches and Methodologies in the Social Sciences: A Pluralist Perspective* (Cambridge: Cambridge University Press).

Denney, D. (2005) *Risk and Society* (London: Sage).

Denzin, N. K. and Lincoln, Y. S. (eds.) (2005) *Handbook of Qualitative Research*, 3rd edn (London: Sage).

Devereux, E. (2007) *Understanding the Media*, 2nd edn (London: Sage).

Diddon, R., Scholte, R. H. J., Korzilius, H., De Moor, J. M. H., Vermeaulen, A., O'Reolly, M., Lang, R. and Lancioni, G. E. (2009) 'Cyberbullying among students with intellectual and developmental disability in special educational settings', *Developmental Neurorehabilitation*, Vol. 12 (3), pp. 146–151.

Dines, G. (2010) *Pornland: How Porn Has Hijacked Our Sexuality* (Boston: Beacon Press).

Ding, S. and Littleton, K. (2005) *Children's Personal and Social Development* (Oxford: Blackwell, in association with the Open University Press).

Dorling, D. (2012) 'Inequality constitutes a particular place', *Social and Cultural Geography* Vol. 13 (1), pp. 1–9.

Dorling, D. (2013) 'Fairness and the changing fortunes of people in Britain', *Journal of the Royal Statistics Society*, Vol. 176 (1), pp. 97–128.

Drotner, K. (2000) 'Difference and diversity: trends in young Danes' media uses', *Media Culture and Society*, Vol. 22 (2), pp. 146–166.

Drotner, K. (2011) 'Children and digital media: online, on site, on the go' in Qvortrup, J., Corsaro, W. A. and Honig, M. S. (eds.) *The Palgrave Handbook of Childhood Studies* (Basingstoke: Palgrave Macmillan).

du Gay, P., Evans, J. and Redman, P. (2000) 'General Introduction' in du Gay, P., Evans, J. and Redman, P. (eds.) *Identity: A Reader* (London: Sage).

Duerager, A. and Livingstone, S. (2012) *How Can Parents Support Children's Internet Safety?* (London: EU Kids Online).

Dugdale, A. (1999) 'Materiality: juggling sameness and difference' in Law, J. and Hassard, J. (eds.) *Actor Network Theory and After* (Oxford: Blackwell).

Durkin, K. (2001) 'Developmental social psychology' in Hewstone, M. and Stroebe, W. (eds.) *Introduction to Social Psychology* (Oxford: Blackwell).

Dutton, W. H. (2013) 'Internet studies: the foundations of a transformative field' in Dutton, W. H. (ed.) *The Oxford Handbook of Internet Studies* (Oxford: Oxford University Press).

Elias, N. (1994) 'Introduction' in Elias, N. and Scotson, J. L. (eds.) *The Established and the Outsiders: A Sociological Enquiry into Community Problems* (London: Sage).

Ellison, N. B. and Boyd, D. (2013) 'Sociality through social network sites' in Dutton, W. H. (ed.) *The Oxford Handbook of Internet Studies* (Oxford: Oxford University Press).

Epstein, M. (2012) 'Introduction to the philosophy of science' in Seale, C. (ed.) *Researching Culture and Society*, 3rd edn (London: Sage).

Etheredge, L. S. (1998) 'Editor's Introduction' in Etheredge, L. S. (ed.) *Politics in Wired Nations: Selected Writings on Ithiel De Sola Pool* (Somerset NJ: Transaction).

Facer, K., Joiner, R., Stanton, D., Reidz, J., Hullz, R. and Kirk, D. (2004) 'Savannah: mobile gaming and learning?', *Journal of Computer Assisted Learning, Vol. 20*, pp. 399–409.

Fenton, N. (2012) 'The Internet and social networking' in Curran, J., Fenton, N. and Freedman, D. (eds.) *Misunderstanding the Internet* (London: Routledge).

Fenwick, T. (2010) '(un)Doing standards in education with actor-network theory', *Journal of Educational Policy, Vol. 25 (2)*, pp. 117–133.

Fenwick, T. and Edwards, R. (2010) *Actor-Network Theory and Education* (London: Routledge).

Fischer, C. S. (1988) 'Gender and the residential telephone, 1890–1940: technologies of sociability', *Sociological Forum, Vol. 3 (2)*, pp. 211–233.

Fischer, C. S. (1992) *America Calling: A Social History of the Telephone to 1940* (Berkeley, CA: University of California Press).

Fischer, H. (2008) 'Ecology of the media and hyperhumanism' in Uzelac, A. and Cvjetičanin, B. (eds.) *Digital Culture: The Changing Dynamics* (Zagreb: Institute for International Relations).

Foucault, M. (1979) [1990] *The History of Sexuality, Volume 1: An Introduction* (Harmondsworth: Penguin).

Foucault, M. (1977) *Discipline and Punish: The Birth of the Prison.* Translated by Alan Sheridan (London: Allen Lane, Penguin).

France, A. (2007) *Understanding Youth in Late Modernity* (Maidenhead: McGraw-Hill).

Frankenberg, R. (ed.) (1997) *Displacing Whiteness: Essays in Social and Cultural Criticism* (Berkeley: Duke University Press).

Frankfort-Nachmias, C. and Nachmias, D. (1996) *Research Methods in the Social Sciences*, 5th edn (London: Arnold).

Freudenburg, W. R. (1993) 'Risk and recreancy: Weber, the division of labour, and the rationality of risk perceptions' in *Social Forces, Vol. 71 (4)*, pp. 909–932.

Frosh, S., Phoenix, A. and Pattman, R. (2002) *Young Masculinities* (Cambridge: Polity Press).

Frost, L. (2005) 'Theorizing the young woman in the body', *Body and Society, Vol. 11 (1)*, pp. 63–85.

Furedi, F. (2002) *Paranoid Parenting: Why Ignoring the Experts May Be Best for Your Child* (Chicago: Chicago Review Press).

Furlong, A. and Cartmel, F. (1997) *Young People and Social Change: Individualization and Risk in Late Modernity* (Buckingham: Open University Press).

Gaffney, P. (2011) *Constructions of Childhood and Youth in Old French Narrative* (Franham: Ashgate).

Gaiser, T. J. and Schreiner, A. E. (2009) *A Guide to Conducting Online Research* (London: Sage).

Galis, V. (2011) 'Enacting disability: how can science and technology studies inform disability studies?', *Disability and Society, Vol. 26 (7)*, pp. 825–838.

Gallacher, L. and Kehily, M. J. (2013) 'Childhood: a sociocultural approach' in Kehily, M. J. (ed.) *Understanding Childhood: A Cross-Disciplinary Approach* (Bristol: Policy Press, in association with the Open University).

Gallagher, B. (2005) 'New technology: helping or harming children?' *Child Abuse Review, Vol. 14 (6)*, pp. 367–373.

Gane, M. (2004) *The Future of Social Theory* (London: Continuum International Publishing Group Ltd).

Garcia, A. and Morrell, E. (2013) 'City youth and the pedagogy of participatory media', *Learning Media and Technology, Vol. 38 (2)* pp. 123–127.

García-Montes, J. M., Caballero-Muñoz, D. and Pérez-Álvarez, M. (2006) 'Changes in the self resulting from the use of mobile phones', *Media Culture and Society, Vol. 28 (1)*, pp. 67–82.

Gauntlett, D. (2004) 'Web studies: what's new' in Gauntlett, D. and Horsley, R. (eds.) *Web Studies*, 2nd edn (London: HodderArnold).

Giddens, A. (1976) *New Rules of Sociological Method* (London: Hutchinson).

Giddens, A. (1990) *The Consequences of Modernity* (Cambridge: Polity Press).

Giddens, A. (1991) *Modernity and Self-Identity: Self and Society in the Late Modern Age* (Cambridge: Polity Press).

Giddens, A. (1992) *The Transformation of Intimacy: Sexuality, Love and Eroticism in Modern Societies* (Cambridge: Polity Press).

Giddens, A. (1999) *Runaway World: How Globalisation Is Shaping Our Lives* (London: Profile Books Ltd).

Giddens, A. (2006) *Sociology*, 5th edn (Cambridge: Polity Press).

Gilbert, N. (2008) *Researching Social Life*, 3rd edn (London: Sage).

Giles, D. (2006) 'Constructing identities in cyberspace: the case of eating disorders', *British Journal of Social Psychology, Vol. 45 (3)*, pp. 463–477.

Gillespie, M. (1995) 'Technology and tradition: audio-visual culture among South Asian families in West London' in Jackson, S. and Moores, S. (eds.) *The Politics of Domestic Consumption Critical Readings* (London: Prentice Hall Harvester Wheatsheaf).

Gillette, Y. and DePompei, R. (2004) 'The potential of electronic organisers as a tool in the cognitive rehabilitation of young people', *NeuroRehabilitation, Vol. 19 (3)*, pp. 233–243.

Gillies, V. (2003) *Families and intimate relationships: a review of the sociological literature*, online Families and Social Capital ESRC Research Group Working Paper No. 2, London: South Bank University. Available from: http://www.lsbu.ac.uk/families/workingpapers/familieswp2.pdf.

Gillies, V. and Robinson, Y. (2012) 'Developing creative research methods with challenging pupils', *International Journal of Social research Methodology*, *Vol. 15 (2)*, pp. 161–173.

Gillis, J. (2011) 'Transitions to modernity' in Qvortrup, J., Corsaro, W. A. and Honig, M. S. (eds.) *The Palgrave Handbook of Childhood Studies* (Basingstoke: Palgrave Macmillan).

Gittins, D. (2009) 'The historical construction of childhood' in Kehily, M. J. (ed.) *An Introduction to Childhood Studies*, 2nd edn (Maidenhead: Open University Press).

Goffman, E. (1959) *The Presentation of Self in Everyday Life* (Garden City, New York: Doubleday).

Goffman, E. (1971) *Relations in Public: Microstudies of the Public Order* (New York: Basic Books).

Goggin, G. (2006) *Cell Phone Culture Mobile Technology in Everyday Life* (London: Routledge).

Goggin, G. and Newell, C. (2007) 'The business of digital disability', *The Information Society, Vol. 23 (3)*, pp. 159–168.

Goldson, B. (1997) ' "Childhood": an introduction' in Scraton, P. (ed.) *'Childhood' in 'Crisis'?* (London: UCL Press), pp. 1–25.

Gomart, E. and Hennion, A. (1999) 'A sociology of attachment: music amateurs, drug users' in Law, J. and Hassard, J. (eds.) *Actor Network Theory and After* (Oxford: Blackwell).

Goodenough, T., Williamson, E., Kent, J. and Ashcroft, R. (2003) 'What do you think about that? Researching children's perceptions of participation in a longitudinal genetic epidemiological study', *Children and Society, Vol. 19 (2)*, pp. 113–125.

Goodley, D. (2011) *Disability Studies: An Interdisciplinary Introduction* (London: Sage).

Grant, L. (2011) ' "I'm a completely different person at home": using digital technologies to connect learning between home and school', *Journal of Computer Assisted Learning, Vol. 27 (1)*, pp. 292–302.

Green, E. (2001) 'Technology, leisure and everyday practices' in Green, E. and Adam, A. (eds.) *Virtual Gender Technology, Consumption and Identity* (London: Routledge).

Green, J. (1997a) 'Risk and the construction of social identity: children's talk about accidents', *Sociology of Health and Illness, Vol. 19 (4)*, pp. 457–479.

Green, J. (1997b) *Risk and Misfortune: The Social Construction of Accidents* (London: UCL Press).

Green, N. and Smith, S. (2004) ' "A spy in your pocket"? The regulation of mobile data in the UK', *Surveillance and Society, Vol. 1 (4)*, pp. 573–587.

Greene, S. and Hogan, D. (eds.) (2005) *Researching Children's Experience: Approaches and Methods* (London: Sage).

Greig, A., Taylor, J. and MacKay, T. (2012) *Doing Research with Children: A Practical Guide* (London: Sage).

Grey, A. (2011) 'Cybersafety in early childhood education in Australasia', *Journal of Early Childhood, Vol. 36 (2)*, pp. 77–81.

Grover, S. (2004) 'Why won't they listen to us? On giving power and voice to children participating in social research', *Childhood, Vol. 11 (1)*, pp. 81–93.

Hagerman, M. A. (2010) ' "I like being interviewed!": kids' perspectives on participating in social research' in Johnson, H. B. (eds.) *Children and Youth Speak for Themselves: Sociological Studies of Children and Youth Volume 13* (Bingley: Emerald).

Hall, S. [1996] (2000) 'Who needs "identity"?' in du Gay, P., Evans, J. and Redman, P. (eds.) *Identity: A Reader* (London: Sage).

Hall, S. [1980] (2006) 'Encoding/decoding' in Durham, M. G. and Kellner, D. M. (eds.) *Media Studies KeyWorks* (Oxford: Blackwell).

Halliday, J. (2011) 'London riots: how BlackBerry Messenger played a key role', *The Guardian* (Monday 8 August 2011), available from: http://www.guardian.co.uk/media/2011/aug/08/london-riots-facebook-twitter-blackberry.

Hamilton, K. (2012) 'Low-income families and coping through brands: inclusion or stigma?', *Sociology, Vol. 46 (1)*, pp. 74–90.

Hammersley, M. and Atkinson, P. (2007) *Ethnography Principles in Practice*, 3rd edn (London: Routledge).

Hannemyr, G. (2003) 'The Internet as hyperbole', *The Information Society, Vol. 19 (2)*, pp. 111–121.

Hanson, E. (2011) 'The child as pornographer', *The South Atlantic Quarterly, Vol. 110 (3)*, pp. 673–692.

Haraway, D. (1991) 'A cyborg manifesto: science, technology, and socialist-feminism in the late twentieth century' in Haraway, D. *Simians, Cyborgs and Women: The Reinvention of Nature* (New York: Routledge).

Harden, J. (2000) 'There's no place like home: the public/private distinction in children's theorizing of risk and safety', *Childhood, Vol. 7 (1)*, pp. 43–59.

Harshbarger, J. L., Ahlers-Schmidt, C. R., Mayans, L., Mayans, D. and Hawkins, J. H. (2009) 'Pro-anorexia websites: what a clinician should know', *International Journal of Eating Disorders, Vol. 42 (4)*, pp. 367–370.

Hart, C. (1998) *Doing a Literature Review* (London: Sage).

Hart, G. (1997) 'Introduction' in Green, J. (ed.) *Risk and Misfortune: The Social Construction of Accidents* (London: UCL Press).

Hart, R. (1992) *Children's Participation: From Tokenism to Citizenship* (London: Earthscan/UNICEF).

Hart, R. (2011) 'Introduction and the meaning of children's participation' in Rutgers, C. (ed.) *Creating a World Fit for Children: Understanding the UN Convention on the Rights of the Child* (New York: Idebate Press).

Hasebrink, U., Livingstone, S., Haddon, L. and Ólafsson, K. (2009) *Comparing Children's Online Opportunities and Risks across Europe: Cross-National Comparisons for EU Kids Online* (LSE, London: EU Kids Online).

Hasinoff, A. A. (2012) 'Sexting as media production: rethinking social media and sexuality', *New Media and Society*, published online at DOI: 10.1177/1461444812459171.

Hay, J. (2001) 'Locating the televisual', *Television and New Media, Vol. 2 (3)*, pp. 205–234.

Heath, S. and Walker, C. (eds.) (2012) *Innovations in Youth Research* (Basingstoke: Palgrave Macmillan).

Hendrick, H. (2011) 'The evolution of childhood in Western Europe' in Qvortrup, J., Corsaro, W. A. and Honig, M. S. (eds.) *The Palgrave Handbook of Childhood Studies* (Basingstoke: Palgrave Macmillan).

Hester, S. and Francis, D. (1994) 'Doing data: the local organization of a sociological interview', *British Journal of Sociology, Vol. 45 (4)*, pp. 675–694.

Hetherington, K. (1998) *Expressions of Identity: Space, Performance, Politics* (London: Sage).

Heywood, C. (2005) *A History of Childhood* (Cambridge: Polity Press).

Higbed, L. and Fox, J. R. E. (2010) 'Illness perceptions in anorexia nervosa: a qualitative investigation', *British Journal of Clinical Psychology, Vol. 49 (3)*, pp. 307–325.

Hill, M. (2005) 'Ethical considerations in researching children's experiences' in Greene, S. and Hogan, D. (eds.) (2005) *Researching Children's Experience: Approaches and Methods* (London: Sage).

Hill, M. (2006) 'Children's voices on ways of having a voice', *Childhood, Vol. 13 (1)*, pp. 69–89.

Hill, M., Laybourn, A. and Borland, M. (1996) 'Engaging with primary-aged children and their emotions and well-being: methodological considerations', *Children and Society, Vol. 10*, pp. 129–144.

Hine, C. (2005) *Virtual Methods: Issues in Social Research on the Internet* (Oxford: Berg).

Hirsch, D. (2013) *A Minimum Income Standard for the UK in 2013* (JRF, available from: http://www.jrf.org.uk/sites/files/jrf/income-living-standards-full.pdf).

Hobbs, N. (2011) 'Anorexic women targeted by "super-skinny" porn websites', *The Guardian* (Wednesday 6 April 2011).

Hogan, D. (2005) 'Researching "the child" in developmental psychology' in Greene, S. and Hogan, D. (eds.) *Researching Children's Experience: Approaches and Methods* (London: Sage).

Holland, P. (1996) 'Children, childishness and the media in the ruins of the twentieth century' in Pilcher, J. and Wagg, S. (eds.) *Thatcher's Children? Politics, Childhood and Society in the 1980s and 1990s* (London: Falmer Press), pp. 155–171.

Hollander, J. A. (2004) 'The social context of focus groups', *Journal of Contemporary Ethnography, Vol. 33 (5)*, pp. 602–637.

Holloway, L. and Valentine, G. (2000) *Children's Geographies* (London: Routledge).

Holloway, S. L. and Valentine, G. (2003) *Cyberkids: Children in the Information Age* (London: RoutledgeFalmer).

Holmes, M. (2010) 'The emotionalization of reflexivity', *Sociology, Vol. 44 (1)*, pp. 139–154.

Holt, L. (2011) 'Introduction: geographies of children, youth and families: disentangling the socio-spatial contexts of young people across the globalizing world' in Holt, L. (ed.) *Geographies and Children, Youth and Families: An International Context* (London: Routledge).

Honig, (2011) 'How is the child constituted in childhood studies?' in Qvortrup, J., Corsaro, W. A. and Honig, M.-S. (eds.) *The Palgrave Handbook of Childhood Studies* (Basingstoke: Palgrave Macmillan).

Hood, S., Kelley, P., Mayall, B., Oakley, A. and Morrell, R. (1996a) *Children, Parents and Risk* (London: Social Science Research Unit).

Hood, S., Kelley, P. and Mayall, B. (1996b) 'Children as research subjects: a risky enterprise', *Children and Society, Vol. 10 (2)*, pp. 117–128.

Hopkins, P. (2010) *Young People, Place and Identity* (London: Routledge).

Hughes, R. and Hans, J. D. (2001) 'Computers, the Internet, and families a review of the role new technology plays in family life', *Journal of Family Issues, Vol. 22 (6)*, pp. 778–792.

Hutchby, I. (2001a) *Conversation and Technology from the Telephone to the Internet* (Bristol: Polity Press).

Hutchby, I. (2001b) 'Technologies, texts and affordances', *Sociology, Vol. 35 (2)*, pp. 441–456.

Hutchby, I. and Moran-Ellis, J. (2001) 'Introduction: relating children technology and culture' in Hutchby, I. and Moran-Ellis, J. (eds.) *Children, Technology and Culture: The Impacts of Technologies in Children's Everyday Lives* (London: RoutledgeFalmer).

Inglis, D. (2009) 'Cultural studies and everyday life tapping hidden energies' in Jacobsen, M. H. (ed.) *Encountering the Everyday: An Introduction to the Sociologies of the Unnoticed* (Basingstoke: Palgrave Macmillan).

Ito, M. (2009) *Engineering Play: A Cultural History of Children's Software* (Massachusetts: MIT Press).

Ito, M., Okabe, D. and Matsuda, M. (2005) *Personal, Portable, Pedestrian: Mobile Phones in Japanese Life* (Cambridge, MA: MIT Press).

Jackson, S. and Scott, S. (2004) 'Sexual antinomies in late modernity', *Sexualities, Vol. 7 (2)*, pp. 233–284.

Jacobsen, M. H. (2009) 'Introduction the everyday: an introduction to an introduction' in Jacobsen, M. H. (ed.) (2009) *Encountering the Everyday: An Introduction to the Sociologies of the Unnoticed* (Basingstoke: Palgrave Macmillan).

James, A. (2007) 'Giving voice to children's voices: practices and problems, pitfalls and potentials', *American Anthropologist, Vol. 109 (2)*, pp. 261–272.

James, A. (2010) 'Competition or integration? The next steps in childhood studies?', *Childhood, Vol. 17 (4)*, pp. 485–499.

James, A. and James, A. (2004) *Constructing Childhood: Theory, Policy and Social Practice* (Basingstoke: Palgrave Macmillan).

James, A. and James, A. (2008) *Key concepts in Childhood Studies* (London: Sage).

James, A. L. and James, A. (2001) 'Tightening the net: children, community and control', *British Journal of Sociology, Vol. 52 (2)*, pp. 211–288.

James, A., Jenks, C. and Prout, A. (2010) *Theorizing Childhood* (Cambridge: Polity Press).

Jamieson, L. (1999) 'Intimacy transformed? A critical look at the "pure relationship"', *Sociology, Vol. 33 (3)*, pp. 477–494.

Jary, D. and Jary, J. (1995) 'The transformations of anthony giddens – the continuing story of structuration theory', *Theory, Culture and Society, Vol. 12 (2)*, pp. 141–160.

Jenkins, H. (2006) *Convergence Culture: Where Old and New Media Collide* (New York: New York University Press).

Jenks, C. (1996) *Childhood* (London: Routledge).

Jenks, C. (2005) *Childhood, 2nd Edn.* (London: Routledge).

Jensen, M. (2006) 'Mobility among young urban dwellers', *Young, Vol. 14 (4)*, pp. 343–361.

Jin, Z. (2011) *Global Technological Change: From Hard Technology to Soft Technology* (Bristol: Intellect Books).

Jones III, J. P. (2010) 'Introduction: social geographies of difference' in Smith, S. J., Pain, R., Marston, S. A. and Jones III, J. P (eds.) *The Sage Handbook of Social Geographies* (London: Sage).

Jones, L. (2002) 'Derrida goes to nursery school: deconstructing young children's stories', *Contemporary Issues in Early Childhood, Vol. 3 (1)*, pp. 139–146.

Jordon, P. W. (2000) *Designing Pleasurable Products: An Introduction to the New Human Factors* (London: Taylor Francis).

Joseph, J. (2003) 'Cyberstalking: an international perspective' in Jewkes, Y. (ed.) *Dot.Cons Crime, Deviance and Identity* (Cullompton: Willan Publishing).

Juarascio, A. S., Shaoib, A. and Timko, C. A. (2010) 'Pro-eating disorder communities on social networking sites: a content analysis', *Eating Disorders, Vol. 18 (5)*, pp. 393–407.

Judge, S., Puckett, K. and Cabuk, B. (2004) 'Digital equity: new findings from the early childhood longitudinal study', *Journal of Research on Technology in Education, Vol. 36 (4)*, pp. 383–396.

Kamel Boulos, M. N., Anastasiou, A., Bekiaris, E. and Panou, M. (2011) 'Geoenabled technologies for independent living: examples from four European projects', *Technology and Disability, Vol. 23*, pp. 7–17.

Katz, J. E. and Aakhus, M. A. (2002) *Perpetual Contact: Mobile Communication, Private Talk, Public Performance* (Cambridge: Cambridge University Press).

Kearney, M., Schuck, S., Burden, K. and Aubusson, P. (2012) 'Viewing mobile learning from a pedagogical perspective', *Research in Learning Technology, Vol.20*, DOI 10.3402/rlt/2010.14406.

Keating, M. (2008) 'Culture and social science' in della Porta, D. and Keating, M. (eds.) *Approaches and Methodologies in the Social Sciences A Pluralist Perspective* (Cambridge: Cambridge University Press).

Keen, A. (2007) *The Cult of the Amateur* (London: Nicholas Brealey Publishing).

Kehily, M. J. (1999) 'More sugar/ teenage magazines, gender displays and sexual learning', *European Journal of Cultural Studies, Vol. 2 (1)*, pp. 65–89.

Kellett, M. (2005a) *How to Develop Children as Researchers* (London: Paul Chapman Publishing).

Kellett, M. (2005b) *Children as Active Researchers: A New Research Paradigm for the 21st Century?* (ESRC, UK: available from http://oro.open.ac.uk/7539/1/).

Kellet, M. (2010) *Rethinking Children and Research: Attitudes for Contemporary Society* (Continuum: London).

Kellett, M., Forrest, R., Dent, N. and Ward, S. (2004) 'Just teach us the skills please, we'll do the rest: empowering ten-year-olds as active researchers', *Children and Society, Vol. 18*, pp. 329–343.

Kellner, D. (1992) 'Popular culture and the construction of postmodern identity' in Lash, S. and Freidman, J. (eds.) *Modernity and Identity* (Oxford: Blackwell).

Kellner, D. (1995) *Media Culture* (London: Routledge).

Kent, T. (2005) 'Ethical perspectives on the erotic in retailing', *Qualitative Market Research: An International Journal, Vol. 8 (4)*, pp. 430–439.

Kidd, P. S. and Parshall, M. (2000) 'Getting the focus and the group: enhancing analytical rigour in focus group research', *Journal of Qualitative Health, Vol. 10 (3)*, pp. 293–308.

Kim, P. and Sawhney, H. (2002) 'A machine-like new medium – theoretical examination of interactive TV', *Media Culture and Society, Vol. 24 (2)*, pp. 217–233.

Kim, P., Hagash, T., Carillo, L., Gonzales, I., Makany, T., Lee, B. and Gàrate, A. (2011) 'Socioeconomic strata, mobile technology, and education: a comparative analysis', *Education Technology Research Development, Vol. 59 (4)*, pp. 465–486.

Kimmel, A. J. (1988) *Ethics and Values in Applied Social Research* (London: Sage).

Kirby, P. (2002) 'Involving young people in research' in Franklin, B. (ed.) *The New Handbook of Children's Rights Comparative Policy and Practice* (London: Routledge).

Kitzinger, J. (1994) 'The methodology of focus groups: the importance of interaction between research participants', *Sociology of Health, Vol. 16 (1)*, pp. 103–121.

Kline, R. and Pinch, T. (1999) 'The social construction of technology' in MacKenzie, D. and Wajcman, J. (eds.) *The Social Shaping of Technology*, 2nd edn (Maidenhead: Open University Press).

Kline, S. J. [1985] (2003) 'What is technology?' in Scharff, R. C. and Dusek, V. (eds.) *Philosophy of Technology: The Technological Condition – An Anthology* (Oxford: Blackwell).

Kohl, U. (2007) *Jurisdiction and the Internet* (Cambridge: Cambridge University Press).

Konkka, K. (2003) 'Indian needs – cultural end-user research in Mombai' in Lindhom, C., Keinonen, T. and Kiljander, H. (eds.) *Mobile Usability: How Nokia Changed the Face of the Mobile Phone* (London: McGraw-Hill).

Kontogianni, S. (2012) *Children and New Technologies: The Digital Divide among Children with Special Needs* unpublished Master's Thesis (National and Kapodistrian University of Athens: Faculty of Communication and Mass Media Studies).

Kozinets, R. V. (2010) *Netnography: Doing Ethnographic Research Online* (London: Sage).

Kozlovsky, R. (2008) 'Adventure playgrounds and postwar reconstruction' in Gutman, M. and de Coninck-Smith, N. (eds.) *Designing Modern Childhoods: History Space, and the Material Culture of Children* (London: Rutgers University Press), pp. 171–192.

Krug, G. (2005) *Communication, Technology and Cultural Change* (London: Sage).

Küng, L., Picard, R. G. and Towse, R. (2008) *The Internet and the Mass Media* (London: Sage).

Lancaster, Y. P. (2003) *Listening to Young Children: Promoting Listening to Young Children – The Reader* (Maidenhead: Open University Press).

Lancy, D. (2008) *The Anthropology of Childhood Cherubs, Chattel, Changelings* (Cambridge: Cambridge University Press).

Lange, A. and Mierendorff, J. (2011) 'Method and methodology in childhood research' in Qvortrup, J., Corsaro, W. A. and Honig, M. S. (eds.) *The Palgrave Handbook of Childhood Studies* (Basingstoke: Palgrave Macmillan).

Lansdown, G. (2011) *Every Child's Right to Be Heard* (London: UNICEF and Save the Children).

Larson, L. C. (2010) 'Digital readers: the next chapter in e-book reading and response', *The Reading Teacher, Vol. 64 (1)*, pp. 15–22.

Latour, B. (1991) 'Materials of power: technology is society made durable' in Law, J. (ed.) *A Sociology of Monsters: Essays on Power, Technology and Domination* (London: Routledge).

Latour, B. (1993) *We Have Never Been Modern* (Hemel Hempstead: Harvester Wheatsheaf).

Latour, B. (1994) 'Where are the missing masses? The sociology of a few mundane artefacts' in Bijker, W. E. and Law, J. (eds.) *Shaping Technology/Building Society: Studies in Sociotechnical Change* (Cambridge, MA: MIT Press).

Latour, B. (1999) 'On recalling ANT' in Law, J. and Hassard, J. (eds.) *Actor Network Theory and After* (Oxford: Blackwell).

Latour, B. (2005) *Reassembling the Social: An Introduction to Actor-Network-Theory* (Oxford: Oxford University Press).

Law, J. (1991) 'Introduction: monsters, machines and sociotechnical relations' in Law, J. (ed.) *A Sociology of Monsters: Essays on Power, Technology and Domination* (London: Routledge).

Law, J. (1994) *Organising Modernity* (Oxford: Blackwell).

Law, J. (1999) 'After ANT: complexity, naming and topology' in Law, J. and Hassard, J. (eds.) *Actor Network Theory and After* (Oxford: Blackwell).

Law, J. and Hassard, J. (eds.) (1999) *Actor Network Theory and After* (Oxford: Blackwell).

Lee, L. M. (1998) 'Childhood and self-representation: the view from technology', *Anthropology in Action, Vol. 5 (3)*, pp. 13–21.

Lee, N. (2001a) 'The extensions of childhood technologies, children and independence' in Hutchby, I. and Moran-Ellis, J. (eds.) *Children, Technology and Culture: The Impacts of Technologies in Children's Everyday Lives* (London: RoutledgeFalmer).

Lee, N. (2001b) *Childhood and Society* (Buckingham: Open University Press).

Lee, N. (2008) 'Awake, asleep, adult, child: an a-humanist account of persons', *Body and Society, Vol. 14 (4)*, pp. 57–74.

Lee, N. M. (2005) *Childhood and Human Value: Development, Separation and Separability* (Buckingham: Open University Press).

Lee, N. and Brown, S. (1994) 'Otherness and the actor network: the undiscovered continent (humans and others: the concept of "agency" and it's attribution)', *American Behavioural Scientist, Vol. 37 (6)*, pp. 772–790.

Lee, N. and Stanner, P. (1999) 'Who pays? Can we pay them back' in Law, J. and Hassard, J. (eds.) *Actor Network Theory and After* (Oxford: Blackwell).

Lehman-Wilzig and Cohen-Avigdor (2004) 'The natural life cycle of new media evolution', *New Media and Society, Vol. 6 (6)*, pp. 707–730.

Leung, L. and Wei, R. (1999) 'Who are the mobile phone have-nots?', *New Media and Society, Vol. 1 (2)*, pp. 209–226.

Lewis, C. (2009) 'Children's play in the later medieval English countryside', *Childhood in the Past, Vol. 2*, pp. 86–108.

Lewis, J. (2002) 'Mass communication studies' in Miller, T. (ed.) *Television Studies* (London: British Film Institute).

Liang, J. K., Liu, T. C., Wang, H. Y., Chang, B., Deng, Y. C., Yang, J. C., Chouz, C. Y., Ko, H. W., Yang, S. and Chan, T. W. (2005) 'A few design perspectives on one-on-one digital classroom environment', *Journal of Computer Assisted Learning, Vol. 21* pp. *181–189*

Lindholm, C., Keinonen, T. and Kiljander, H. (2003) *Mobile Usability: How Nokia Changed the Face of the Mobile Phone* (London: McGraw Hill).

Lindstand, P. and Brodin, J. (2004) 'Parents and children view ICT', *Technology and Disability, Vol. 16*, pp. 179–183.

Ling, R. (1999) ' "We release them little by little": maturation and gender identity as seen in the use of mobile telephony' presented at the International Symposium on Technology and Society (ISTAS'99), *Women and Technology: Historical, Societal and Professional Perspectives* 29–31 July (New Jersey: Rutgers University, New Brunswick).

Ling, R. (2000) 'We will be reached: the use of mobile phone telephony among Norwegian youth', *Information Technology and People, Vol. 13 (3)*, pp. 102–120.

Ling, R. (2004) *The Mobile Connection: The Cell Phone's Impact on Society* (San Francisco: Morgan Kaufman Publications).

Ling, R. (2012) *Taken for Grantedness: The Embedding of Mobile Communication into Society* (London: MIT Press).

Ling, R. and Yttri, B. (2002) 'Hyper-coordination via mobile phones in Norway' in Katz, J. E. and Aakhus, M. (eds.) *Perpetual Contact: Mobile Communication, Private Talk, Public Performance* (Cambridge: Cambridge University Press).

Livingstone, S. (1998) 'Mediated childhoods: a comparative approach to young people's changing media environment in Europe', *European Journal of Communication, Vol. 13 (4)*, pp. 435–456.

Livingstone, S. (1999) 'New media, new audiences?', *New Media and Society, Vol. 1 (1)*, pp. 59–66.

Livingstone, S. (2002) *Young People and New Media* (London: Sage).

Livingstone, S. (2009) *Children and the Internet* (Cambridge: Polity Press).

Livingstone, S. and Bober, M. (2004) *UK Children Go Online: Surveying the Experiences of Young People and Their Parents* [online] (London: LSE Research online).

Livingstone, S., Görzig, A. and Ólafsson, K. (2011B) *Disadvantaged Children and Online Risk: EU Kids Online Network* (LSE, London: EU Kids Online).

Livingstone, S., and Haddon, L. (2009) *EU Kids Online: Final Report* (LSE, London: EU Kids online).

Livingstone, S. and Haddon, L. (2012) *EU Kids Online II: Enhancing Knowledge Regarding European Children's Use, Risk and Safety Online EU Kids Online, Deliverable D1.6.* (LSE, London: EU Kids online).

Livingstone, S., Haddon, L., Görzig, A., and Ólafsson, K. (2011a) *Risks and Safety on the Internet: The Perspective of European Children Full Findings and Policy Implications from the EU Kids Online Survey of 9–16 year Olds and their Parents in 25 Countries* (LSE, London: EU Kids online).

Livingstone, S., Haddon, L., & Görzig, A. (eds.) (2012) *Children, Risk and Safety on the Internet: Kids Online in Comparative Perspective* (Bristol: The Policy Press).

Livingstone, S., Haddon, L., Görzig, A. and Ólafsson, K. (2010) *Risks and Safety for Children on the Internet: the UK Report Full Findings from the EU Kids Online Survey of UK 9–16 year olds and Their Parents* (LSE, London: EU Kids online).

Livingstone, S., Haddon, L., Görzig, A. and Ólafsson, K. (2011a) *Risks and Safety on the Internet: The Perspective of European Children Full Findings and Policy Implications from the EU Kids Online Survey of 9–16 year Olds and Their Parents in 25 Countries* (LSE, London: EU Kids online).

Livingstone, S. and Helsper, E. (2010) 'Balancing opportunities and risks in teenagers' use of the internet: the role of online skills and internet self-efficacy', *New Media and Society, Vol. 12 (2)*, pp. 309–329.

Livingstone, S. Kirwil, L. Ponte, C. and Staksrud, E. (2013) *In their Own Words: What Bothers Children Online? With the EU Kids Online Network* (EU Kids Online,

London School of Economics & Political Science, London, UK)Lohmann, I. and Mayer, C. (2009) Lessons from the history of education for a 'century of the child at risk', *Paedagogia Historica, Vol. 45 (1–20)*, pp. 1–16.

Long, J. (2006) 'The socio-economic return to primary schooling in Victorian England', *The Journal of Economic History, Vol. 66 (4)*, pp. 1026–1053.

Longhurst, B. (2007) *Cultural Change and Ordinary Life* (Buckingham: Open University Press).

Looi, C. K., Zhang, B., Chen, W., Seow, P., Chia, G., Norris, C. and Soloway, E. (2010) 'Mobile inquiry learning experience for primary science students: a study of learning effectiveness', *Journal of Computer Assisted Learning, Vol. 27 (3)*, pp. 269–287.

Love, S. (2005) *Understanding Mobile Human-Computer Interaction* (Oxford: Elsevier).

Luckin, R., Bligh, B., Manches, A., Ainsworth, S., Crook, C. and Noss, R. (2012) *Decoding Learning Report: The Proof, Promise and Potential of Digital Education*, available from: http://www.nesta.org.uk/home1/assets/features/decoding_learning_report.

Lyon, D. (1995) 'The roots of the information society idea' in Heap, N., Thomas, R., Einon, G., Mason, R. and Mackay, H. (eds.) *Information Technology and Society* (London: Sage, in association with Open University Press).

Mackenzie, D. and Wajcman, J. (eds.) (1999) *The Social Shaping of Technology*, 2nd edn (Buckingham: Open University Press).

MacNaughton, G., Rolfe, S. and Siraj-Blachford (eds.) (2001) *Doing Early Childhood Research: International Perspectives on Theory and Practice* (Buckingham: Open University Press).

Madden, M., Lenhart, A., Duggan, M., Cortesi, S. and Gasser, U. (2013) *Teens and Technology 2013* (Washington: Pew Research Centre).

Mah, D. C. H. (2006) 'Explaining internet connectivity', *The Information Society: An International Journal, Vol. 21 (5)*, pp. 353–366.

Mahon, A., Glendinning, C., Clarke, K. and Craig, G. (1996) 'Researching children: methods and ethics', *Children and Society, Vol. 10 (2)*, pp. 145–154.

Mand, K. (2012) 'Giving children a voice: arts-based participatory research activities and representation', *International Journal of Social Research Methodology, Vol. 15 (2)*, pp. 149–160.

Marvin, C. (1988) *When Old Technologies Were New* (York: Oxford University Press).

Mascheroni, G. and Ólafsson, K. (2013) *Mobile Internet Access and Use among European Children: Initial Findings of the Net Children Go Mobile Project* (Milano: Educatt

Mascheroni, G. and Ólafsson, K. (2014) *Net Children Go Mobile: Risks and Opportunities* (Milano: Educatt).

Massey, D. (2005) *For Space* (London: Sage).

Matthewman, S. (2011) *Technology and Social Theory* (Basingstoke: Palgrave Macmillan).

Matthews, H. and Tucker, F. (2007) 'On both sides of the tracks: British rural teenagers' views on their ruralities' in Panelli, R., Punch, S. and Robson, E. (eds.) *Global Perspectives on Rural Childhood and Youth: Young Rural Lives* (New York: Routledge).

Maurás, M, (2011) 'Public policies and child rights: entering the third decade of the convention on the rights of the child', *Annals, Vol. 633*, pp. 52–66.

Maus, M. (2002) *The Gift* (London: Routledge).

Mavrou, K. (2011) 'Assistive technology as an emerging policy and practice: processes, challenges and future directions', *Technology and Disability, Vol. 23*, pp. 41–52.

May, T. (2011) *Social Research Issues, Methods and Research*, 4th edn (Buckingham: Open University Press).

May, V. (2011) 'Self, belonging and social change', *Sociology, Vol. 45 (3)*, pp. 363–378.

McCracken, G. (1990) *Culture and Consumption: New Approaches to the Symbolic Character of Consumer Goods and Activities* (Bloomington: Indiana University Press).

McGuire, M. R. (2012) *Technology, Crime and Justice: the Question Concerning Technomia* (London: Routledge).

McKechnie, J. and Hobbs, S. (1999) 'Child labour: the view from the north', *Childhood, Vol. 6*, pp. 89–100.

McKendry, P. C. and Price, S. J. (2005) 'Families coping with change: a concpetual overview' in McKendry, P. C. and Price, S. J. (eds.) *Families and Change* (London: Sage).

McLuhan, M. (1964) *Understanding Media* (London: Routledge).

McLuhan, M. and Fiore, Q. (1967) *The Medium Is the Message: An Inventory of Effects* (London: Penguin).

Mcnair, B. (1996) *Mediated Sex: Pornography and Postmodern Culture* (London: Arnold).

Medak, T. (2008) 'Transformations of cultural production, free culture and the future of the Internet' in Uzelac, A. and Cvjetičanin, B. (eds.) *Digital Culture: The Changing Dynamics* (Zagreb: Institute for International Relations).

Meneses, J. and Mominó, J. M. (2010) 'Putting digital literacy in practice: how schools contribute to digital inclusion in the network society', *The Information Society, Vol. 26 (3)*, pp. 197–208.

Mercer, J. (2010) *Child Development Myths and Misunderstandings* (London: Sage).

Merritt, R. (2006) *Full of Grace: A Journey through the History of Childhood* (Bologna: Damiani publishing).

Miles, M. B. and Huberman, A. M. (1994) *Qualitative Data Analysis* (London: Sage).

Miller, T. (2002) 'Introduction' in Miller, T. (ed.) *Television Studies* (London: British Film Institute).

Milman, N. (2012) 'The flipped classroom strategy: what is it and how can it be best used?', *Distance Learning, Vol. 9 (3)*, pp. 85–87.

Mol, A. (1999) 'Ontological politics. a word and some questions' in Law, J. and Hassard, J. (eds.) *Actor Network Theory and After* (Oxford: Blackwell).

Montgomery, H. (2009) 'Children, young people and poverty in the UK' in Montgomery, H. and Kellet, M. (eds.) *Children and Young People's Worlds: Developing Frameworks for Integrated Practice* (Bristol: Polity Press, in association with the Open University).

Montgomery, H. (2013) 'Childhood: an anthropological approach' in Kehily, M. J. (ed.) *Understanding Childhood: A Cross-Disciplinary Approach* (Bristol: Policy Press, in association with the Open University).

Moran, A. (1994) 'The technology of television' in Green, L. and Guinery, R. (eds.) *Framing Technology Society, Choice and Change* (St. Leonards, NSW: Allen and Unwin).

Morgan, D. L. (1998) *Focus Groups as Qualitative Research* (London: Sage).

Morgan, M., Gibbs, S., Maxwell, K. and Britten, N. (2002) 'Hearing children's voices: methodological issues in conducting focus groups with children aged 7–11 years', *Qualitative Research, Vol. 2 (1)*, pp. 5–20.

Morley, D. (1986) *Family Television: Cultural Power and Domestic Leisure* (London: Routledge).

Morley, D. (1995) 'The gendered framework of family viewing' in Jackson, S. and Moores, S. (eds.) *The Politics of Domestic Consumption: Critical Readings* (London: Prentice Hall).

Morley, D. [1995] (2008) 'Theories of consumption in media studies' in Ryan, M. (ed.) *Cultural Studies: An Anthology* (Oxford: Blackwell Publishing).

Morrow, V. (2009) 'Children, young people and their families' in Montgomery, H. and Kellet, M. (eds.) *Children and Young People's Worlds: Developing Frameworks for Integrated Practice* (Bristol: Polity Press, in association with the Open University).

Morrow, V. and Pells, K. (2012) 'Integrating children's human rights and child poverty debates: examples from young lives in Ethiopia and India', *Sociology, Vol. 46 (5)*, pp. 905–920.

Morrow, V. and Richards, M. (1996) 'The ethics of social research with children: an overview', *Children and Society, Vol. 10 (2)*, pp. 90–105.

Moser, I. (2000) 'Against normalization: subverting norms of ability and disability', *Science as Culture, Vol. 9 (2)*, pp. 201–240.

Moser, I. and Law, J. (1999) 'Good passages, bad passages' in Law, J. and Hassard, J. (eds.) *Actor Network Theory and After* (Oxford: Blackwell).

Moyal, A. (1995) 'The feminine culture of the telephone: people, patterns and policy' in Heap, N., Thomas, R., Einon, G., Mason, R. and Mackay, H. (eds.) *Information Technology and Society* (London: Sage, in association with Open University Press).

Murdoch, J. (1997) 'Towards a geography of heterogeneous associations', *Progress in Human Geography, Vol. 21 (3)*, pp. 321–337.

Murdoch, J. (2001) 'Ecologising sociology: actor-network theory, co-construction and the problem of human exemptionism', *Sociology, Vol. 35 (1)*, pp. 111–133.

Murthy, D. (2012) 'Towards a sociological understanding of social media: theorizing Twitter', *Sociology, Vol. 46 (6)*, pp. 1059–1073.

Myerson, G. (2001) *Heidegger, Habermas and the Mobile Phone* (Cambridge: Icon Books).

Newman, M., Woodcock, A. and Dunham, P. (2006) ' "Playtime in the borderlands": children's representations of school, gender and bullying through photographs and interviews', *Children's Geographies, Vol. 4 (3)*, pp. 289–302.

Neyland, D. (2006) 'Dismissed content and discontent: an analysis of the strategic aspects of actor-network theory', *Science, Technology and Human Values, Vol. 31 (1)*, pp. 29–51.

Nielssen, O., O'Dea, J., Sullivan, D., Rodriguez, M., Bourget, D. and Large, M. (2011) 'Child pornography offenders detected by surveillance of the Internet and by other methods', *Criminal Behaviour and Mental Health, Vol. 21 (3)*, pp. 215–224Norris, M. L., Boydell, K. M., Pinhas, L. and Katzman, D. K. (2006) Ana and the Internet: A review of pro-anorexia websites. *International Journal of Eating Disorders, Vol. 39(6)*, pp. 443–447.

Oakley, A. (1990) 'Interviewing women: A contradiction in terms' in Roberts, H. (ed.) *Doing Feminist Research* (London; Routledge).

O'Brien, C. (2003) 'The nature of childhood through history revealed in art-works', *Childhood, Vol. 10 (3)*, pp. 362–378.

O'Brien, M., Jones, D. and Sloan, D. (2000) 'Children's independent spatial mobility in the urban public realm', *Childhood, Vol. 7 (3)*, pp. 257–277.

O'Connel Davidson, J. and Layder, D. (1994) *Methods, Sex and Madness* (London: Routledge).

O'Connell, R., Price, J. and Barrow, C. (2004) *Cyber Stalking, Abusive Cyber Sex and Online Grooming: A Programme of Education for Teenagers*, available online from Cyberspace Research Unit: http://www.FKBKO.net.

Ofcom, (2012a) *Adults' Media Use and Attitudes Report*, available from: http://stakeholders.ofcom.org.uk/binaries/research/media-literacy/media-use-attitudes/adults-media-use-2012.pdf.

Ofcom (2012b) *Children and Parents' Media Use and Attitudes Report*, available from: http://stakeholders.ofcom.org.uk/binaries/research/media-literacy/oct2012/main.pdf.

Ofcom (2012c) *Communications Market Report 2012*, available from: http://stakeholders.ofcom.org.uk/binaries/research/cmr/cmr12/CMR_UK_2012.pdf.

Ofsted (2010) *The Safe Use of New Technologies*, available from: http://www.ofsted.gov.uk.

Okuyama, Y. (2013) 'A case study of US deaf teens' text messaging: their innovations and adoption of textisms', *New Media and Society*, DOI: 10.1177/1461444813480014.

Ólafsson, K., Livingstone, S. and Haddon, L. (2013a) *How to Research Children and Online Technologies? Frequently Asked Questions and Best Practice* (LSE, London: EU Kids Online).

Ólafsson, K., Livingstone, S. and Haddon, L. (2013b) *Children's Use of Online Technologies in Europe: A Review of the European Evidence Base* (LSE, London: EU Kids Online).

O'Leary, Z. (2004) *The Essential Guide to Doing Research* (London: Sage). O'Leary, Z. (2010) *The Essential Guide to Doing Research*, 2nd edn (London: Sage).

Oliver, M. (2009) *Understanding Disability: From Theory to Practice*, 2nd edn (Basingstoke: Palgrave Macmillan).

O'Neill, B. and McLaughlin, S. (2010) Report D7.1 *Recommendations on Safety Initiatives* (LSE, London: EU Kids Online).

ONS (2013) *Internet Access Quarterly Update, Q4 2012*, available from: http://www.ons.gov.uk/ons/dcp171778_300874.pdf.

Orme, N. (2001) *Medieval Children* (New Haven: Yale University Press).

Osgerby, B. (2004) *Youth Media* (London: Routledge).

Oudshoorn, N., Rommes, E. and Stienstra, M. (2004) 'Configuring the user as everybody: gender and design cultures in information and communication technologies', *Science Technology and Human Values, Vol. 29 (1)*, pp. 30–36.

Pahl, R. (2000) *On Friendship* (Cambridge: Polity Press).

Pain, R., Grundy, S., Gill, S., Towner, E., Sparks, G. and Hughes, K. (2005) ' "So long as I take my mobile": mobile phones, urban life and geographies of young people's safety', *International Journal of Urban and Regional Research, Vol. 29 (4)*, pp. 814–830.

Parker, E. B. (1973) 'Implications of new information technology', *The Public Opinion Quarterly, Vol. 37 (4)*, pp. 590–600.

Pawson, R. (1999) 'Methodology' in Taylor, S. (ed.) *Sociology Issues and Debates* (Basingstoke: MacMillan).

Penn, H. (2005) *Unequal Childhoods: Young Children's Lives in Poor Countries* (London: Routledge).

Peter, J. and Valkenburg, P. M. (2006) 'Adolescents' exposure to sexually explicit material on the Internet', *Communication Research, Vol. 33 (2)*, pp. 178–204.

Philo, C. (2000) ' "The corner-stones of my world": editorial introduction to special issue on spaces of childhood', *Childhood, Vol. 7 (93)*, pp. 243–256.

Pilcher, J. (1996) 'Children and sex in the 1980s and 1990s' in Pilcher, J. and Wagg, S. (eds.) *Thatcher's Children? Politics, Childhood and Society in the 1980s and 1990s* (London: Falmer Press), pp. 77–93.

Pimlott-Wilson, H. (2012) 'Visualising children's participation in research: Lego Duplo, rainbows and clouds and moodboards', *International Journal of Social Research Methodology, Vol. 15 (2)*, pp. 135–148.

Pinchbeck, I. and Hewitt, M. (1973) *Children in English Society Volume II: From the Eighteenth Century to the Children Act 1948* (London: Routledge and Kegan Paul).

Pink, S. (2007) *Doing Visual Ethnography*, 2nd edn (London: Sage).

Pink, S. (2012) *Situating Everyday Life* (London: Sage).

Plant, S. (2000) *On the Mobile: The Effects of Mobile Telephones on Social and Individual Life*, Motorola: available from: www.motorola.com/mot/doc/0/234Motdoc.pdf.

Plowden, L., McPake, J. and Stephen, C. (2010) 'The technologisation of childhood? Young children and technology in the home', *Children and Society, Vol. 24 (1)*, pp. 63–74.

Plummer, K. (1995) *Telling Sexual Stories: Power, Change and Social Worlds* (London: Routledge).

Plummer, K. (2001) *Documents of Life 2: An Invitation to Critical Humanism* (London: Sage).

Pool, De Sola, I., Decker, C., Lizard, S., Israel, K., Rubin, P. and Weinstein, B. (1998) 'Foresight and hindsight: the case of the telephone' in Etheredge, L. S. (ed.) *Politics in Wired Nations: Selected Writings on Ithiel de Sola Pool* (Somerset, NJ: Transaction).

Popović, H. and Hromadžić, H. (2008) 'Media users: from readership to co-creators' in Uzelac, A. and Cvjetičanin, B. (eds.) *Digital Culture: The Changing Dynamics* (Zagreb: Institute for International Relations).

Poster, M. (1999) 'Underdetermination', *New Media and Society, Vol. 1 (1)*, pp. 12–18.

Poster, M. (2006) 'Postmodern virtualities' in Durhman. M. G. and Kellner, D. M. (eds.) *Media and Cultural Studies Key Works* (Oxford: Blackwell).

Postman, N. (1983) *The Disappearance of Childhood* (London: W. H. Allen).

Prensky, M. (2001) 'Digital natives, digital immigrants Part 1', *On the Horizon, Vol. 9 (5)*, pp. 1–6.

Priestley, M. (2003) *Disability: A Life Course Approach* (Cambridge: Policy Press).

Primorac, J. and Jurlin, K. (2008) 'Access, privacy and culture: the implications of digitalization in South Eastern Europe' in Uzelac, A. and Cvjetičanin, B. (eds.) *Digital Culture: The Changing Dynamics* (Zagreb: Institute for International Relations).

Prout, A. (1996) 'Actor-network theory, technology and medical sociology: an illustrative analysis of the metered dose inhaler', *Sociology of Health and Illness, Vol. 18 (2)*, pp. 198–219.

Prout, A. (2000) 'Children's participation: Control and self-realisation in British late modernity', *Children and Society Vol. 14*, pp. 304–315.

Prout, A. (2003) 'Participation, policy and changing conditions of childhood' in Hallett, C. and Prout, A. (eds.) *Hearing the Voices of Children* (London: Falmer/Routledge).

Prout, A. (2005) *The Future of Childhood* (London: RoutledgeFalmer).

Punch, K. (2005) *Introduction to Social Research: Quantitative and Qualitative Approaches* (London: Sage).

Qvortrup, J. (ed.) (2005) *Studies in Modern Childhood: Society, Agency, Culture* (Basingstoke: Palgrave Macmillan).

Qvortrup, J. (2011) 'Childhood as structural form' in Qvortrup, J., Corsaro, W. A. and Honig, M. S. (eds.) *The Palgrave Handbook of Childhood Studies* (Basingstoke: Palgrave Macmillan).

Qvortrup, J., Corsaro, W. A. and Honig, M. S. (eds.) (2011) *The Palgrave Handbook of Childhood Studies* (Basingstoke: Palgrave Macmillan).

Rakow, L. F. (1999) 'The public at the table: form public access to public participation', *New Media and Society, Vol. 1 (1)*, pp. 74–82.

Rapoport, T. (1992) 'Two patterns of girlhood: inconsistent sexuality-laden experiences across institutions of socialisation and socio-cultural milieux', *International Sociology, Vol. 7 (3)*, pp. 329–346.

Rappert, B. (2003) 'Technologies, texts and possibilities: a reply to Hutchby', *Sociology, Vol. 37 (3)*, pp. 565–580.

Read, J. (2010) 'Gutter to garden: historical discourses of risk in interventions in working class children's street play', *Children and Society, Vol. 25 (6)*, pp. 421–434.

Renolds, E. (2005) *Girls, Boys and Junior Sexualities: Exploring Children's Gender and Sexual Relations in the Primary Classroom* (London: RoutledgeFalmer).

Rheingold, H. (2002) *Smart Mobs: The Next Social Revolution* (Cambridge, MA: Basic Books).

Ribbens McCarthy, J., Doolittle, M. and Day Sclater, S. (2008) *Understanding Family Meanings: A Reflective Text* (Bristol: Polity Press, in association with the Open University).

Rice, R. E. (1999) 'Artefacts and paradoxes in new media', *New Media and Society, Vol. 1 (1)*, pp. 24–32.

Rideout, V., Saphir, M., Rudd, A., Pai, S. and Bozdech, B. (2012) *Social Media, Social Life: How Teens View Their Digital Lives* (online: Common Sense Media), available from: http://www.commonsensemedia.org/sites/default/files/research/socialmediasociallife-final-061812.pdf.

Ringrose, J., Gill, R., Livingstone, S. and Harvey, L. (2012) *A Qualitative Study of Children, Young People and 'Sexting': A Report for the NSPCC*, available from: http://www.nspcc.org.uk/Inform/resourcesforprofessionals/sexualabuse/sexting-research-report_wdf89269.pdf.

Roberts-Holmes, G. (2011) *Doing Your Early Years Research Project* (London: Paul Chapman Publishing).

Roberts, J. M. and Sanders, T. (2005) 'Before, during and after: realism, reflexivity and ethnography', *The Sociological Review, Vol. 53 (2)*, pp. 294–313.

Robinson, J. P. and Kestnbaum, M. (1999) 'The personal computer, culture, and other uses of free time', *Social Science Computer Review, Vol. 17 (2)*, pp. 209–216.

Robson, C. (2011) *Real World Research: A Resource for Social Scientists and Practitioner Researchers*, 3rd edn (Oxford: Blackwell).

Roche, J. (1999) 'Children: rights, participation and citizenship', *Childhood, Vol. 6 (4)*, pp. 475–493.

Roehl, A., Reddy, S. L. and Shannon, G. J. (2013) 'The flipped classroom: an opportunity to engage millennial students through active learning', *Journal of Family and Consumer Sciences, Vol. 105 (2)*, pp. 44–49.

Rousseau, J. J. [1762] (2009) *Emile* translated by Foxley, B. (Las Vegas: IAP).

Rule, J. B. (2002) 'From mass society to perpetual contact: models of communication technologies in social context' in Katz, J. E. and Aakhus, J. (eds.) *Perpetual Contact: Mobile Communication, Private Talk, Public Performance* (Cambridge: Cambridge University Press).

Rutgers, C. (2011) Chapter 3: 'Participation and the right to be heard' in Rutgers. C. (ed.) *Creating a World Fit for Children: Understanding the UN Convention on the Rights of the Child* (New York: Idebate Press).

Ryan-Flood, R. and Gill, R. (2010) 'Introduction' in Ryan-Flood, R. and Gill, R. (eds.) *Secrecy and Silence in the Research Process* (London: Routledge).

Safford, E. and Safford, P. (1996) 'Dimensions of a "new history"' published originally as 'A history of childhood and disability teachers', College Press, pp. 286–300 in Morrison, H. (ed.) (2012) *The Global History of Childhood Reader* (London: Routledge), pp. 183–196.

Sarantakos, S. (2005) *Social Research*, 3rd edn (Basingstoke: Palgrave Macmillan).

Savirimuthu, J. (2011) 'The EU, online child safety and media literacy', *International Journal of Children's Rights, Vol. 19*, pp. 547–569.

Schroeder, R. (2010) 'Mobile phones and the inexorable advance of multimodal connectednes', *New Media and Society, Vol. 12 (1)*, pp. 75–90.

Schwarzt Cowan, R. (1999) 'The industrial revolution in the home' in MacKenzie, D. and Wajcman, J. (eds.) *The Social Shaping of Technology*, 2nd edn (Maidenhead: Open University Press).

Scott, S. and Jackson, S. (2000) 'Childhood' in Payne, G. (ed.) *Social Divisions* (Basingstoke: Palgrave Macmillan).

Scott, S., Jackson, S. and Backett-Milburn, K. (1998) 'Swings and roundabouts: risk anxiety and the everyday worlds of children', *Sociology, Vol. 32 (4)*, pp. 689–705.

Scourfield, J., Dicks, B., Drakeford, M. and Davies, A. (2006) *Children, Place and Identity: Nation and Locality in Middle Childhood* (London: Routledge).

Scratton, P. (1997) 'Preface' in Scratton, P. (ed.) *Childhood in 'Crisis'?* (London: UCL Press).

Selwyn, J. (2000) 'Technologies and environments: new freedoms, new constraints' in Boushel, M., Fawcett, M. and Selwyn, J. (eds.) *Focus on Early Childhood: Principles and Realities* (Oxford: Blackwell Science).

Selwyn, N. (2003) 'Doing IT for the kids: re-examining children, computers and the information society', *Media, Culture and Society, Vol. 25 (3)*, pp. 351–378.

Selwyn, N. (2004) 'Exploring the role of children in adults' adoption and use of computers', *Information Technology and People, Vol. 17 (1)*, pp. 53–70.

Selwyn, N. (2005) 'An immobile minority? A study of middle-class non-users of mobile phones' paper presented at the First European Communication Conference, KIT Amsterdam 24/11/05–26/11/05.

Selwyn, N. (2011a) *Education and Technology: Key Issues and Debates* (London: Continuum).

Selwyn, N. (2011b) 'Editorial: in praise of pessimism—the need for negativity in educational technology', *British Journal of Educational Technology, Vol. 42 (5)*, pp. 713–718.

Shahar, S. (1990) *Childhood in the Middle Ages* (London: Routledge).

Shapiro, S. (1998) 'Places and spaces: the historical interaction of technology, home, and privacy', *The Information Society, Vol. 14 (4)*, pp. 275–284.

Siapera, E. (2012) *Understanding New Media* (London: Sage).

Sibley, D. (1995) *Geographies of Exclusion* (London: Routledge).

Sikes, P. (2004) 'Methodology, procedures and ethical concerns' in Opie, C. (ed.) *Doing Educational Research* (London: Sage).

Silverman, D. (2012) 'Research and theory' in Seale, C. (ed.) *Researching Society and Culture* (London: Sage).

Silverstone, R. (1994) *Television and Everyday Life* (London: Routledge).

Silverstone, R. (1999) 'What's new about new media?', *New Media and Society, Vol. 1 (1)*, pp. 10–12.

Silverstone, R. (2007) *Media and Morality on the Rise of the Mediapolis* (Cambridge: Polity Press).

Singh, S. (2001) 'Gender and the use of the internet at home', *New Media and Society, Vol. 3 (4)*, pp. 395–416.

Slater, D. (1998) 'Public/private' in Jenks, C. (ed.) *Core Sociological Dichotomies* (London: Sage).

Smart, B. (1992) *Modern Conditions, Postmodern Controversies* (London: Routledge).

Smith, R. (2000) 'Order and disorder: the contradictions of childhood', *Children and Society, Vol. 14*, pp. 3–10.

Smith, P., Mahdavi, J., Carvalho, M. and Tippett, N. (2005) *An Investigation into Cyberbullying, its Forms, Awareness and Impact, and the Relationship between age and Gender in Cyberbullying: A Report to the Anti-Bullying Alliance*, available from: http://www.anti-bullyingalliance.org.uk/downloads/pdf/cyberbullyingre portfinal230106_000.pdf.

Smoreda, Z. and Licope, C. (2000) 'Gender-specific use of the domestic telephone' *Social Psychology Quarterly, Vol. 63 (3)*, pp. 238–252.

Smoreda, Z. and Thomas, F. (2001) *Social Networks and Residential ICT Adoption and Use.* Paper presented at the EURESCOM summit meeting, Heidelberg, available from: http://www.cost269.org/Committee/linksmoreda/ Smoreda%20&%20Thomas.pdf.

Snee, H. (2012) 'Youth research in web 2.0: a case study in blog analysis' in Heath, S. and Walker, C (eds.) *Innovations in Youth Research* (Basingstoke: Palgrave Macmillan).

Society for Study of Childhood in the Past (online) – SSCIP, available from: http:// www.sscip.org.uk/.

Söderström, S. (2009) 'Offline social ties and online use of computers: a study of disabled youth and their use of ICT advances', *New Media and Society, Vol. 11 (5)*, pp. 709–727.

Sonck, N. Livingstone, S., Kuiper, E. and de Haan, J. (2011) *Digital Literacy and Safety Skills* (LSE, London: EU Kids Online).

Spencer, S. (2004) 'Reflections on the "site of struggle": girls' experience of secondary education in the late 1950s', *History of Education, Vol. 33 (4)*, pp. 437–449.

Spiker, P. (1995) *Social Policy: Themes and Approaches* (London: Prentice Hall).

Stainton Rogers, W. (2011) *Social Psychology*, 2nd edn (London: McGraw Hill).

Stalder, F. (2006) *Manual Castells* (Cambridge: Polity Press).

Steeves, V. and Jones, O. (2010) 'Editorial: surveillance and children', *Surveillance and Society, Vol. 7 (3/4)*, pp. 187–191.

Steinfield, C., Ellison, N. B. and Lampe, C. (2008) 'Social capital, self-esteem, and use of online social network sites: a longitudinal analysis', *Journal of Applied Developmental Psychology, Vol. 29*, pp. 434–445.

Stendal, K., Balandin, S. and Molka-Danielsen, J. (2011) 'Virtual worlds: a new opportunity for people with lifelong disability?', *Journal of Intellectual and Developmental Disability, Vol. 36 (1)*, pp. 80–83.

Sterling, B. (1995) 'US telephone network' in Heap, N., Thomas, R., Einon, G., Mason, R. and Mackay, H. (eds.) *Information Technology and Society* (London: Sage, in association with Open University Press).

Stevens, I. and Hassett, P. (2007) 'Applying complexity theory to risk in child protection practice', *Childhood, Vol. 14 (1)*, pp. 128–144.

Stöber, R. (2004) 'What media evolution is a theoretical approach to the history of new media', *European Journal of Communication, Vol. 19 (4)*, pp. 483–505.

Stokes, P. J. G. (2010) 'Young people as digital natives: protection, perpetration and regulation', *Children's Geographies, Vol. 8 (3)*, pp. 319–323

Stone, J. (2004) 'Buzz in the playground: mobile phone brands say they don't target under-16s but phone ownership by children as young as seven is on the rise. Are youths being exploited?', *Marketing Week, Vol. 27 (39)*, p. 37.

Stone, L. (1977) *The Family, Sex and Marriage in England 1500–1800* (New York: Harper and Row).

Strasburger, V. C., Wilson, B. J. and Jordan, A. B. (2014) *Children, Adolescents, and the Media*, 3rd edn (London: Sage).

Strathern, M. (1999) 'What is intellectual property after' in Law, J. and Hassard, J. (eds.) *Actor Network Theory and After* (Oxford: Blackwell).

Tapscott, D. (1998) *Growing Up Digital: The Rise of the Net Generation* (New York: McGraw Hill).

Taylor, A. and Harper, R. (2002) *Age-old Practices in the 'New World': A Study of Gift-Giving between Teenage Mobile Phone Users*, available from: http://www.dwrc.surrey.ac.uk/Portals/0/GiftGiving.pdf.

The Royal College of Psychiatrists [online], available from: www.rcpsych.ac.uk/mentalhealthinfoforall/problems/eatingdisorders/eatingdisorders.aspx.

Thomas, N. and O'Kane, C. (1998) 'The ethics of participatory research with children', *Children and Society, Vol. 12*, pp. 336–348.

Thomas, N. and O' Kane, C. (2000) 'Discovering what children think: connections between research and practice', *British Journal of Social Work, Vol. 30*, pp. 819–835.

Thomson, R. (2007) 'Belonging' in Kehily, M. J. (ed.) *Understanding Youth: Perspectives, Identities and Practices* (London: Sage, in association with Open University Press).

Thorne, B. [1987] (2012) 'Re-visioning women and social change: where are the children?' in Morrison, H. (ed.) *The Global History of Childhood Reader* (London: Routledge).

Thornton, S. (1995) *Club Cultures. Music, Media and Subcultural Capital* (Hanover and London: Wesleyan).

Thorogood, N. (2000) 'Sex education as disciplinary technique: policy and practice in England and Wales', *Sexualities, Vol. 3 (4)*, pp. 425–438.

Thurlow, C. and McKay, S. (2003) 'Profiling "new" communication technologies in adolescence', *Journal of Language and Social Psychology, Vol. 22 (1)*, pp. 94–103.

Tiller, J. M., Sloane, G., Schmidt, U. and Troop, N. (1997) 'Social support in patients with anorexia nervosa and bulimia nervosa', *International Journal of Eating Disorders, Vol. 21*, pp. 31–38.

Trigg, A. B. (2001) 'Veblen, Bourdieu and conspicuous consumption' in *Journal of Economic Issues, Vol. 35 (1), pp.* 99–115.

Truman, C. (2000) 'New social movements and social research' in Truman, C. and Mertens, D. (eds.) *Research and Inequality* (London: Routledge).

Tudor, A. (1995) 'Culture, mass communication and social agency', *Theory Culture and Society, Vol. 12 (5)*, pp. 81–107.

Turmel, A. (2008) *A Historical Sociology of Childhood: Developmental Thinking, Categorization and Graphic Visualization* (Cambridge: Cambridge University Press).

Ungar, S. (2001) 'Moral panic versus the risk society: the implications of the changing sites of social anxiety', *British Journal of Sociology, Vol. 52 (2)*, pp. 271–291.

UNICEF (2012) *The State of the World's Children 2012: Children in an Urban World*, available from: http://www.unicef.org/sowc2012/pdfs/SOWC%202012-Main%20Report_EN_13Mar2012.pdf.

Uzelac, A. (2008) 'How to understand digital culture: digital culture – a resource for a knowledge society?' in Uzelac, A. and Cvjetičanin, B. (eds.) *Digital Culture: The Changing Dynamics* (Zagreb: Institute for International Relations).

Valentine, G. (1996) 'Children should be seen and not heard? The role of children in public space', *Urban Geography, Vol. 17 (3)*, pp. 205–220.

Valentine, G. and Holloway, S. (2001) ' "Technophobia": parents' and children's fears about information and communication technologies and the transformation of culture and society' in Hutchby, I. and Moan-Ellis. J. (eds.) *Children Technology and Culture: The Impacts of Technologies in Children's Everyday Lives* (London: Routledge).

Valkenburg, P. M., Schouten, A. P. and Peter, J. (2005) 'Adolescents' identity experiments on the internet', *New Media and Society, Vol. 7 (3)* pp. 383–402

Van Avermat, E. (2001) 'Social influence in small groups' in Hewstone, M. and Stroebe, W. (eds.) *Introduction to Social Psychology* (Oxford: Blackwell).

Varbanova, L. (2008) 'The online power of users and money: can culture gain?' in Uzelac, A. and Cvjetičanin, B. (eds.) *Digital Culture: The Changing Dynamics* (Zagreb: Institute for International Relations).

Veale, A. (2005) 'Creative methodologies in participatory research with children' in Greene, S. and Hogan, D. (eds.) *Researching Children's Experience: Approaches and Methods* (London: Sage).

Veblen, T. (1994) *The Theory of the Leisure Class* (New York: Dover Publications).

Vincent, J. (2004) *'11–16 Mobile' Examining Mobile Phone and ICT Use amongst Children Aged 11 to 16* (Guildford: DWRC), available from: http://www.dwrc.surrey.ac.uk/portals/0/11-16Mobiles.PDF.

Vicente, M. R. and López, A. J. (2010) 'A multidimensional analysis of the disability digital divide: some evidence for Internet use', *The Information Society, Vol. 26 (1)*, pp. 48–64.

Vitak, J. and Ellsion, N. (2012) ' "There's a network out there you might as well tap": exploring the benefits of and barriers to exchanging informational and support-based resources on Facebook', *New Media and Society, Vol. 13 (7)*, pp. 1161–1179.

Wajcman, J. (1994) 'Technological a/genders: technology, culture and class' in Green, L. and Guinery, R. (eds.) *Framing Technology Society, Choice and Change* (St. Leonards, NSW: Allen and Unwin).

Walsham, G. (1983) 'Telephone systems in the Third World: a research project', *The Journal of the Operational Research Society, Vol. 34 (3)*, pp. 225–231.

Warde, A., Martens, L. and Olsen, W. (1999) 'Consumption and the problem of variety: cultural omnivorousness, social distinction and eating out', *Sociology, Vol. 33 (1)*, pp. 105–127.

Warschauer, M. (2003) *Technology and Social Inclusion: Rethinking the Digital Divide* (Cambridge, MA: MIT Press).

Weber, M. (1964) *The Theory of Social and Economic Organisation* (New York: Free Press).

Weightman, A. P. H., Preston, N., Holt, R., Allsop, M., Levesley, M. and Bhakta, B. (2010) 'Engaging children in healthcare technology design: developing rehabilitation technology for children with cerebral palsy', *Journal of Engineering Design, Vol. 21 (5)*, pp. 579–600.

Weller, S. (2012) 'Evolving creativity in qualitative longitudinal research with children and teenagers', *International Journal of Social Research Methodology, Vol. 15 (2)*, pp. 119–133.

Wellman, B. and Tindall, D. (1993) 'How telephone networks connect social networks' in Wellman, B. (ed.) *Progress in Communication Sciences: Advances in Communication Network Analysis* (Norwood, NJ: Ablex).

Wells, K. (2009) *Childhood in a Global Perspective* (Cambridge: Polity Press).

Wilkinson, I. (2001) *Anxiety in a Risk Society* (London: Routledge).

Williams, K. (2003) *Understanding Media Theory* (London: Arnold).

Williams, S. and Reid, M. (2010) 'Understanding the experience of ambivalence in anorexia nervosa: the maintainer's perspective', *Psychology and Health, Vol. 25 (5)*, pp. 551–567.

Williams, S. and Williams, L. (2005) 'Space invaders: the negotiation of teenage boundaries through the mobile phone', *The Sociological Review, Vol. 53*, pp. 315–330.

Willmore, L. (2002) 'Government policies toward information and communication technologies: a historical perspective', *Journal of Information Science, Vol. 28 (2)*, pp. 89–96.

Winter, K. and Connolly, P. (1996) ' "Keeping it in the family": Thatcherism and the Children Act 1989' in Pilcher, J. and Wagg, S. (eds.) *Thatcher's Children? Politics, Childhood and Society in the 1980s and 1990s* (London: Falmer Press), pp. 29–42.

Wong, M. E. and Tan, S. S. K. (2012) 'Teaching the benefits of smart phone technology to blind consumers: exploring the potential of the iPhone', *Journal of Visual Impairment and Blindness, October–November 2012*, pp. 646–649.

Wood, E. (2009) 'Saving childhood in everyday objects', *Childhood in the Past, Vol. 2*, pp. 151–162.

Woods, M. (2005) 'Introduction to early childhood studies' in Taylor, J. and Woods, M. (eds.) *Early Childhood Studies: An Holistic Introduction* (London: Arnold).

Wyness, M. (2012) *Childhood and Society*, 2nd edn (Basingstoke: Palgrave Macmillan).

Wynne, B. (1996) 'May the sheep safely graze? A reflexive view of the expert–lay knowledge divide' in Lash, S., Szerszinski, B. and Wynne, B. (eds.) *Risk, Environment and Modernity: Towards a New Ecology* (London: Sage).

Zelizer, V. (1985) *Pricing the Priceless Child: The Changing Social Value of Children* (Chichester: Princeton University Press).

Zimmerman Umble, D. (1992) 'The Amish and the telephone resistance and reconstruction' in Silverstone, R. and Hirsch, E. (eds.) *Consuming Technologies: Media and Information in Domestic Spaces* (London: Routledge).

Zurita, G. and Nussbaum, M. (2007) 'A conceptual framework based on activity theory for mobile CSCL', *British Journal of Educational Technology*, Vol. 38 (2), pp. 211–235.

Index

Printed and bound in the United States of America

DATE DUE
